THE GREAT TIME-KILLER

THE WORLD PUBLISHING COMPANY · CLEVELAND &

The Great Time-Killer

by

HAROLD MEHLING

NEW YORK

Published by The World Publishing Company
2231 West 110th Street, Cleveland 2, Ohio

Published simultaneously in Canada by
Nelson, Foster & Scott Ltd.

Library of Congress Catalog Card Number: 62-9044

FIRST EDITION

WP562

Together with a large-screen, full-color,
spectacular observation of Thoreau's,
*"As if you could kill time
without injuring eternity . . ."*
this book is dedicated to
my children, Rodney and Linda.

CONTENTS

THE GREAT TIME-KILLER

FOREWORD
THE GREAT TIME-KILLER

"Show me an unhappy home and I'll show you a home that doesn't like television."—A Madison Avenue philosopher.

To borrow a phrase from Bob Hope: "Remember how great?" Remember how great television used to be? Remember how television excited people, and how they *talked* about it?

Along Madison Avenue these days, the merchandise-movers will tell you—they have told me, anyway—that such nostalgia is nonsensical. Old times, they say, are gone forever, and, besides, they were a bore. In those days, they explain, we were an audience that "confused bewilderment with profundity, lack of craftsmanship with art—an audience that was willing to bore itself in pursuit of what it mistakenly considered culture."

Nevertheless, I have a persistently recurring recollection of countless mornings on which men and women exchanged thoughts that had been born during a television program the evening before.

They discussed, for example, a play about an ugly duckling—a clumsy butcher-boy who thought no girl could ever care for him. It was written in a way that revealed the sensitivity, the enormous capacity for pain and joy, that resides in everyone, including those who are apt to be thought of as clods.

That was *Marty.*

It is impossible to forget, too, that millions were taken up with *The Catered Affair, Visit to a Small Planet, The Bachelor Party, Patterns, Twelve Angry Men,* and other original television dramas. They talked about adaptations, too—*She Stoops to Conquer, The Corn Is Green, Emperor Jones, Ah, Wilderness!* and others.

They had something to talk about.

It is conceivable that a person could still strike up a conversation about what he saw on television the night before. "Well," he might say, "this mother was raising her children to avenge the death of their father, and when she had trouble keeping them in line, she horsewhipped the son and shot the daughter in the back." Or, "This father is lovable but dumb, and his wife and kids know it, so they have to get him out of all the jams he gets himself into. In this one, he decides he's going to make a fortune . . ."

There is no law against such conversation, of course, but on the other hand there is no conversation, either. "I don't need tranquilizers," Groucho Marx has said. "I watch television."

The outstanding difference between television during the early 1950's and the early 1960's is that the young model, while light-years from perfection, showed promise of attaining decency. Today, grown-up television shows certainty of becoming a major national scandal. The truth is that the scandal is already upon us, but theft from the mind is less glaring than from the wallet.

We have been robbed—deliberately, there is no doubt of that—by the television networks, by sponsors and their Madison Avenue advertising agencies, and by the hired hands in the Hollywood laugh-laugh mills. Together, and profitably, they have transformed television into a peddler, a genial good-time Charlie with holes in his head.

The spoilers have defenses for their conduct, of course—an infinite number of defenses. They assume many forms and are dizzying in their diversity. One industry executive explains that television is really a continuous electronic psychiatrist: "We are bringing relaxation and relief and escape, mental and emotional catharsis, to more millions of people than have ever before simultaneously experienced the benefit of such therapy." Another allies himself with the downtrodden against the filthy rich: "This is a working-class medium. While the well-to-do are attending plays or visiting each other at parties, the workers, who can't afford to go out, are being entertained at home." An executive defends the common man against brainwashing by intellectuals and bureaucrats: "It's about time someone spoke up for the people against the cultural kick of the high 'n' mighty in Washington." An advertising man suggests that discordant family life and a distaste for trash-can programming are synonymous: "Show me an unhappy home and I'll show you a home that doesn't like television." And, finally, another advertising man warns that dissenters may simply wreck America. "Tampering with television programming can derail the economy," he declares.

I like to juxtapose these comments with a remark voluntarily uttered by one Jules Bungdus, who has produced a radio soap opera in his time but is now a vice-president of an advertising agency known as Kastor, Hilton, Chesley, Clifford & Atherton. "Of course," Bungdus said, "both the advertisers and the viewing public need pulp television, even if that seems a derogatory way of referring to many of the mass-audience shows."

Such candor, however, is hardly the rule. On most sunny, cloudy, or partly cloudy days, the television and/or advertising executive can be relied on to retreat to his best line of defense—outright distortion. The malcontents, he says, want to wrest the common man's beer can from his hand, knock his tired feet off the top of the television, and make him sit at attention while he ingests *Antigone, Parsifal,* and Bernstein three hours a night, seven nights a week.

Television executives employ such desperate tactics because their programming is so lousy, to put it plainly. They are not only losing their audiences' enthusiasm, but the audiences themselves; thus they are fretty and incoherent.

Considering their vigorous combat for advertising dollars, it is odd that they should so completely abandon restraint and promulgate a doctrine that seems downright suicidal. Anyone who doesn't like television, they say, has an immediate and drastic form of relief at his fingertips. He can turn the damned thing off. Aside from the self-destructive aspects of this advice, there is a ring of the ludicrous; I visualize a burglar palming the silverware and explaining, with annoyance, "If you don't like me in your house, get out of the house."

Television *is* our house. We own it. Without *our* air waves —an incredibly valuable national resource—there would be no television. We allow broadcasters to use our air waves in order to serve us, and in return, we permit them to earn a profit. Instead, they are refusing to serve, insisting on unlimited profits, implying that critics are somehow un-American, and ordering us out. The nineteenth century would have admired their arrogance.

It is less than bright to contend that, despite all this, television is merely a reflection of our general condition and can improve only with that condition. This is a convenient argument often heard at intellectual cocktail parties; when delivered with a sneer, it relieves the haughty of concern with the fact that television today is a national soma-dispenser, delivering a population into blissful vacuousness, teaching automatic response to the Pavlovian command to buy, buy, buy. Many intellectuals regard culture as their private preserve, resent intrusions, and feel that television is just right for the lowbrow.

But the power of the living-room screen is too great for sneering. In other days and with other mediums, investigation of its anesthetizing influence might be a function of academic high priests. But these are not other days—*those* are the days that are gone forever—and we are not dealing with mere comic books. Rather, while the world experiences radical upheaval that demands perception and understanding, the gurgle-gurgle box insulates us from that world and substitutes a narcoticland in which we sit, stare, and kill time, while everything always turns out all right in the end.

Except that everything is not turning out all right, is it?

Every once in a while, an intelligent broadcaster—and there are some—is struck by that reality. One such man, Donald H. McGannon, president of the Westinghouse Broadcasting Company, has pondered the relationship of broadcasting to international events and concluded, "Many intelligent people believe we now face the choice of all of us keeping up with the world—or abruptly leaving it." McGannon's company sponsors public service conferences at which broadcasters expose themselves to pleas that they join the world, and at one of these gatherings, Archibald MacLeish told them:

> What you do matters. A man could even argue—and I should be prepared to—that what you do matters more over the long run (if our civilization has a long run ahead of it) than what anybody else does, because you are more persistently shaping the minds of more people than all the rest of us put together.

Whereupon broadcasting continued to broadcast as if broadcasting didn't matter, except to the stockholders.

Television also matters very much to a large number of men and women who work in it. These are the people, creative and administrative, who light up the picture tube each day, hoping that this day will be more honest than the last.

Many of them have contributed to this book; they have, in fact, made it possible. They are demoralized and embittered; they want the story of television's degeneration told in the hope that the medium can be rescued.

That is the story in this book.

1 ARE YOU A SNOB OR SOMETHING?

"If we listened to the eggheads, we'd be out of business in six months."—Robert W. Sarnoff, chairman, National Broadcasting Company.

These pages are not addressed to the men who direct the television industry; they know all about television. They are addressed, rather, to those who are dissatisfied with television but are not sure why, and to those who would be dissatisfied, or perhaps outraged, if they understood how, to what extent, and with what deliberate cynicism they were being victimized.

Both the dissatisfied and the potentially dissatisfied are members of a technologically created species of American who was classified only a dozen years ago as the *viewer*. As the ideal viewer's function is conceived by the men of television, he is a biological miracle. He is capable of earning a living, eating, sleeping, and participating in his family's activities while still finding time to devote approximately five hours of each day to his major function—sitting before a television set and staring at pictures that have been made by advertisers (commercials) or at pictures that have been inspired by advertisers (programs).

If in this rigorous schedule a moment can be reserved for thinking, the men of television hope that the viewer will think pleasant thoughts, such as "What are Ozzie and Harriet *really* like?" rather than unpleasant thoughts, such as "What is *really* wrong with television?" In order to be rid of dangerous illusions, it should be conceded at the outset that in this race for our attention Ozzie and Harriet are currently in the lead by, roughly, five lengths.

Research, polls, surveys, studies, and other modern alchemy that transmutes humans into numbers tell us that the species *viewer,* often referred to in the trade as the "market," is now made up of over 160,000,000 Americans. While this is a grandly inclusive lot of people, it does not include the men who run television. They are excluded because outside of the demands of business they rarely watch television—a fact less strange than it may at first seem. They don't watch because they know what's going to be on. These men, despite their expressions of surprise and shock, understood what Newton Minow, the chairman of the Federal Communications Commission, was talking about when he referred to their landscape as a "vast wasteland."

Television executives are not given to publicizing their abstinence for the same reason that heroin growers rarely criticize heroin—there is no percentage in knocking the product. Occasionally, however, to their embarrassment, a member of the brotherhood obstreperously speaks up. In this spirit, Arthur Godfrey has said, "I don't understand how people tolerate the junk on television. How often do I watch? With the exception of a few interviews on Sunday afternoon, I never look at the damn thing." And Fairfax M. Cone, head of the Foote, Cone & Belding advertising agency, has volunteered the information that "I agree with most critics about most popular television programming. I abhor it. And I rarely look at it—except professionally."

It should be understood, however, that we are not dealing here with unremitting Philistines. When television and advertising executives are safely out of the office, many of them act much like run-of-the-mine intelligent human beings. They —steady, now—would even like to see *good television.* They owned up to this when *Broadcasting,* a trade magazine, asked them to make up hypothetical program schedules based not on fusty rating numbers but on their personal preferences. They immediately seeded the wasteland, irrigated it, and produced a garden of fresh, crunchy good taste.

They'd program "quality drama," the executives said, and concerts, and "great circus" programs, and operas, and variety revues spotlighting talented performers new to television. They'd present biographical dramas based on the lives of Disraeli, Theodore Roosevelt, and other intriguing figures (for the children's hour: Charlemagne and Helen of Troy). Suspense and mystery drama would be of the Edgar Allan Poe caliber, without so much unimaginative gunfire. There would be live music, too, from Benny Goodman to the ballet. And the news would be discussed unhurriedly by educators, diplomats, historians, and government officials.

When the executives were asked, conversely, which programs they could cheerfully do without, their candidates were disturbingly familiar. *The Untouchables,* they said, and *Adventures in Paradise, Surfside Six, Hawaiian Eye, The Roaring Twenties, Pete and Gladys, Bringing Up Buddy,* and so on. What were they nostalgic for? *Philco Playhouse, Omnibus, Wide Wide World, Producer's Showcase, Kukla, Fran & Ollie, Playhouse 90,* Sid Caesar and Imogene Coca.

After displaying such vibrantly fine taste, the broadcasting and advertising men returned to their workaday routines of fashioning programs for the mob that were anathema to them.

People who present the public with entertainment they themselves wouldn't watch are well suited to disseminate peculiar ideas, which they may or may not believe themselves. Among such notions propagated by the men of television is the contention that those who complain about programming are either intellectual snobs (subspecies *egghead*), neurotic malcontents, guided or misguided enemies of the American Way of Life, or a misanthropic hybrid of these unsavory types. Television executives have alleged, implied, or endorsed this startling idea on numerous occasions—in conversation, in public addresses, and in solemn, sworn testimony before our leaders in Washington. Odd notion or no, it is their most-played recording of the past decade.

Are you a snob, a malcontent, or a subversive? You may vigorously think not, but we all make mistakes. To find out if you have made a mistake, at least in the view of television's operators, cast yourself for a few moments in the role of a typical breadwinner who comes home tired after a day of contention with the world and would like to take off his shoes and be entertained or relaxed.

You say that's no role—that *is* you? Splendid; now we have a real-life drama peopled by familiar figures just like the folks we all know. Who needs theatrics?

So your tired feet are comfortably elevated and your television set is tuned and your can of beer or cup of coffee is in hand and all's right with the world again. "Life's not so bad after all, honey," you may murmur to your wife during the three commercials that precede the program and the first commercial of the show itself. (Admittedly, that's a scanty line to carry you through four commercials, but you feel a guilty obligation to listen to a *little* of the sponsors' messages, don't you? Good Americans don't cheat!)

But on with the show. The story concerns a detective agency run by two young clean-cuts played by actors you never heard of before *TV Guide* devoted an *entire article* to their high-school days and their jobs in a garage and what their mothers think of all this television acting . . . and land sakes! Truth to tell, they aren't actually actors, but they *are* Hollywood lovely-boys; one with blond hair, twinkly blue eyes, and a devil-with-it grin; the other with glistening, black, wavy hair, a magnificent chest, and a dedicated, anti-nonsense manner. Neither, in addition, has hips; their bodies, like four-month fetuses, are only partly formed.

So you're watching the action—this is what is known as an action show, which means the actors must move around as in perpetual motion, preferably via sports cars or convertibles, but also by foot, plane, ship, or train; or by punching their way through other actors. Well, anyway, as Mort Sahl would say after so many detours, these two youths amble into an Acapulco night club and encounter a very drunk young lady whose cleavage is threatening her navel, whose petulant lower lip is shining wet with gin, and who is quarreling with the night-club owner, instantly recognized as the heavy because he is fat, short, surly, and simply not clean-cut.

"Say," you mutter to your wife, "I've seen this before. The blond guy says let's help her and the other guy says let's stay away from her—she's poison—and the blond guy convinces his partner that they ought to get her out of there and find out what's bothering her. I've seen it before, I tell you!"

Your wife corrects you. "You're thinking of that other show, *Easthampton Eleven,*" she says. "This is *Sunnyside Seven.* Shush."

Having erred, you subside. It was in *Easthampton Eleven* that one eye wanted to get the very drunk young lady with the cleavage and the wet lip out of the fat, short, surly villain's night club, despite the fact that the other eye wanted to stay away from her because she was poison. *This* show is *Sunnyside Seven.*

Two minutes later, in *Sunnyside Seven,* after two tables and six chairs have been smashed, the eyes have got the young lady with the cleavage and the wet lip out of the fat, short, surly villain's night club, despite the fact that one partner wanted to stay away from her because he thought she was poison.

"How about that?" you venture. "The same thing. That must be why I thought I'd already seen it."

"In the other one, in the fight," your wife notes, "they only broke one table and three chairs."

Despite this distinction, you become uneasy. And after the next commercial, during which someone shatters the laxative habit, or annihilates the hot cigarette habit, or banishes the armpit-odor habit, you become downright vexed. For now you discover that wet-lip has come to Acapulco to track down her younger sister, who she suspects has met foul play at the greasy hands of the night-club owner. But wasn't that the fate of that other young lady in Miami? And the one in Las Vegas? And the one in Saskatchewan? Yes, it was.

Well, as someone once said wisely, you don't have to eat the last spoonful of a can of cyanide to appreciate the flavor of cyanide. Before another commercial disturbs the peace, you realize that *Sunnyside Seven* is a bare-handed reshuffle of *Easthampton Eleven, Southport Six, Twenty-Two Fishhouse Row,* and *The Unmentionables,* most of which you've seen and the cumulation of which is sufficient to render you inert with boredom.

Now the chances are that you are not a student of Greek drama, nor of modern literature, either, and so you do not articulate your ennui in high-flown terms. You don't compare an action show to *Moby Dick,* a situation comedy to *Pygmalion,* a soap opera to *Antigone,* and search within those contexts for what went wrong on television. You simply yawn, and, with squadrons of others, you no longer talk about last night's television program when friends drop in.

But worse, your inquisitive mind gives birth to questions which, by their nature, lead you inevitably into the thicket of reasoned discontent. *What has happened to television?* you wonder. *Why don't I get a kick out of it any more? Why do so many shows seem like so many other shows? Why do I usually know what's coming next? Why don't these shows* entertain *me?*

And being endowed with a basic wisdom the operators of the National Broadcasting Company, the Columbia Broadcasting System, and the American Broadcasting Company do not even suspect, your doubts gradually take on a more definable shape. *Why don't these shows ever give me anything to think about?* you wonder. Are critics right when they contend that "programming for everybody" means programming for nobody but morons? Do mass-appeal shows have to be stupid? Do mass mediums tend to degenerate, the massier they try to be? Shouldn't advertisers stick to advertising and leave programming alone? Isn't most of television advertising just wasteful nonsense, anyway? Is there enough difference between aspirin A and aspirin B or between soap X and soap Y to justify the expenditure of so many millions of dollars for which consumers get the bill?

But most important, the problem of programs: *If adults wouldn't dream of eating Pablum three times a day, why should television feed it to us night after night?*

The fact is that while there is nothing extraordinary about such thinking, it marks you as nothing less than an incipient revolutionary in the eyes of the princes of television and their court jesters in the Madison Avenue advertising agencies. Consider, for example, the depressing position of Frank Stanton, Ph.D., president of CBS and a seasoned bushwhacker of critics. Stanton, with the leverage of an impressive collection of university degrees, has hoisted himself to a rarefied platform as the philosopher, or academic high priest, of the broadcasting industry. Unlike the cruder Robert W. Sarnoff, chairman of NBC, who is fond of such sallies as "If we listened to the eggheads, we'd be out of business in six months," Stanton exorcises the evil spirits of criticism with learned incantations. He employs patience and reason, tirelessly elaborating his concept of "cultural democracy" for the edification of those who have "serious misconceptions, unexamined assumptions, and sheer prejudices about the nature of mass media." For many years, Stanton used as CBS's programming standard the idea that "a mass medium must concern itself with the common denominator of mass interest." This was a useful rationale in that it made money; it justified CBS Radio's role as mother hen of the soap operas, or daytime weepers.

More recently, however, Stanton's reaction to criticism has hardened; he has lost some patience with those who nag him relentlessly for better television programming. And so he has been led, somewhat testily, to suggest that doubters (whom he likes to call intellectuals) would prefer life in such places as the Soviet Union, Nazi Germany, or perhaps Upper Slobovia. ". . . there is among many intellectuals," he has written, "an uncongeniality with some of the basic ingredients of a democratic society and, in many cases, a real distrust of them. . . . Some sort of hostility on the part of the intellectuals toward the mass media is inevitable, because the intellectuals are a minority, one not really reconciled to some basic features of democratic life."

Those who dissent from Stanton's premise will of course have to decide for themselves, hopefully after a thorough family discussion, whether they would prefer life elsewhere. I, for one, choose to remain in the United States, and to pray that *Pete and Gladys, Shotgun Slade,* and *Cain's Hundred* will go elsewhere.

Sarnoff, on the other hand, is earthier. Much criticism of television, he has darkly stated, emanates from "certain arcane regions." The NBC chairman confines himself to simplicity in dealing with critics, as would a candidate for village dog-catcher. We're here to serve the peepul, he says. They must like what they're being served because they take it, don't they? When he is able to, which is almost always, Sarnoff attempts to stand on this platform; it omits scores of pertinent planks and therefore serves him well.

But anyone who rejects both Stanton's elegant slickness and Sarnoff's primitivism has several more rivers to cross. He must face a battalion of television loyalists whose good livelihoods depend on the maintenance of the status quo but who do not exhibit Stanton's intellectual sheen in defending it. There is, for instance, Merrill Panitt, the editor of *TV Guide,* a magazine that deals with television exclusively and somewhat orgiastically —it once introduced a recipe for a "TV snack" with the words, "Early in the day, melt butter in a skillet . . ." Panitt knows what television's critics are up to; their deviltry is a "wonderful method of gaining attention and getting your do-good organization's name in the papers." And there is Charles Alicoate, publisher of *Radio-TV Daily,* a trade paper, who regards critics as "spokesmen for special interest groups, disgruntled competitors, the fringe intelligentsia, the do-gooder, the self-appointed guardians of the arts." It is difficult to converse with these people because they do not speak clearly while looking under their beds.

But all defenses of television are not so heavy-handed. Some members of the club, lacking originality, can at least recognize a bright epigram and rephrase it in endless variation. In April, 1961, *TV Guide* remarked, "Apparently nobody likes the current TV season but the viewers." If one could tag such a phrase with radioactive isotopes, he would see it skip along Madison Avenue. Five weeks after it appeared in *TV Guide,* Henry Schachte of Lever Brothers, one of television's heaviest users, said, "Nobody loves you broadcasters, except the people who live in 50,000,000 American homes." And hardly had six more weeks passed than Bud Collyer, the perennially cheerful master of ceremonies, was commenting, "If you believe most of what you read and hear about television, nobody likes it. Except the people."

Some excommunicated critics commit even worse crimes than condemning programming; they do not wholeheartedly accept television advertising as an irreplaceable feature of the American dream. They are the ones who couldn't care less whether television sells more bottles of Mr. Clean than of Lestoil, and who wonder why *they* should pay the enormous bills of this private fracas. They must face an inspection of their true, or devious, motives. One advertising man has succinctly declared, "An attack on advertising is an attack on the American way of life, of which advertising is an essential part." An equally blunt gentleman, Harry W. Chesley, president of the D'Arcy advertising agency, has exposed the downright treasonable nature of criticism. "Let's recognize," he told a meeting of appreciative colleagues, "that the fuzzy thinking of some of our critics both inside and outside government has already placed us at a disadvantage—that it already represents an even more serious threat than anything Russia can do abroad or than inflation or recession can do at home."

I warned you, didn't I, about subversion?

But if dissenters are suspect, at least they are in good company. In 1960, President Eisenhower's Commission on National Goals considered the state of broadcasting and reeled in horror. "It is too easy to say that people are getting what they want," the Commission noted. "The fact that large audiences are attracted by fourth-rate material does not acquit the broadcasting companies or the government, which has ultimate responsibility for the use of this valuable and scarce resource, from asking whether the public interest is being adequately served. . . . Thus far, television has failed to use its facilities adequately for educational and cultural purposes and reform in its performance is urgent."

It is conceivable, however, that all such comments and ripostes are too general to indicate the depth of broadcasting's hostility toward criticism. To gain this understanding, interested parties should consult the words of Max Banzhaf, director of advertising for the Armstrong Cork Company, another prominent television advertiser. *Broadcasting,* the most prominent journal of the industry, reported a Banzhaf speech in this way:

> Criticism is merely a means to an end when people in government, educators, and writers attack advertising, Mr. Banzhaf said.
>
> "The end," he explained, is "the control of business. They seek to control advertising as a means of shackling private enterprise and placing greater control in the hands of govern-

> ment. Advertising is under attack because it represents a skirmish which must be fought in the battle of big government versus private enterprise—the battle between the advocates of state socialism and the advocates of free enterprise, the free market economy, and individual liberty."

As someone who has expressed discontent with the overabundance of commercials on television, with deceptive and poppycock claims, with shrieking, shouting, and diagrams of internal human plumbing, and with oatmeal instead of steak as programming, were you aware that you were trying to promote state socialism?

If you were not, then you would not logically surmise, either, that people who believe that most of television programming is dreadful are hypocrites or eccentrics. Those descriptives have been employed by Max Wylie, one of television's most bare-faced defenders. But Wylie, who has been both a network and advertising agency executive, found "hypocrite" and "eccentric" altogether inadequate in referring to John Crosby, who was probably the most widely read and outspoken television columnist in the land until he abandoned the field out of boredom. In a magazine article ("Maybe he needed the money," Wylie suggested), Crosby had remarked on the various methods employed by advertising agencies and sponsors to tamper with and emasculate writers' work. A possible solution for this state of affairs, the critic proposed, was the creation of a program advisory board consisting of noted figures of the rank of Herbert Hoover, Pearl Buck, Walter Lippmann, Leonard Bernstein, and others.

This seemingly mild suggestion provoked Wylie to enter print with the observation that Crosby's mind was bordering on "psychiatric disorientation." He used the same forum to proclaim a basic plank of his own cultural platform: "There is nothing wrong with mediocrity if you are mediocre. Mediocrity is exactly right. Most television critics never take this into account."

But mediocrity is not revered for its own sake, of course; it is merely the inescapable product of formularized programming. The case for spontaneity and freshness was best made, perhaps, by that phenomenon of midnight impetuousness, Jack Paar. For five years, Paar demonstrated that one of television's mightiest weapons is unpredictability. With comedy, tears, venom, hero worship, naïveté, and petulance, he revealed himself to be a human being, with strengths and frailties, rather than a bloodless stamping made in Hollywood. Deified or dismissed, Paar proved that television is electric when it deals with actuality instead of artificiality.

It is a revelation, too, to know that the television industry's aforementioned outbursts were directed almost entirely at criticisms of *entertainment.* Almost none of the malcontents had sinned, at least in these instances, by suggesting that our evenings should be dominated by documentary studies of life among the Croatians, or discussions of cubist art, or presentations of *Tristan und Isolde.* They were simply lamenting that the show business segment of television had laid an egg.

But such are the financial stakes involved that any threat to television's enormous profits is translated into a threat to motherhood, flag, church, and the American collie. If we did not understand that this is merely a defensive pose, we might be led to suspect—borrowing from a way of thinking previously cited—that the men of television were bordering on psychiatric disorientation.

It is true, though, that while the network operators are in absolute control of their faculties, they are nevertheless indicating symptoms of incipient paranoia. Bedeviled by congressmen (who have shown themselves, however, to be harmless), by imprecations from government regulators, and by newspaper columnists who forever seem to be carping, they are reacting with extreme defenses that tend to stifle meaningful discourse. They are even frightened by books—specifically, by this book. And thereby hangs one of those personal tales which normally would not be worth reporting but occasionally take on enough significance to justify recording.

The writing of this book was preceded by approximately one year of research, which was made easier by a passing familiarity gained from having written a number of shows for CBS. In the course of this work, it became clear that the worst starting point for research was at the high network level; corporate sensitivity and corporation-man fear was too acute. Accordingly, I canvassed the thinking of advertising agency men, sponsors, rating services personnel, producers, directors, writers, and network employees not on the high executive level. But the moment eventually arrived when time could be saved by formally requesting statistics, data, and discussion from the networks themselves.

Shortly before requests for information were directed to the ABC and NBC networks, the publisher of this book had announced its preparation through a news release based on notes I supplied. The announcement made clear that the book would attempt to initiate a fruitful discussion of television as a formidable problem in American life. It said, in part:

> We sit each evening, blinkered from family and conversation, and see and hear television sell: drugs, cosmetics, soaps, cars, cigarettes, breakfast foods. We see, and we are beginning to sense, that because of a primary devotion to the job of selling, this marvelous means of communication has been forced to adopt one of selling's primary tenets—appeal to as many as possible, offend as few as possible, and don't argue about politics, religion, or other controversial matters such as what we should do with our lives between the time we are born and the time we die. . . .
>
> In the light of a crucial world situation . . . television has cast the viewer in the role of Nero, fiddling happily while Rome burns. . . .

This release, having been made public, found its way into the offices of a vice-president of the ABC television network, where it caused distress. "I don't know why I should even see you," he said in a telephone conversation. "I will, but you'd better be able to explain this release away. You'll have to make quite a case."

The following afternoon, the vice-president made *his* case. Pointing to the description of the projected book, he said it was "full of misinformation and misstatement," by which he meant he did not agree with its opinions. During a lecture that consumed the next twenty minutes, he repeated almost every industry alibi I had encountered over the previous year, and added several that related specifically to the ABC network. In addition, he revealed that he had discussed the release with a vice-president of NBC and would also discuss it with a CBS vice-president.

Entranced by a feeling of self-importance that is downright ridiculous for a writer to entertain, I ventured a few defenses of my position, then asked for copies of a number of speeches that had been delivered by ABC executives, and for an interview with Oliver Treyz, then president of ABC. The vice-president rewarded me with printed copies of speeches but added that he would recommend that Treyz not see me. "You'll only quote him out of context," he said. "Maybe I'll be overruled, but that will be my recommendation." Treyz has not seen me.

My illusion of self-importance was heightened at NBC, where not one vice-president, but two, directed their attention to this book. Said one, over the telephone, "I've read the release on your book, and frankly it almost knocked me out of my chair." He added that, as a consequence, NBC might have to reassess its relationship with me. This was a reference to an earlier meeting I had had with a lower-level executive, at which arrangements were made for me to interview certain NBC personnel. The vice-president said he thought it would be wise if we got together and talked. "But I want you to understand that we're not reacting out of fear," he pointed out. "We're not afraid of this kind of thing."

During the courageous meeting that followed, the troublesome release was read to me (I began to tire of it, somehow), after which I was asked if it fairly represented what this book would say.

I replied that the book's contents would be much broader than the release suggested, but that its tone accurately reflected my approach. Some remarks were exchanged, the repetition of which will not advance an understanding of the issues involved, but eventually I was asked if I could indicate why I should expect NBC's assistance, since I seemed to have made up my mind in advance. I explained that I sought only factual information and comment on matters that had been discussed many times, and that the purpose was a public discussion of a major national problem. Emboldened by my own logic, I then requested an interview with NBC's chairman, Robert W. Sarnoff, and information on how many times each NBC affiliate had carried a particular network public affairs program during the preceding season. As for my seeing Sarnoff, one of the vice-presidents said, "We'll see." As for the record of affiliates carrying a public affairs program (one of the most serious problems in television), they said they'd "have to kick it around" and would call me in a few days.

"We've kicked it around," said one of the vice-presidents, when the call came, "and we've decided you'd better go it alone. Helping you would be like contributing to our own downfall."

A letter to the upper levels of CBS has gone unanswered, except for a reply stating that the addressee, another vice-president, was out of town and would contact me when he returned. Perhaps he has never returned; in any event, he has not contacted me.

Such is the atmosphere that prevails. Fortunately, it made research only more difficult, not impossible. And unfortunately, it contributed to a distressing apprehension: that the broadcasting industry is in no condition to participate in a meaningful dialogue on its performance. It will not even concede that the long honeymoon is over, that television is losing its vast, habituated audience, particularly during prime evening time. The decline began in the fall of 1958, when the medium had become saturated with Hollywood's paste entertainment. Some estimates hold that by the fall of 1961, between five and six million fewer people were watching with their earlier regularity.

The industry reacted to these figures with resourcefulness. Perhaps recalling some of its commercials, it said that the Asian Flu epidemic of the fall of 1957 had imprisoned an abnormally high number of people with their picture tubes and that, therefore, succeeding years should not be compared with this period. "Where can you go from a peak except down?" asked Jay Eliasberg, CBS's research director, thus arguing that television's future lay in dwindling audiences. The network finally rested on the grumble that, anyway, the decline was "so slight as to be negligible."

Advertising agency executives, whose commissions have been rising as television increases the cost of ad budgets, hurried to the defense of their favorite medium. Richard A. R. Pinkham, who was a senior vice-president of the Ted Bates agency, observed that television "fits so perfectly into our hedonistic way of life that even if it continues to slide, it will still command most of the leisure time of most Americans and it will remain a superb advertising medium."

But even if this assumption were granted, it would not solve the networks' increasing problems with some advertisers, who are beginning to worry that their selling messages are no longer reaching the higher-income "thought leaders." As *Variety* pointed out in the spring of 1961, "There's no way to verify it by the ratings, but nevertheless there's a growing concern among some top TV thinkers that the medium has lost a vital segment of its audience—the professional class of doctors, lawyers, teachers, and business leaders. In short, the opinion-makers. . . . One CBS executive in the pubaffairs area (once *Variety's* shorthand is mastered, reading it is almost fun) spelled it out shortly after *CBS Reports* aired its excellent and provocative 'A Real Case of Murder.' He went to a dinner party at which nine of the fifteen guests were lawyers. None of the fifteen had seen the show; none of the lawyers had even heard about it. Contrast that, the executive said, with some of the response accorded the old *See It Now* series. . . ."

To such observations, more standard rebuttals from Madison Avenue. A Kenyon & Eckhardt agency executive said, "What thought leaders? They're self-styled. They don't lead anybody. They just think they do. They were the last to buy television sets and the first to leave them." And a voice from the Foote, Cone & Belding agency: "As for thought leaders, well, they're the first to tire of everything. Now they're all home listening to their stereophonic fm sets."

These pouting contentions lose standing, though, when advertising agencies that handle huge accounts take a contrary view. During 1961, for example, the Campbell-Ewald agency of Detroit, which represents Chevrolet, initiated a study of the television audience from which emerged a bristling new creature known as the "restless viewer." He is the one who isn't taking his television with a nipple as unprotestingly as he used to; he is showing signs of maturity.

And since the networks are offering the same non-entertainment that they have been insisting is "what the people want" but evidently is only another figment from the Madison Avenue fig tree, the panic is on. *TV Guide* reflects the gravity of the problem when it becomes shrill in demanding that people get down to business and *view*. "Now is the time for all good eggheads to come to the aid of their programs," it said a few months after the "thought leader" alarm was sounded. "Those who were loudest in their demands for serious, cultural, educational, uplifting, enlightening, broadening television shows will now kindly tune in or shut up." A month later the magazine banished fetching girls and lovely-boy actors from its cover and substituted a bold directive: THIS IS THE WEEK TO WATCH.

None of which necessarily suggests that the broadcasting-advertising industry will change its ways; it hasn't changed them in thirty years. It feels that critics are poachers on its private preserve and in any event are simply not qualified to comment on such complexities as exist in broadcasting. Not even this position is original. It has been lifted from the archaic defenses of the Hollywood movie makers, whose sensitivity reached such heights that it inspired jokes—instructive jokes—such as the one surrounding Cecil B. De Mille and one of his crashingly pious epics:

> It seems that De Mille's super-colossal movie, which had taken twelve years to produce at a cost of $50,000,000 and was populated with thirty-eight of Hollywood's brightest stars, was being sneak-previewed one evening at a Los Angeles suburb. When the film ended, the legendary producer strode out to the sidewalk, where he was surrounded by his faithful coterie—almost as numerous as the cast.
>
> "Marvelous, Cecil," said a press agent. "An absolute extravaganza!"
>
> "Tremendous, Cecil," said a cost accountant.
>
> "Stupendous, Cecil," said one of the film's nine directors. "This will positively *make* the Bible!"
>
> Triumphantly De Mille accosted a small boy who was just then emerging from the theater. "Son," he asked, "what did you think of my movie?"
>
> "It stunk," the boy responded.
>
> De Mille exploded. "It stunk? Are you crazy? Who do you think you are, you little louse, to say my epic picture stunk?"
>
> The boy mulled the question briefly, then replied: "Gee, Mr. De Mille, who do you have to be?"

A LUST FOR LOOT

"I personally cannot believe that you . . . could . . . not know what was going on." —Representative Peter F. Mack, to Robert E. Kintner, president of NBC, during an investigation of television quiz shows.

On the evening of October 16, 1956, Daniel Enright, impresario of a television quiz-opera company, visited a young New Yorker, Herbert Stempel, and before an hour had passed asked if he would like to make $25,000. Stempel replied: "Who wouldn't?"

That rejoinder was neither original nor extraordinary, but it was fervent; Stempel had compelling reasons for coveting a windfall. A student at the City College of New York at the age of twenty-nine, he was oppressed by financial dependence on his wife's wealthy parents. He had been a poor boy, moreover, and had been forced to advance himself "the hard way," as he explained later.

So he accepted Dan Enright's proposition and became a contestant, if that is the word, on the quiz show *Twenty-One,* which was then one of the most popular television shows catering to human infatuation with large sums of money. Stempel appeared on *Twenty-One,* over the NBC network, eight consecutive times and won $49,500 (including a bonus for diligent ham acting) by consistently answering more questions correctly than any of several opponents. He did not find these victories particularly difficult because Enright gave him the questions and answers before the shows went on the air, a practice Stempel acquiesced in. Enright made the feat even simpler by coaching one of Stempel's opponents, too, but in such a way that he was doomed to lose.

Through this practical arrangement, two important purposes were served. Stempel, a highly emotional character, made money and basked in the national limelight; and television was able to deliver millions of viewers to an advertiser, under shady but profitable conditions.

There came a day, however, when Stempel's usefulness to *Twenty-One* diminished; Enright had found another so-called contestant with still another rationale that would overcome an aversion to swindling. This was Charles Lincoln Van Doren, the Columbia University instructor who felt that a masquerade as a human data-processing machine would constitute "a great service to the intellectual life, to teachers and to education in general, by increasing public respect for the work of the mind. . . ."

But for Van Doren to replace Stempel, the student had to lose at the game of *Twenty-One,* and that is where the canker gnawed. Stempel, exalted by his elevation from nobody to somebody, did not want to lose, especially to Van Doren, who seemed to him to represent and possess everything that Stempel didn't. Van Doren, he explained, "had a fancy name, Ivy League education, parents all his life, and I had just the opposite. . . ."—the classic offering of the disinherited slum kid caught at the till.

So Stempel fretted, pouted, and balked before taking the long count in favor of Van Doren. But his decision, a voluntary one only in the narrowest sense, left a residue of bitterness that ultimately exploded into the tawdry quiz-show scandals. Actor Edward Hilgemeier, Jr., who was involved with a different outbreak of the quiz epidemic, CBS Television's

Dotto, is usually considered to be "the man who blew the whistle on the quiz shows," but for reasons that go to the heart of the television problem to this day, Hilgemeier would still be whistling to himself if it had not been for Herbert Stempel. It is intriguing to speculate on the possibility that the public might never have learned of the dishonesty of the quiz shows at all. The testimony of network executives, given during the exposé, indicates that television's controllers would have made this scandal the best-kept secret of a most talkative industry.

For all the benefit the public has derived, however, the affair might as well have remained a secret. With the passage of time, the networks' role has receded in public recollection while remembrance has remained vivid of such personalities as Stempel and Van Doren, Hank Bloomgarden and Gino Prado, Teddy Nadler and Patty Duke. Names do make news, but not necessarily news of substance, and the substance of this matter is that forgetfulness of the networks' major responsibility allows them to get off the hook—again.

Exposure of quiz-show, and industry, corruption during the congressional investigation of late 1959 put television in the worst light in broadcasting's history. The networks prettified themselves afterward with patch-up cosmetics. They scheduled more public affairs shows—on Saturdays, on Sunday afternoons, or at the tail end of weekday prime time, where their sober content would not hamper the building of all-important "evening viewing blocs." Reform ended there; any additional programming of public affairs shows was a necessity of a presidential election year. Entertainment programs continued their descent into simple-mindedness and the hypocrisy of it all provoked an official of the Batten, Barton, Durstine & Osborn advertising agency to say: "The networks put the public service shows on . . . to get the government off their backs. It worked. Now the networks are sneaking them out as fast as they can."

In short, the thinking that inspired the quiz-show sickness

is the same thinking that is crippling television today, and the debacle that followed the scandal is the debacle on the picture tube before us. That is why a careful recapitulation of the quiz-show mess will serve many more purposes than sensationalism.

In the beginning there was not Dan Enright and *Twenty-One,* but Louis G. Cowan and *The $64,000 Question.* Cowan, sometimes described as the fall guy of the quiz debacle, was a television producer who took pains not to burden the public with his own considerable thoughtfulness. He was in the publicity business in Chicago when he developed the famous *Quiz Kids* show for radio, and then *Stop the Music,* which was popular and noisy during radio's noisiest period.

Cowan's foresight showed him the direction television was taking in the mid-1950's, and he was early in stride; he constructed a television adaptation of radio's *Take It or Leave It,* the show that coined the immortal phrase "the $64 question." He added three zeros to give the sum true television dimension, found a sponsor, and placed the program on the CBS network, where *The $64,000 Question* burst into public view one evening in early June, 1955. When it quickly achieved first place in the rating polls and made the front pages of newspapers, Cowan became the brightest man on Madison Avenue. Seven weeks after the show's première, he sold out his interest in its producing company to become a vice-president of CBS, where he was attached to Frank Stanton's supreme headquarters. Not long afterward, Cowan replaced a bright man of an earlier period and became president of CBS Television. He landed the job because of a quiz show, and he lost it four years later because of a quiz show, although he has resolutely maintained that *The $64,000 Question* was never fixed while he was associated with it.

More pertinent to the affair than Cowan was a pair of hard-headed manufacturers, the brothers Charles and Martin Revson, of Revlon, Inc. Charles Haskell Revson, a debonair man of middle age who was once a Calvert Whisky "Man of Distinction," was the personification of what is frequently merchandised as a wholesome American success story. He and Martin grew up in New Hampshire under economic adversity, from which they developed a "consuming ambition," as *Fortune* has described it, "to break into the big time and, especially on Charles's part, an inflexible determination not to let themselves be pushed around." The fact that in 1950 Charles was knighted with a Horatio Alger Award, a quaint baronetcy of the market place, indicates that he was not pushed around too much or too often. The basis of the award is not completely clear, but it probably had something to do with Charles's efforts to improve the lot of American women by selling them lipsticks and nail polishes.

Martin Elliot Revson, four years junior to Charles but no less blunt-minded, was known in the lip- and nail-paint industry as an imaginative head. He is supposed to have made advertising history, or at least cocktail chatter, with a Revlon magazine advertisement that pictured a sensational young brunette clothed in sheath and vacuous expression and adorned with a cape whose color, the ad promised, would suit (in a cosmetic) women who could answer yes to such questions as "Have you ever danced with your shoes off? Do you think any man really understands you? Do you secretly hope the next man you meet will be a psychiatrist?"

The business that this yearning, burning approach to women brought to the Revsons was good, but is good ever good enough? The brothers had tinkered with television sponsorship in an effort to improve sales still further, but in Charles's words, they had merely backed "one stiff after another." Unlike some other businessmen, the Revsons did not fawn before the might of the new medium; their interest was in sales, not electronic miracles.

The $64,000 Question, however, looked like a Willy Loman in his prime when it was presented to them by Norman, Craig & Kummel, Revlon's advertising agency at the time.

(Revlon holds a Madison Avenue record for engaging and discarding the greatest number of ad agencies in the least time.) But the Revsons were not utterly entranced from the start. It is said that when Charles met with two of the ad agency's owners in a New York night club after the first show was aired, he pronounced it a flop with the unquenchable confidence of an amateur in show business. He changed his mind not long afterward, to put it mildly, and soon he was walking out of plays and sneaking away from banquets in order not to miss a broadcast. Before long, English television was exhibiting a 64,000 shilling show and Mexico a 64,000 peso show, both sponsored by woman's best friend, Revlon. While it seemed to take a lot to impress Charles Revson, an increase in sales was all that was really necessary. For a decade, the firm's sales had been increasing at the rate of \$2,000,000 to \$3,000,000 a year, but in 1955, when the alluring Revlon girls appeared on *The \$64,000 Question,* sales rose 54 per cent, or \$19,000,000 worth; dealers sold some Revlon products at a faster pace than they could be supplied. For the Revsons, this show was no stiff.

But, as is often heard in business circles, you can't afford to stand still—you'll wind up going backward. The task of the producers of *The \$64,000 Question* was to insure that their salesman didn't stand still. This absolute necessity was made painfully plain in a series of weekly meetings held in the Revlon offices, with brother Martin in the chair, Revlon's advertising director, George J. Abrams, as his subaltern, and producers and advertising agency people in attendance. At the congressional investigation of the quiz scandals, these high-tension klatches were portrayed as grand inquisitions, with Martin Revson inflicting "picturesque" language on heretics who had departed from his dicta. The meetings, according to a producer, provided Revlon with a direct voice in "every possible phase of the show."

The brothers Revson found the congressional hearings taxing, inasmuch as Revlon's reputation, and quite possibly its sales, were at stake. A company study had disclosed that 85 per cent of persons questioned were able to associate Revlon's name with its quiz shows. Charles Revson appeared appropriately sad, therefore, when he claimed that he was "absolutely flabbergasted" to learn that both *The $64,000 Question* and the imitative *The $64,000 Challenge,* whose sponsorship Revlon had shared with P. Lorillard, had been fixed. Brother Martin insisted to congressmen that sponsor pressure never leaped the bounds of propriety. Of the producers of *Question* and *Challenge,* he said: "They had the last word on everything about the shows. If we didn't like it, there was nothing we could do about it. . . . I never suggested that a particular contestant win or lose. It never entered my mind that the producer could control the winning or losing."

But producer Merton Koplin contradicted this version as he offered a glimpse of sponsor tactics during the weekly roastings. Koplin answered the investigators' questions in this way:

Q. At any meeting, did the sponsor indicate a desire that certain contestants should continue on the program and certain should not?

A. Yes. They had definite opinions as to the value of all contestants.

Q. In what way did they manifest these desires to you?

A. They spoke glowingly of them or they criticized them. They did not like some.

Q. Did they ever say, "It would be good for the show if this contestant continued?"

A. Yes, they did.

Q. Did they ever say it would be good for the show if this contestant went off?

A. Yes.

Q. If the producer . . . did not achieve the desired result in the next program through failure of control, or your methods were too general, what was the reaction of the sponsor at the next meeting?

A. The reaction was one of extreme displeasure.

The manner of sponsor persuasion was described more philosophically, but no less explicitly, when the congressional committee heard testimony from Steven Carlin, executive producer of the two shows:

> Q. Would you say that it would have been hard, if not impossible, to say "No" to a suggestion made by Revlon, the sponsor?
>
> A. There is a tradition in television, at least to my knowledge, of trying to please the client. If you have a . . . very persuasive client, pleasing him becomes far more difficult. . . . We were willing to please the client.

Robert L. Foreman, who sat in on the Revlon meetings on behalf of Batten, Barton, Durstine & Osborn, made these facts of television life starker yet when he testified. After much shadowboxing with congressmen over precise words on which they could agree, Foreman's testimony shook down this way:

> Q. As far as you know, the sponsor did not tell the producer how long a contestant should stay on or whether he should be taken off?
>
> A. Not in those words.
>
> Q. Did he do it in some other words?
>
> A. Unless you take the implication that a good contestant should remain on and a bad contestant is not good for the show.

What was good for Revlon was good for the show. The controls that guaranteed "goodness" stemmed from a desire to get rid of contestants who had legitimate knowledge but whose personality would not attract viewers, and in their place, to populate the isolation booths with contestants who might not have the requisite knowledge but did have "audience appeal." Revlon's advertising director, George Abrams, explained the arrangement: "If a contestant was interesting, it was generally the consensus of opinion that he should continue on the show. If he was dull, we would suggest to the producer that it would be desirable that the contestant not continue in the future." The shows' producers, Abrams agreed, "did not have to be hit over the head" to get the sponsor's message.

"Interesting" contestants meant high ratings, which meant large numbers of viewers, which in turn meant high lipstick and nail polish sales. The formula worked: In 1956, Revlon's sales increased by 66 per cent over the previous big year; its net earnings after taxes were over $8,000,000, as compared with $1,300,000 in pre-quiz 1954. By 1958, Revlon's sales were $51,000,000 a year ahead of its closest competitor, whereas five years earlier the lead had been only $9,000,000. Asked if this runaway record could be attributed to the quiz-show bonanza, Martin Revson replied, "It helped. It helped."

The ratings of both *Question* and *Challenge* were treated with reverence and in minute detail at the weekly meetings in the Revlon offices. "The primary purpose of these meetings," explained ad man Abrams, "was to discuss methods of keeping the ratings high, or raising them." The show's "pull" was exhibited on wall charts that showed the week-by-week ratings and then broke them down contestant by contestant, to see who was doing the most for lip and nail.

The Revlon people "attempted to draw conclusions" from these analyses, producer Koplin testified; while some of what resulted may be written off as low comedy, it also provides clues to the behavior of humans who are bitten by the rating adder. Koplin explained:

> If we had a man with a beard on, the conclusion was that we should get more men with beards. If we had someone with an exotic category, the feeling was expressed that we should get more exotic categories. If we had a younger contestant, the cry went up that we should have a young contestant on every show.

And so it went, week by week over a period of almost three and a half years. The public was led to believe in the breathtaking wisdom of such children as Robert Strom, the "scientist," and Leonard Ross, the stock market "expert"; and in such freakish knowledge as that of Mrs. Myrt Power on baseball, Joyce Brothers on boxing, Marine Captain Richard McCutcheon on food, and policeman Redmond O'Hanlon on Shakespeare. Their encyclopedic exploits were celebrated in headline and picture; and their sweating, groaning, mumbling, and muttering were absorbed by somewhere between thirty and fifty million viewers each week.

The significance of the size of this audience, or again, market, was not lost on Daniel Enright, who had already perpetrated such spectacles as *Life Begins at Eighty,* in which octogenarians made a case for obscurity in old age, and *Juvenile Jury,* in which some young people demonstrated that they should neither be seen nor heard.

Enright was also aware, as was everyone else in the television industry, that NBC had reacted to CBS's success with *The $64,000 Question* with the grace of a predatory boy attracted to another's prize immie; it had tried to take the show away. *Variety,* observing the frantic maneuvering that commenced shortly after *Question* became successful, called it "the most fantastic criss-cross pattern and chain reaction of events . . . that vets in the business can recall." With the brothers Revson happily in the middle, network executives alternately outbid each other with offers of time slots, rates, and other enticements. The net result was that Revlon obtained the most favorable financial terms possible from CBS while NBC was left with fleck on its chin and a savage sadness in its corporate heart.

It is not known exactly when Dan Enright discovered the remedy for this condition, but a filmed dry run of his *Twenty-One* was shown in March, 1956, nine months after the première of *Question,* to representatives of Pharmaceuticals, Inc., which was also active in the remedy business. Pharmaceuticals manufactured Geritol, a balm for iron deficiency anemia ("We call it tired blood"), Zarumin, for "arthritic-like" pain, and Sominex, a sleeping tablet "like a doctor's prescription." The drug firm, which was spending approximately 40 per cent of its income on advertising, was no stranger to Enright's creativity, having sponsored both his *Life Begins at Eighty* and *Juvenile Jury* during the early 1950's.

And so, in September, 1956, the company brought *Twenty-One* to the American people, complete with *two* isolation booths (television is forever trumping aces), and with Enright's partner, Jack Barry, as master of ceremonies. More stage directions were issued and more rehearsed groaning and grunting emerged from contestants. Air-conditioning units in the solitary confinement booths were kept off and more beads of perspiration popped out on foreheads. And for over two years more people were led to the retail counters after having been emotionally drawn to shows masquerading as honest contests. Geritol was happy, Enright was overjoyed, and NBC was ecstatic. That network's glee must have become boundless, in fact, when in March, 1956, the day after Charles Van Doren was given $129,000, CBS's *The $64,000 Question* was moved to announce that it would henceforth award prizes up to $250,000 "to keep up with the trend of the times." To avoid misunderstanding, though, it should be made clear that such glee did not stem from the fact that the opposition was actually being forced to spend more money; the astronomical sums that were advertised leveled out rather modestly when subjected to budgetary pressures.

First, though, a word about our sponsor, Pharmaceuticals, Inc., which sold over $25,000,000 worth of Geritol while *Twenty-One* was on the air. Edward Kletter, the firm's advertising vice-president, was in concert with the Revson brothers in expressing confidence in the certitude of his own producer. As Charles Revson was "absolutely flabbergasted" to learn that his shows were fixed, Kletter was "shocked" to discover that *his* programs were, too. He didn't know this, he said, until he read about it in a newspaper. Asked by congressional investigators if he had ever requested that any contestant's tenure be prolonged on *Twenty-One* "because of their pulling appeal to the public," he replied, "Never." Asked if he had ever told Dan Enright, "Well, I certainly hope that so-and-so won't be on that program too long," he repeated, "Never."

When Kletter was questioned about the curious circumstances in which contestants (Van Doren, Stempel, and others) were allowed to draw advances on their prize money when they could still lose all but a consolation prize if the contest were being conducted honestly, he intimated a relationship of contestant to sponsor that most of the contestants probably would have found surprising. "I don't believe," he said, "that advances in themselves would indicate that the program was fixed in any way, no more than if an employee would come to me and say, 'I would like an advance on my salary. I need $10 more this week. Would you advance it until I get paid at the end of the month?' That is all it meant to us at that time."

Similar wordsmithing surrounded the congressional committee's generally inept attempts to get witnesses representing sponsors to agree that the quiz shows had been fixed at all. Even after countless contestants had entered their confessions, witnesses found themselves preferring the genteel word "controlled" to the down-to-earth expression "rigged." It took Dan Enright, a non-elusive man when faced with reality, to supply a definition that explained, in its first part, how *Twenty-One* was usually rigged, and in its second, how *The $64,000 Question* and *The $64,000 Challenge* were often fixed. Enright declared:

> I think it is fair to say that any process by which a contestant is given an advantage over another contestant known by the staff which produces the show is rigging. Rigging can go to the extent we did in furnishing actual questions and answers. But suppose you are a contestant . . . and you came into my office and, say, your specialty was the law, and I sat down and started to question you about the law, and made certain notations on the side as to what questions you can answer and what questions you can't answer, and then you go on the air and if I want you to continue, I will ask only the questions I know you will answer. If I want you to lose, I will ask you the questions which you can't answer.

Is that any less unfair than actually sitting down and giving you questions and answers? It amounts to the same thing.

Except in the service of melodrama, there would be little point in reconstructing what has been called this "melancholy business," unless it had some greater meaning. That meaning may be found by anyone who cares to ponder a question that has never been answered satisfactorily: Is it possible that the CBS and NBC television networks did not know what was going on under their noses for three years?

The presidents of these networks testified that this was actually the case. CBS's Frank Stanton said that at least two incidents had taken place on quiz shows that moved him to ask questions of his subordinates. But when he received assurances that everything was aboveboard, he didn't expand his curiosity. Thus it was, according to the network's general attorney, Thomas K. Fisher, that CBS was not privy to the wholesale misconduct until August 8, 1958, when, oddly, it became almost the last to know.

It was on that date that the network was called by the Ted Bates advertising agency and told that charges of rigging had been leveled at the morning *Dotto* quiz show. Bates was the agency for the sponsor, the Colgate-Palmolive Company, which had heard the charge a day earlier from actor Edward Hilgemeier, Jr., who now plays his role in the story. Hilgemeier had been a stand-by contestant on *Dotto* during May, 1958, when he picked up a contestant's notebook and read answers to questions that were being asked on the air at that moment. When the show ended, he shared his discovery with the young woman who had been defeated by the owner of the notebook, and together they confronted the producers, who at first expressed both amazement and chagrin that such an unfortunate incident had occurred. After prolonged and bitter negotiation, Hilgemeier was paid $1,500 as a settlement for what he considered to be unfair treatment, but by that time he had become incensed enough to reveal the story to a reporter for the *New York Post,* and to submit an affidavit to the Federal Communications Commission. When the FCC's response appeared to him to be a "cold shoulder," he said, he took his affidavit to Colgate-Palmolive, where a lather developed that ended in calls to the advertising agency and to CBS; a week later *Dotto* was canceled.

CBS then embarked on an investigation of other quiz shows on its network; borrowing a page from Perry Mason, or Peter Gunn, or perhaps Mike Hammer, it also called in a private eye. With his assistance, other discrepancies were found, including a machine rigged so that contestants on *For Love or Money* had almost no chance of winning the advertised amount in prizes.

At NBC, comprehension of the true nature of the quiz-show frauds remained on an even lower level. When NBC's nighttime version of *Dotto* was also canceled by Colgate-Palmolive, the network opened an investigation of its other quiz shows in a demonstration of the power of self-policing. A former FBI man was placed in charge of the examination, and according to Robert E. Kintner, NBC's president, he "made a detailed survey of the procedures used in these shows—how contestants were selected, how questions and answers were processed, who had contact with the contestants, and the like."

Although it seemed that everything was thrown into the investigation but J. Edgar Hoover and Allen Dulles, the remarkable finding was reached, on its conclusion, that there was "no evidence of any improprieties in the programs."

As of late August, 1958, therefore, the only casualty to the networks' quiz-show bonanza was *Dotto,* a relatively minor nugget. The rich lode, containing *Question, Challenge,* and *Twenty-One,* was still being mined.

But on August 28, Herbert Stempel, Dan Enright's disaffected answer man, dropped the bomb whose echoes are still tormenting the television industry. He recounted for the newspapers the entire story of his participation in the rigging of *Twenty-One*. And when he revealed that he had been under orders to lose to Charles Van Doren, the intellectual kingdom's self-appointed ambassador to the great unwashed, the days of the quiz shows became numbered. Desperate efforts were made to save them, though, and as a result, viewers of *Twenty-One* were exposed one night to one of television's most peculiar spectaculars. With NBC's permission, Jack Barry announced:

> Before the program starts, there is something I must say to all of you. I am talking about the stories that you have read attacking my partner, Dan Enright, and me. All I want to say is this:
>
> The stories are wholly untrue. I repeat, they are wholly untrue. At no time has any contestant ever been given advance information about any questions ever used on this program . . . we have not betrayed your trust in us. We never will.

But when the district attorney of New York County announced that a grand jury would investigate the mess, and more contestants revealed that they had been rigged, the shows were plainly marked for extinction. First to go was *Challenge* (which was canceled by CBS just before it was to jump to NBC), then *Twenty-One*, which NBC had bought from Barry & Enright for over $2,000,000; and finally, the model for programming copycats, *The $64,000 Question*. (A postscript for Louis G. Cowan, originator of *Question*, was his ouster, a year later, as head of the CBS television network.)

Despite this rather striking chronology, NBC's Robert Kintner was able to say of the congressional investigation that opened *over a year after these revelations:* "These hearings gave the public, and also NBC, the first established evidence of quiz-show rigging."

One congressman found declarations of this kind too much for his composure. Peter F. Mack of Illinois told Kintner bluntly: "I personally cannot believe that you, with all of your experience, could serve in television and radio work for this length of time and not know what was going on."

Others may decide for themselves, but in doing so it is not necessary to become bogged in various dates of August, 1958, the month in which most network executives said they first learned of quiz-show irregularities. If anyone wanted to look for a fire in his own home, smoke signals were evident as much as sixteen months earlier:

1. In the April 22, 1957, issue of *Time,* the lead article in the television section was entitled "The $60 Million Question," and the opening sentence asked, "Are the quiz shows rigged?" *Time* did not yet know the extent of the corruption, but it did venture to say, "The producers of many shows control the outcome as closely as they dare—without collusion with contestants, yet far more effectively than most viewers suspect."

CBS's Stanton said he had not seen this article; he was out of the country at the time and no one called it to his attention when he returned. Kintner and all of his associates must have missed that issue of *Time,* too, because he said he did not read the article and it was not mentioned to him.

2. At about the same time, Harriet Van Horne, television columnist of the New York *World-Telegram and Sun,* interviewed a former producer of *The $64,000 Question,* and wrote that the show was controlled. CBS interrogated neither the producers nor any of the celebrated contestants who had appeared on the program.

3. In the August 20, 1957, issue of *Look,* the title of an article asked, "Are TV Quiz Shows Fixed?" This article, although it discussed shows then appearing on the networks, also escaped the attention of both Stanton and Kintner and, presumably, any of their associates who might have mentioned it.

4. In September, 1957, Stempel told his story to the New

York *Journal-American.* Dan Enright, learning of this and employing offense as defense, informed two NBC vice-presidents of the possibility that a derogatory story would appear, at the same time denying Stempel's charges and implying that the contestant was unbalanced. The vice-presidents notified NBC's legal department and another meeting was held with Enright.

Shortly afterward, when the newspaper shied from the story, out of a fear of libel action, it is supposed, the vice-presidents dropped the matter. "Our NBC staff people," Kintner said, "wrote off the incident as the claim of an eccentric and did not report it to Mr. Robert Sarnoff, chairman of the board of NBC, or to me."

Those were the most discernible smoke signals, but were they even needed? Dan Enright found it difficult to assume that television industry sophisticates would not realize that "controls" were being used. And Robert Foreman, BBD&O's representative on *The $64,000 Question* for almost two years, said he always "assumed they had certain controls which they could exercise." (In 1958, a novel by Foreman, *The Hot Half Hour,* told how an advertising agency official explained "controls" to the planner of a "spontaneous" quiz show: "You've control over the questions, the contestants, the timing, the spacing of the contestants, and therefore, as complete control over the results as does the director of a dramatic show.")

In view of all this, from what source did the startling ignorance of the network officials spring? Many attempts have been made to answer this question. A congressman tried, for example, by asking a witness if he thought "the executives of CBS were aware of the fact that a wee bit of dishonesty would make them more money?"

A publicity man for *Twenty-One* had an engaging theory of why NBC did not act more quickly than it did: "Well, it struck me then as sort of a situation where a husband may suspect a wife, but he loves her too much to even want to really know. . . . NBC loved Barry & Enright in those days."

A producer had a simpler explanation. "No one seemed to care," he said.

The critical question of the networks' responsibility would probably recede in importance if their presidents had indicated a realization of their own guilt in catering to a lust for loot, which is what the quiz-show sickness represented. But one of the industry's early actions after the congressional hearings ended was the retention of Elmo Roper, the public opinion surveyor, to find out how much of a black eye television had sustained in the debacle. Roper did his field work in a week's time and returned the reassuring verdict that people were "properly critical of abuses but they have not lost confidence in the medium as a whole." He also predicted that "barring some other disclosures of other kinds of misconduct, the number of people critical of television will be reduced six months or a year from now." Then he appeared before the Federal Communications Commission in Washington and testified:

> Perhaps the public is more aware than they have been given credit for of the fact that most of the headlines they have been reading about dishonesty in television have been in newspapers, and they recognize newspapers as being locked in a violent competitive struggle with television for the advertising dollar. . . .

This view was not shared, however, by Walter Lippmann, the eminent columnist who could not easily be labeled as a competitor's hatchet man. Lippmann thought there was much more to the exposé than jealousy. "Television," he said, "has been caught perpetrating a fraud which is so gigantic that it calls into question the foundations of the industry. . . . There has been, in fact, an enormous conspiracy to deceive the public in order to sell profitable advertising to the sponsors."

A similar view was expounded in some of the harshest words of the congressional investigation when Representative Walter Rogers of Texas told a witness:

> No one realizes more than I do that some people would very well destroy this government in order to earn a dollar, and when you talk about letting those people self-discipline themselves, it is like making an agreement with a bunch of tigers not to eat a bunch of lambs, and then going off and leaving them. . . . They will do everything they can to make a dollar and it has been exhibited on this witness stand by everyone that has appeared. . . .

The television industry has done little of a convincing nature to indicate that Congressman Rogers was overstating the case. This despite the fact that warm hearts were prepared to believe the best. Harriet Van Horne, for one, wrote, "If nothing else emerges from the scandals, you can bet some new programs will—high-minded, high-budgeted programs aimed to the discriminating audience that began to snap off the set long before the scandals and subsequent mass revulsion." A year and a half later, Miss Van Horne was totally disenchanted: "Boy, was I a fool to believe the pious declarations made by the networks. I thought they'd have the decency to make amends for the lives they shattered with their sordid schemes that even involved children. The most disgraceful part of the whole thing is that the top executives learned absolutely nothing. . . ."

3 THE MEDDLERS

"It's the better part of valor to avoid controversy."—Gail Smith, director of advertising and research, General Motors Corporation.

When the quiz-show scandals erupted in 1958, the television networks hurried most of their counterfeits off the air. "Look, public," the broadcasters exclaimed, "clean hands! *Cleaner* than clean!"

But all that had been scrubbed up were television's fingernails; its soul had escaped purification. As a result, the vast majority of today's entertainment programs are just as fixed, rigged, or "controlled," as were *Twenty-One* and *The $64,000 Question.*

An astounding contention? Perhaps; but no television executive waits in dread of his indictment. District attorneys and congressional committees are prone to investigate the superficial and currently sensational, which is one reason why fraud has become so deeply embedded in our broadcasting.

If fraud consists of "an intentional perversion of truth to induce another to part with some valuable thing," as the dictionary says, then that word is fitting and irreplaceable, and there is no more authoritative starting point, in presenting evidence of such deception, than with the words of Frank Stanton, president of the Columbia Broadcasting System.

Many hopeful auditors of television were cheered when Stanton enunciated a broadcaster's Declaration of Integrity at the peak of the quiz-show debacle in October, 1959. He revealed then that his company was "taking a fresh, hard look at our basic operational theories and practices as they affect the whole pattern of everything that appears on the CBS television network—and I mean everything."

Shortly afterward, when Stanton testified during the congressional investigation of quiz-show rigging, he was even more specific, comprehensive, and encouraging. Every television program, he said, "must clearly be what it appears to be." Again Stanton closed up the loopholes. "The test in every case," he said, "must be whether any substantial number of the viewing audience is likely, in the given circumstances, to be deceived or misled as to the true nature of the program being offered."

Less than two weeks later, James T. Aubrey, Jr., head of the CBS television network, issued a memo ("To: The Organization") in which he translated Stanton's brave credo into working rules. At the same time, he declared that he would not be content to rely on rules alone. "The issuance of memoranda and the observance of the rules embodied in them," Aubrey pointed out, "cannot be considered as the full measure of the responsibility and obligations of those concerned with programming. The only true assurance is an affirmative philosophy among all persons concerned that all programs, no matter what their type, must have integrity and respect for the viewer."

Considering the sharply competitive relationship between CBS and the National Broadcasting Company, it would be grossly unfair to imply that NBC did not also leap to the task of fumigating the Augean stables. Despite some standard blatherskite about the tremendous accomplishments of his television network, President Robert E. Kintner assured congressmen: "We intend to safeguard the integrity of our service by all possible measures. . . ." He pledged NBC's vigilance toward "any area of possible deceptive practices in our programs or broadcast operations," and he revealed that he and ever-watchful Robert Sarnoff had established a policing agency to root out deception. "Finally," Kintner said, "I earnestly express the hope that the incidents of quiz-show rigging, which were utterly without conscience, will not be regarded as representative of the television business as a whole."

On the day that Frank Stanton issued his declaration, and on the days that he and Robert Kintner testified, the television industry was deceiving the public. Most of the programs transmitted by CBS, NBC, and the American Broadcasting Company, and carried by their hundreds of affiliated stations, were not at all what they appeared to be. A substantial portion of the viewing audience was deceived because it was not aware that these programs were rigged either by advertisers and advertising agencies or by the networks themselves on behalf of those clients.

Never before has entertainment been so thoroughly and painstakingly doctored so that huge numbers of people can be manipulated to perform a desired function—in this case the dutiful purchase of advertised goods. The job is done by those whom Marya Mannes has called the "intruders," who "come between nearly every program the broadcasters put on television and the viewing public."

The manipulation of the audience has as its goal the mass conditioning of a people—a process that can take place only in a carefully constructed fantasy-land which is devoid of racial, religious, and political problems; and of unemployment, sickness, and other depressing conditions. It is a land of scrubbed-up, faceless somnambulists, rather than one of Americans who have been striving for scores of years to find solutions to these very problems. This anomaly does not seem to concern sponsors, who, in fact, are aggressively outspoken about their purposes. Gail Smith, director of advertising and research for General Motors, has been explicit in explaining why his firm opposes querulousness and favors joy. "We're interested in maintaining the good will of all the viewers and we see no reason why we should jeopardize this good will," he said. "It's the better part of valor to avoid controversy." Not to be outdone, Smith's opposite number at the Chrysler Corporation, R. E. Forbes, has come out four-square for programs with a "good climate." He dislikes shows that might create a "wrong commercial mood."

Altogether, these methods make up what only a broadcaster, an advertising man, or a quibbler could deny is commercial brainwashing—or, to be precise, fraud.

People who still read are by now familiar with anecdotes that illustrate meddling by sponsors. National jokes have been inspired by Chrysler's reluctance to allow mention of a man named L – – – – – – – (he signed the Emancipation Proclamation), by Westinghouse's distate for Rudyard Kipling's thoughtless title, "The L – – – – – That Failed," by the cigarette maker who recoiled at the word camel, and by a competitor who regarded *lucky* as a dirty word and would not even allow a character to ask, "Are you an American?" To these specimens of corporate thought may now be added General Electric's objection to a photograph of Franklin D. Roosevelt in a drama set in the depression days of the 1930's, and General Mills's ban against references to " 'competitive' horses such as 'Trigger,' 'Silver,' et al." Lest we forget, too, the Aluminum Company of America transformed the locale of an unhappy drama from a "mobile home atmosphere" to a "shantytown," and a cigarette-sponsored segment of *Do You Trust Your Wife?* was re-filmed because a man, asked his wife's astrological sign, replied, "Cancer." In the new version, the reply was, "Aries."

Many of Madison Avenue's finest are willing to extend largesse in such cases and concede that big sponsors sometimes act like small boys. But that is about all the largesse that is available. When a vice-president of the Ted Bates advertising agency testified before the Federal Communications Commission, he dismissed these monstrosities as "merely little taboos" that did not affect "the quality of the script." But as he rambled on, he revealed the mentality of people who are capable of such tinkering. He told of two cigarette firms that sponsored similar programs. One sponsor, the ad man explained, manufactured a filter cigarette, "and his policy indicated that the heavy must smoke *non*-filter cigarettes."

"The heavies are villains?" he was asked.

"Villains," he said. "Whereas, the manufacturer of the non-filter cigarette insisted that the heavy smoke a *filter* cigarette. It sounds ridiculous, but it's not at all. . . . The association of a product . . . with a villain, a murderer, or whatever, is certainly something to be avoided."

Another ad man explained: "We review scripts in advance for violations of company policy. For example, if a sponsor's product is sold in supermarkets, we would not want the villain to be a supermarket manager."

A vice-president of Compton Advertising, a veteran Procter & Gamble agency, went further. ". . . if you have a client who sells bulk soap to laundries," he said, "you don't put on a show which shows a laundry carefully tearing buttons off shirts—the laundries don't like it; if you are selling boxed shortening to bakers, you don't put on a show which shows nefarious bakers who poisoned bread—bakers don't like that. Similarly, if you have an automobile client, you scarcely put on a show in which the oil is shown to be of horrible quality so that machinery grinds to a halt halfway across the Atlantic. These seem to be obvious, but they aren't. I have known all three to happen in my own agency, passed by my own associates who didn't know they would be offensive to people who are major customers and clients."

Some of these examples may amuse, in a vinegary way, but at a certain point their implications become only grim. That point arrives when the networks submit to sponsors who must believe that the American people are senseless. The public, as Newton Minow has said, is "treated with contempt." A case in point involves the much publicized incident (Frank Stanton later called it a "regrettable mistake") that marred the drama, "Judgment at Nuremberg," an episode of CBS's deceased *Playhouse 90* series.

The play dealt with the trials of German judges who had lent the weight of their offices to the Nazis' extermination campaign against Jews. In the course of the drama, a leading character shouted his scorn for the jurists who had helped send innocent men and women into gas ovens. But instead of the words "gas ovens," the home audience heard only silence. A sound engineer had spiked the audio portion of the program just long enough to delete the phrase. Many persons who noticed the interruption regarded it as an electronic lapse, but the truth soon emerged. The sponsor, the American Gas Association, had censored the words "gas ovens" on grounds that the Nazis had used cyanide gas, not cooking gas.

Nicholas E. Keesely, a senior vice-president of the Lennen & Newell advertising agency, which handled "Judgment at Nuremberg" for the gas association, subsequently gave this version of the incident:

> In going through the scripts, we noticed gas referred to in a half dozen places that had to do with the death chambers. This was just an oversight on somebody's part. We deal with a lot of artistic people in the creative end, and sometimes they do not have the commercial judgment, or see things as we are paid to see [them], and we raised the point with CBS and they said they would remove the word 'gas,' and we thought they would, and they did in some cases, and at the last minute we found that there were some still left in. As a result—and this was just, I think, stupidity—the show went on the air, where the word 'gas' was deleted by the engineer rather than rehearsing the talent.

The ad man pointed out that "this didn't change anything as far as the plot was concerned," and, unfortunately, most criticism of the incident has focused on this razor-edged point. What the gas association's action revealed, as a symbol of sponsor attitudes, was its incredible fear that if the American people thought Hitler had used cooking gas, they would cook all future hamburgers on electric stoves.

The gas association's exhibition of panic was duplicated when the du Pont company was told that one of its shows had committed a grave offense. In this drama, flowers were waived in favor of a scholarship fund for a boy who had been killed; the National Florist Association objected to this threat to the institution of flower-laden funerals, and the National Florist Association buys cellophane from du Pont. When Selig Seligman, a vice-president of the ABC network, was subsequently asked: "Should the American public be deprived of this story because the Flower Association objects?" he replied that "if the sponsor feels it hurts the image he's trying to accomplish to sell his product, it should be deprived." And du Pont has since declared that television programming "has suffered not through too much [sponsor] acceptance of responsibility, but too little."

Responsibility is one of the most elastic phrases in the television business, and du Pont is expert in the field of elastics. It can be counted on to apply pressure against "sad and stressful" programs, which is what it called *Ethan Frome,* a drama it sponsored and which, it said, "did not make as effective an environment for commercials as more pleasant vehicles, such as *Harvey.*"

Other euphemisms for censorship are rampant in the business, chief among them being "good taste," "good judgment," and "business policy." But as a congressman once remarked to Revlon's Charles Revson, quiz-show sponsor and advocate of a heavy advertiser's hand, "There has never been an act of censorship committed without someone feeling that he was exercising good judgment." When Revson preferred the phrase "opportunity to suggest," the congressman retorted: "The suggestion from the man who pays the bill, you must admit, has a certain persuasive ring to it, does it not?" Revson didn't agree. Not long afterward, he used the "opportunity to suggest" in dealing with Harry Belafonte; the singer's relations with Revson were quickly terminated. And as for Revlon's conception of "business policy," it discourages the depiction of a druggist as a narcotics user or of a prostitute as an excessive user of facial make-up.

Television producers who are given to defending The System point to instances in which they have successfully resisted the sponsor or his ad agency lieutenants, but their anecdotes are not very heavy when weighed against the ad men's matter-of-fact comments on the fate of un-cooperative producers. C. Terence Clyne, when he was senior vice-president of the McCann-Erickson agency, revealed that when a producer balks, "We simply do not renew that program. In most cases, that show goes off the air."

But clash and gnash between front office and assembly line is hardly the rule, as NBC's executive vice-president, Walter Scott, has indicated. Since the producers who grind out the series "know what these problem areas are," Scott said, "they represent no hardships."

To remove nagging doubt from producers' and writers' lives, some advertisers promulgate censorship manuals that cover every situation that might occur in this life and the next. Procter & Gamble, television's No. 1 sponsor, is the most diligent disseminator of these taboo lists, which are guaranteed to kill a decent script on contact. This should surprise no one who is familiar with the background of Cincinnati's favorite company. P&G has always aspired to be all things to all men, all women, all children, and any animals with enough money to buy soap. One of its turn-of-the-century advertisements for I – – – – showed a well-dressed matron at a store counter with a tattered old granny behind her; the caption read: "It knows no class distinction. The rich find it most satisfactory, the poor the most economical." P&G is out to cleanse the world, and, in the words of a trade magazine, is "convinced that television was invented for it, and has acted accordingly." As might be expected of the medium's heaviest financial supporter, it enforces its "Editorial Policy," a staggering collection of taboos, with meticulous care; this policy prevents P&G entertainment from descending into sloppy entanglements with reality. Behold excerpts from the carved-soap tablets:

> Material dealing with sex perversion, miscegenation and rape is banned.
>
> Ministers, priests, and similar representatives of positive social forces shall not be cast as villains or represented as committing a crime or be placed in any unsympathetic or antisocial role.
>
> If it is necessary in the development of conflict for a character to attack some basic conception of the American way of life, e.g., freedom of speech, freedom of worship, etc., answer must be completely and convincingly made some place in the broadcast.
>
> There will be no material that may give offense, either directly or by inference, to any organized minority group, lodge, or other organizations, institutions, residents of any state or section of the country, or a commercial organization of any sort. This will be taken to include political organizations, fraternal organizations, college and school groups, labor groups, industrial, business and professional organizations, religious orders, civic clubs, memorial and patriotic societies, philanthropic and reform societies (Anti-Tobacco League, for example), athletic organizations, women's groups, etc. . . .
>
> There will be no material for or against sharply drawn national or regional controversial issues.
>
> We will treat mention of the Civil War carefully, mindful of the sensitiveness of the South on this subject.
>
> No written material may be used that might give offense to our Canadian neighbors for any uniquely national reason, e.g., facetious reference to British royalty. . . .
>
> Men in uniform shall not be cast as heavy villains or portrayed as engaging in any criminal activity.
>
> There will be no material on any of our programs which could in any way further the concept of business as cold, ruthless, and lacking all sentiment or spiritual motivation. If a businessman is cast in the role of a villain, it must be made

clear that he is not typical, but is as much despised by his fellow businessmen as he is by other members of society.

Special attention shall be given to *any* mention, however innocuous, of the grocery and drug business, as well as any other group of customers of the company. This includes industrial users of the company's products, such as bakeries, restaurants and laundries.

For obvious reasons, it is essential that no statements be made on any of our shows which could be construed as being unfavorable to any special group of the company's customers or which would favor one type of customer over another. For example, no reference should be made to any difference in the prices charged by supermarkets as compared to independents or to the economy of using laundromats instead of regular commercial laundries.

If there is any question whatever about such material, it should be deleted.

When Albert N. Halverstadt, Procter & Gamble's general advertising manager, was asked to comment on the far-ranging jurisdiction of this code of censorship, he said that "although this may seem to be quite broad and comprehensive, we make no apology for that, and if there are other groups that should be included here, I'd be happy to add them."

This is a time for wholehearted admiration; without a doubt, the Soap God has writ what may be the most remarkable document since the first Roman Index. From Mount Cincinnati, it has decreed that love and marriage between whites and Asians, or Bantus and Arabs, is to be lumped with carnal lust in the minds of television writers. It has ruled that all clergymen have attained the ultimate state of grace and cannot stumble, that every facet of American life is beyond reproach, that bitter divisions do not exist in the United States, that slavery is an occasion for soft-shoe stepping in the twentieth century, that members of the armed forces never break laws, and that P&G's colleagues in commerce are to be immune from snickers. Altogether, this answers the question of what one can expect in return for being "reasonable" about the right of a sponsor to apply his concepts of "good taste" and "business policy" to our entertainment. Yet, when James T. Aubrey, Jr., head of the CBS television network, was asked if he thought the P&G taboo list "encourages the creative urge in television," he replied, "I don't think it *dis*courages the creative urge in television."

P&G's vacuum-cleaned version of life is so attractive to other sponsors that it has become an informal model in the world of television taboo. General Mills and General Motors use modified versions of the document to guide their program creators, deleting and substituting phrases where their specific problems differ. Thus, General Mills calls for "special attention" to be given not to the grocery and drug business, but to the baking business, and adds a fragment of its own philosophy: "... the moral code of the characters in our dramas will be more or less synonymous with the moral code of the bulk of the American middle class, as it is commonly understood."

Sponsor meddling takes other forms, too. Writer-producer Robert Alan Aurthur has revealed that he presented *What Makes Sammy Run?* in four acts instead of three because a P&G advertising agency wanted more interruptions in which to use commercials for Crest Tooth Paste. Aurthur recalled "begging them not to do it" and being rebuffed. "As I looked into their cold, slitted eyes," he said, "I knew I was fighting a losing fight, because, as they told me, the Crest story was very important, but I wondered why it wasn't advertised, for example, 'Tonight, at 8 o'clock, we present the Crest story.'"

If such travesties depress creative people, they had better not seek sympathy in television's executive suites. Mort Werner, NBC's programming vice-president, says matter of factly that in entertainment programs "we have always gone on the theory that the man who pays the bills has a right to some voice in shaping the product." And Frank Stanton feels that "there are blessings to be had from some of the outside help we've had ... from advertisers and advertising agencies."

It seems almost ungracious to single out P&G for so much comment when it departs from general sponsor methodology only by being explicit, but the company's record is useful in tracing the decline of television. "It has been suggested, in fact," said a trade magazine in 1960, "that the history of P&G over the past ten years is the history of television." The medium's decline has occurred in fairly direct ratio to the increasing investment of major advertisers since 1950, and P&G's own spending illustrates the point:

	Advertising Budget	*Television Budget*	*% to Television*
1950	$ 33,500,000	$ 570,000	1.7
1951	46,228,000	7,579,000	18.5
1952	44,971,000	14,204,000	31.2
1953	43,675,000	14,790,000	33.8
1954	49,316,000	23,701,000	40.8
1955	56,716,000	38,822,000	68.4
1956	78,975,000	60,979,000	77.2
1957	90,439,000	72,962,000	80.6
1958	98,592,000	84,471,000	85.7
1959	105,617,000	95,340,000	90.3
1960	109,562,745	101,491,119	92.6

Other advertisers emulated the acknowledged master of marketing, and their influence grew with the rising total of their cumulative investment. When the big money began to pour in during the early 1950's, more and more thought was directed to the problem of insuring the gamble; by 1953, the networks had made their key decision to surrender a large part of the medium to Hollywood, where entertainment could be placed on film for scrutiny before airing, and where, moreover, it could be controlled in every conceivable way before a single foot of film was shot. Accidents happen only in live television.

The product of this policy is melted mental cheese, which seeps into every corner of television. Everything must be standardized, no disturbing thoughts are allowed, all hail to non-think. Observe this exchange between an attorney for the Federal Communications Commission and a senior vice-president of the McCann-Erickson advertising agency:

Would it be true that a program which raises issues that would be displeasing to some part of the audience would not normally be chosen by you as a vehicle for national television advertising?

Yes.

In other words, there is a limit to the subject matter?

Correct.

You're not in the business of just pleasing any considerable segment of the national audience, is that correct?

That's right.

The result? The tempted Reverend Mr. Davidson of Somerset Maugham's *Rain* was transformed into an unidentifiable politician. Steve Allen might have miffed someone, somewhere, by recommending thought-provoking books, or by his opposition to radioactive fallout, so an auto sponsor became disenchanted with him and his show died. Mort Sahl made jokes about matters other than women's hats, so a tooth paste maker worried that he might create a "bad product image." *The Play of the Week* might have provoked irritation among a pap-conditioned audience, so soap commercials were canceled. The Armstrong Cork Company decided that a program dealing with atomic-bomb destruction might cause "panic," so it was suppressed by the *Armstrong Circle Theater.* General Motors of Canada objected to a stark, moving play about a lynching and withdrew its sponsorship; the Canadian Broadcasting Corporation presented the drama anyway, without GM's sponsorship. And when Kitchens of Sara Lee sponsored a folk music special over a Chicago station, Josh White was not allowed to sing a song about integration, "Free and Equal Blues." Director William Friedkin withdrew and removed his name from the show's credits. "They gave all kinds of reasons for wanting the number removed," he told *Variety,* "but it is obvious why they wanted it cut. I've got to live with myself, and to put up with this kind of thing is to me an ugly way to make money."

Permitting sponsors to act as thought controllers is also an ugly way to run television.

4 THE NATIONAL PACIFIER

"They want a strong, hard-hitting, controversial show that won't offend anybody."—Audrey Gellen, television producer.

Now, from the conditioning laboratories of the merchant princes, comes a new method of banishing sponsor pain! An operation on the truth to remove its intestines! This method has been proved successful in case after case! Watch closely:

A painful historical incident was removed from the *American Heritage* series, sponsored by the Equitable Life Assurance Society, because an advertising agency feared that the truth might offend an Equitable official. The program was to depict the colorful life of industrialist Andrew Carnegie, who, whatever his faults, never allowed a committee to dehydrate his bluntness. The script recorded an uncomplimentary remark Carnegie had directed against John D. Rockefeller, but, in one of those coincidences that crop up under The System, it developed that one of Equitable's current directors was Donald Rockefeller, a grandson of John D. So Carnegie's remark was excised, the head of the ad agency's television department explained, "because it was just good business, not going out of your way to knock the grandfather of one of the men who was paying for the show."

Other insurance companies are interested in history, too. A Prudential vice-president, Henry M. Kennedy, conceded that when it sponsored *You Are There,* there were "controversial" subjects it disliked. As examples of "controversy," Kennedy referred to themes "with a religious or social bias"—a vague phrase which gathered meaning when it was amplified. "We were thinking of doing a show on the bank holiday of 1933," Kennedy said. "But we decided against it because it might cast doubt on all financial institutions. And today all financial institutions are in pretty good shape."

In late September or early October, when America turns its attention to its national game, baseball, might viewers not be interested in a recapitulation of a historic event, the Black Sox scandal of 1919? They might, but the R. J. Reynolds Company wasn't. Reynolds, makers of Camel cigarettes, which sponsors many baseball broadcasts, "didn't see any good in reviving anything as old as that," according to Sam Northcross, vice-president of Reynolds' advertising agency, William Esty. When the re-creation appeared on *Witness,* a series Reynolds was sponsoring, the firm withdrew its commercials and financial support. Are you smoking more and enjoying it less?

The product is mightier even than the sword. As far as television sponsors are concerned, for example, there was no Civil War. Jack Gould, television critic of the *New York Times,* has indicated why: "From the advertiser's point of view the problem is not simply one of giving equal time to the Blue and Gray. All that is required to precipitate an office crisis is a mere mention of the war's resolution. If it is indicated that the North did win, some sensitivities in the South, especially in light of today's difficulties, may be rubbed raw. And the purchasing power of every Southern viewer must be nurtured and solicited. . . . The upshot is that practically all significant TV plans for commemorating the Civil War have been quietly shelved."

The war *was* celebrated, though; NBC did it by throwing

out one historic fairy tale to make room for another. The casualty was a deadly Hollywood series known as *Riverboat,* which depicted life on Mark Twain's Mississippi; the show operated under a rule that no Negroes were ever to be seen, and none were. From MGM, the producer of this Caucasian epic, NBC bought *The Americans,* a Southern western that pictured the slavery conflict as an unfortunate falling out between two otherwise devoted brothers. It was never made crystal clear what Ben and Jeff Canfield's real differences were, although through many tiresome episodes they fought on opposing sides in what *Variety* called "something approximating a 'Rover Boys at War,' a wholly fictional and unbelievable sequence of events that could just as easily have come out of a *Bonanza* or an *Outlaws.*"

If such dime-novel drama hides the significance of the Civil War from young viewers, the effect of sponsor control over important current events—the history of today—is worth assessing. It has not been so long, after all, since an advertiser objected to Alexander Woollcott's radio program, *Town Crier,* because Woollcott chanced offending some listeners with his criticisms of Hitler and Mussolini; the program was killed. The modern problem has been illuminated by William Dozier, a vice-president of Screen Gems, Columbia Pictures' television adjunct. Dozier recalled a program dealing with a political theme to which a sponsor objected "inasmuch as he was selling products to members of both political parties. . . . He did not want to alienate either group." Therefore, it was a matter of policy, he said, "that we should not do this particular show, because the character in it might be identified either as a Republican or a Democrat."

In dealing with social, rather than specifically political, problems, sponsor sensitivities are at their peak. Max Banzhaf, advertising vice-president of the Armstrong Cork Company and a vigorous defender of sponsor "responsibility," told me of an encounter he had with a writer whose treatment of a sex theme Banzhaf considered "indecent":

"I told him, 'You think television is an art form. You say I'm keeping you from expressing yourself. If you feel that way, go to the Broadway theater. Television is too intrusive. It is a guest in millions of living rooms. You have to act as a guest should.'

"That," Banzhaf explained, "is why I want the right of censorship."

If one were tempted again to be "reasonable" and concede the right of censorship to sponsors in *some* cases, it is not difficult, when Banzhaf demonstrates his exercise of the right of censorship, to see that such a concession would be fatal. He related another vivid conversation:

"An interviewer told me: 'They say you won't do controversial subjects on the *Circle Theater*. Will you?'

"I said, 'Yes.'

" 'Will you do a show about segregation?'

"I said, 'No.'

" 'But you said you'd do controversy. Why won't you do segregation?'

"I replied, 'Because with heads being broken and riots taking place, why inflame people more? What good purpose would it serve?' "

Banzhaf summed up: "There are too many irresponsible people in television."

The Southern market for goods and services has remained untouchable even in face of a lynching that shocked the nation. Writer Rod Serling tried over a three-year period to draw a dramatic moral from the 1955 kidnap-murder of Emmett Till, a fourteen-year-old Negro who had allegedly whistled at a white woman in Mississippi. In 1956, Serling dramatized an epitaph to Till in a play called, "Noon on Doomsday," for the *United States Steel Hour*. He recalled that he first took the idea to the show's producer, The Theatre Guild, where president Lawrence Langner told him, he said, "I think you have here the bone structure of a very effective television play, and I don't think you are going to have to dilute it at all. The only problem is that you can't make it black and white." A practical man in face of such minor adversity, Serling took his idea home and fashioned an all-white version of the Negro's lynching in which the victim was Jewish. Then, about a week after he submitted his script, he said, "all hell broke loose. I got a call to come to New York immediately. I went into the offices and everyone in the Theatre Guild was there. . . . Also present was a representative of the agency handling the U.S. Steel account [Batten, Barton, Durstine & Osborn]. They looked at me with blanched features and said, 'You know, the whole thing must be completely altered.'" And when the massive Steel-BBD&O-Theatre Guild homogenizing committee sheathed its merchandising machetes, Mississippi had become New England, the lynching had disappeared, and, according to Serling, "the characters mouthed nothing but platitudes." U.S. Steel explained that it had improved "a pretty superficial story."

In 1958, Martin Manulis, who was executive producer of *Playhouse 90*, suggested that Serling dramatize the plight of a town torn by conscience because it had stood by while a lynching took place. Serling immediately thought of the Till case again, but was understandably bearish toward its prospects. At Manulis's urging, though, he tried once more with "A Town Has Turned to Dust." This time the Till case reached the television audience with the locale moved to the cowboy Southwest, the period changed to the hardy 1870's, and the victim no longer a Negro. The crowning touch was the obliteration of one of Serling's major thematic points. In his original script, the town's sheriff, who had allowed the lynching to take place, committed suicide because he could not live with his conscience. This moral was too realistic for the Allstate Insurance Company, one of the sponsors of *Playhouse 90;* suicides are not to be encouraged in any way. So the sheriff lost his life to a faster draw, just as he might on *Tall Man, Shotgun Slade,* or another factory-made horse opera.

Sponsors do not, of course, admit that they are Philistines

who have transformed television into a national pacifier. On the contrary, they hold a bottomless bag of defenses for their role, which they regard as benevolent at the least and noble at its best. Their position was pleasantly stated in a letter from Armstrong's Banzhaf, who said: "Frankly, I see nothing wrong with a tired businessman or an overworked housewife completely escaping from reality at the end of a hard day by watching a cowboy movie or a whodunit. It requires very little thought and it is relaxation. . . . I cannot agree with those people who would ban all such opportunities for escape. . . ." Banzhaf errs, of course, when he taxes dissenters with opposition to *all* escapism, but his stand is one of the milder on record. Robert L. Foreman, an executive vice-president of BBD&O, adopted a more injured stance when he informed a Federal Communications Commission hearing of his resentment over criticism of sponsors. "There has been an awful lot of conversation about the policies of advertisers," Foreman said, "as if this was some great cross that the public has to bear and in some way makes good programming impossible. I keep hearing this and reading it, and I know that in . . . practically one hundred per cent of the cases the advertisers' aim would be the same as I would interpret the public's . . ."

A colleague from Benton & Bowles, Thomas J. McDermott, was more informative. He believed that the general run of television fare created "a mood in which . . . the people are most prepared to accept the kind of commercials we do."

The commissioners were most edified when C. Terence Clyne, a veteran ad man, testified that the object of broadcasting was to "create as pleasant and favorable an impression on the part of as large an audience as possible for the company or product sponsoring the program." Clyne had explained earlier that "you may have a situation where a large corporation is expending a lot of dollars to bring entertainment to the viewer, and this corporation does not desire to bring such entertainment that, when it's all over, the viewer is pretty sad and depressed about the state of the world . . ."

All of which explains why television is so stuffed with what might be called "itsy-bitsy morality plays," complete with happy, "upbeat" endings. Producer Audrey Gellen documented this inclination to mush when she revealed her difficulties in presenting Horton Foote's "downbeat" play, "Night of the Storm," on du Pont's *Show of the Month.* "Getting it on was half the trouble," she said. "Then came the long letters: Couldn't you put some jokes in it? Couldn't you brighten it up? There was the watchdog attitude. They came to rehearsals. They said, 'We're going to depress people with this.'" Miss Gellen concluded: "They want a strong, hard-hitting, controversial show that won't offend anybody."

By "they," Miss Gellen was referring to BBD&O, whose executives had the text of her remarks in hand the morning after she delivered them. A BBD&O representative confirmed the agency's intervention in the Foote drama and went on to explain: "We usually handle this situation by seeing synopses beforehand. If we see one that might lead to trouble, we just avoid it. We don't let the producer and writer get into it."

To guarantee that creative people don't get off limits, most advertising agencies place men in positions that could be likened to plantation overseers. Grant Tinker, when a vice-president of Benton & Bowles, described this operation as an example of agency efficiency. "For every moment in the progress of every episode of every program, live or film, for every television client we have," he said, "there is a Benton & Bowles program department representative on hand from the first draft of the script through every stage until the final moment of air time. . . ."

Although it is obvious that the choke chain is an effective noose around the necks of television producers, writers, and entertainers, it should be said that not all sponsors are engaged in a great conspiracy to pollute the national intelligence.

Exceptions to this rule include the Standard Oil Company (New Jersey), Hallmark Cards, and Bell & Howell, firms that have been operating in television with what might be called enlightened self-interest. After Standard sponsored *The Play of the Week* in New York, and a Shakespearean series, *An Age of Kings,* in New York and Washington (which inspired 50,000 letters of appreciation), its president, M. J. Rathbone, explained that his business associates "have never demonstrated any special talent for acting or play-writing." Such work, he said, required "skill that businessmen normally do not have. Hence, we are content to leave these matters to the artists. We enjoy their good company and we feel that it is enough to have the opportunity to present our message in association with their efforts. . . ."

Hallmark Cards, which has sponsored the *Hall of Fame* series and has presented, among other good works, *Amahl and the Night Visitors, Hamlet,* and *Macbeth,* is firmly operated by a rugged individualist named Joyce Hall, who has said: "I'd rather hold the attention of 8,000,000 people than bore 28,000,000. A sponsor can't expect commercials to do a job for him if the rest of his program offends the intelligence or good taste of his audience, but a lot of advertisers overlook that principle of merchandising." Nonconforming Hall has also served notice that he'll "never sponsor a western, a private eye, or a situation comedy glamorizing idiots. I can't get a kick out of copying what forty other fellows have done. I want to look people in the eye without cringing the day after a show." And, at the risk of straining a good thing, Hall has further said: "The trouble is, too many sponsors underrate the audience's intelligence and appreciation of culture when it is well done. They forget that the rising level of education has brought a corresponding improvement in public taste. . . . I don't have a philanthropic attitude toward culture. The simple truth is that good television is good business."

And finally, Bell & Howell, which in 1959 veered from sponsorship of pap programming and has since been identified with *Close-Up,* an ABC public affairs series dealing with current events. Peter G. Peterson, the company's president, defines Bell & Howell's policy as "providing sponsorship without censorship," but its contract with ABC does call for the firm's "consultation" in the selection of subject matter. (All networks allow public affairs sponsors to "consult.") *Close-Up!* has treated some sharply controversial themes which brought threats of boycotts, but the company has stood firm. "We only ask that the network present a balanced view of the issues and the viewpoints so that the American people can better arrive at their own point of view," says Peterson.

This stimulating blend of commercial-cultural thinking is laudable; unfortunately, however, it probably causes more problems than it helps solve. First, it creates an abysmally false impression that scores of well-meaning sponsors may lie in the advertiser bins. The "package-goods" manufacturers, the pill and soap men, dominate television. They put in a mass of money for which they want mass circulation and mass sales, regardless of how these are obtained. Second, and more important, the presence of Standard, Hallmark, and Bell & Howell give weight to the disastrous notion that television will improve if advertisers become even more involved, but on a higher plane. LeRoy Collins, the tolerated president of the National Association of Broadcasters, advanced this doomed idea when he requested more "blue-chip" programming and said: ". . . those who use broadcasting as an advertising medium, and profit greatly thereby, should share more of this responsibility." And FCC Chairman Minow, in his search for an escape from the morass, does not foreclose on sponsor involvement. "Many people feel that advertisers should be separated from program content," he has said. "I haven't formed a final judgment about it, but I do know that some of the present excesses are absolutely outrageous. However, when you do see sponsors who want to do fine things, then it makes you pause and wonder whether we should discourage it."

On the other hand, the implication that sponsors should stay home and look after the inventory has come from at least one prominent businessman, Philip Cortney, president of Coty, Inc. This cosmetic manufacturer took full-page newspaper advertisements during the quiz-show investigation to suggest that sponsors keep their hands off programming. Later, he appeared before the FCC and pursued his contention:

> Q. Is it your point here . . . that as long as the sponsors have the right to affect the program material that their advertising or commercial interests will adversely affect the medium? Is that your view?
>
> A. Definitely, because to think otherwise is simply to ask men to behave like angels. . . . It is not right for us to ask that.

(Coty was and is Revlon's competitor, an awkward circumstance that might cause some observers to discount Cortney's view; but the situation is desperate and all defectors are welcome in the wasteland.)

If advertisers have used programming to manipulate the viewer, thus deceiving him "as to the true nature of the program being offered," in Frank Stanton's phrase, wouldn't an absolute rule against sponsor interference do much to rescue television? Logically, yes, for the alternative would be network control. But the networks *already* control an overwhelming majority of evening entertainment shows, which are what most people see most of the time.

Contradictory? Confusing? No doubt, but informative, too, as an illustration of the double-talk of broadcasting. Carrying over their role from radio, television advertisers once produced most of the programming, through their agencies. The networks, operating on David Sarnoff's premise that they were merely "plumbers' pipes," provided transmission facilities.

This *modus operandi* is known as agency control, under which programs are molded, tailored, censored, and butchered to suit sponsors' desires.

Around the mid-1950's, when program costs rose, advertisers began to share programs with "alternate sponsors." Costs continued to rise, leading sponsors to purchase only time; under this arrangement, several sponsors' commercials could be dropped into a show. Naturally, this led to a lessening of a *specific* sponsor's domination over shows, and an increase in the networks' power.

This method is known as network control, under which programs are still molded, tailored, censored, and butchered to suit sponsors' desires. The more things change, the more they remain the same.

For this reason, a pitched battle now being fought on Madison Avenue over network versus agency control promises to have only one loser—the viewer. It is another private dispute, a war of technicalities. If the agencies win, which is doubtful, each ad man will be free to fight for *his* client's best advantage in the advertising jungle. If the networks retain control, they will be able to thwart program raids by other networks, and they will be free to continue building evening "program blocs," the object of which, of course, is to hold onto viewers from the time they leave the dinner table to the time they stagger off to bed. More viewers equal higher ratings equal higher advertising rates—the undying formula.

There is no special cause for alarm, therefore, when BBD&O finances a Hollywood film series itself and comments: "The type of stories we would not want could be initially eliminated. . . ." Nor was there special cause for hope when Oliver Treyz, ABC's former president, said his network didn't sell time to sponsors and then accept whatever programs they sent over. "We first decide on the program," Treyz said, "then find the sponsors." For, as a vice-president of the Ted Bates agency told the FCC, "suggestions" are heeded by producers no matter who controls a program. In fact, the ad man said, it is "a little bit easier" for agency operatives to protect clients' interests under network control because "something that might slip through the agency by chance might be picked up by the network, which has a similar point of view."

"It is just a matter of judgment and interpretation," said Thomas McDermott of Benton & Bowles. "We have no problem with [taboos] because it is a matter of good sense, and most of the producers and writers, once they realize who the sponsors are, do not write these things in the scripts. I think it is that simple."

If something objectionable should find its way onto film despite all these efforts, the producing company can be counted on to delete it. As an example, William T. Orr, executive producer of Warner Brothers' television division, tells of the day he watched a film, made for a cigarette sponsor, in which a character said, "I neither drink, smoke, nor go out with girls."

"He was supposed to be a virtuous gentleman, so the indication was that these were vices," Orr explained. "We changed it before anybody ever got to us to criticize it, because we knew it was not a good business policy to fly in the face of a sponsor with a remark like that."

Some sponsors and ad men attempt to finesse their meddling by pointing out that their contracts with the networks prohibit interference with program content. This is an illusory prohibition, on the word of Dan Seymour, director of radio and television activities for the largest advertising agency in the world, J. Walter Thompson. "By and large," he testified before the FCC, "most contracts . . . do not give the agencies the formal right to change the material in the script. However, we are in a co-operative business, all of us trying to serve the same end, and this is to put on the best possible entertainment we can. . . . In the initial stage, when a script is given to our representatives, we will find areas that we believe are not in the interest of our clients. We will so note them, send them back to the producer, or meet with him, and in the constant give and take of daily activities, we are able to delete by and large the kind of material that we think is not to our best interest. This happens on dramatic show after dramatic show. . . . We are in the advertising business. We are on the air to sell our products."

This "creative interference" is made possible by another feature of The System that might be called "interlock," through which executive personnel of television networks, Hollywood companies, and advertising agencies become interchangeable. Sylvester L. Weaver directed advertising for the American Tobacco Company before he became president of NBC, later went to the McCann-Erickson advertising agency; Thomas J. McDermott moved from Benton & Bowles to Four Star Films in Hollywood, William Dozier from CBS to Screen Gems, Thomas McAvity from NBC to J. Walter Thompson, Peter Levathes from Young & Rubicam to Twentieth Century-Fox television, Jack van Volkenburg from CBS to McCann-Erickson. Mort Werner went from NBC to Young & Rubicam and back to NBC, whereupon he sent for Grant Tinker from Benton & Bowles.

Like all professionals, the players in this game of switch-hat have worked out a number of explanations of why they do what they do. When asked why advertisers should have anything to do with programming, they will reply that viewers hold the sponsor, not the network or station, responsible for the content of television shows. If this is indeed the case, the problem is surely not impossible of solution; many solutions, in fact, have been suggested. One involves the "magazine concept," under which advertisers, instead of "buying a program," would simply buy time for their commercials, which would then be shown by the network or station on a rotating basis. Since sponsors would not be identified with any particular program, they would no longer have to concern themselves with program content. Wouldn't that be a relief?

Evidently not, for the magazine concept is as popular on Madison Avenue as a tax on advertising. Several major sponsors have already stated that if such a system is instituted, they would be forced to "reassess" their use of television. This attitude explains that the headache of responsibility causes no pain at all; it is a pleasurable headache because it allows the sponsor to insure that programs will create a "commercial mood."

It is questionable, however, whether even a magazine concept would be more than a palliative for television's illness. After three decades of catering to advertisers, the networks suffer from an erosion of intelligence. Some of their highest-level men, for example, have indicated that they simply don't understand the social effect of drama. NBC's Robert Sarnoff is an example. During one of his appearances before the Federal Communications Commission, he testified that he would not allow an advertiser to tamper with a news or documentary program, but that the problem was less important in entertainment, "where there is a great deal of make-believe anyhow."

Commissioner Robert T. Bartley asked, "You don't recognize, then, the influence of drama on political action?"

"Influence of drama on political action?" Sarnoff repeated. "I'm not sure I get your meaning."

Bartley pointed out that *Uncle Tom's Cabin,* as an example, originated as a literary work but played a significant role in developing political ferment.

Sarnoff then got the meaning; he said he would not allow an advertiser "to change *Uncle Tom's Cabin.*"

Bartley had more adventures with the problem of sponsor interference. He asked E. V. Huggins, chairman of the executive committee of the Westinghouse Electric Corporation: "With respect to the participation of an advertiser in the content of programs which he is to sponsor, do you think the public should be made aware of that through an announcement at the time of the broadcast?"

Huggins replied, "I wouldn't see any objection to it. I am not sure that I see the necessity of it."

Bartley pursued the question with Donald H. McGannon, president of Westinghouse's subsidiary, the Westinghouse Broadcasting Company. "Do you think the public has been aware of the extent to which advertisers have controlled the content of programs?" McGannon was asked.

"No, I do not," he replied. He said he would not object to such disclosure, but wondered if the practical problems involved would be too great and whether the public, in any event, would be "responsive."

Public response is always an intriguing puzzle, and an important one; the answer would therefore seem worth the chase. At the very least, a full disclosure of the advertiser's role in entertainment would cause Frank Stanton to rest easy in the knowledge that no viewer was being "deceived or misled as to the true nature of the program being offered."

When all the beating about the bush is ended, the problem of television will always return to its source—whether the medium should continue to degenerate into a squawk-box for ads, or be transformed into an exciting, provocative theater to which we could turn for knowledge, stimulation, and truly entertaining relaxation. Worthington Miner, a producer of *The Play of the Week,* has indicated what that kind of television would look and sound like.

"It has been said, and wisely," Miner remarked, "that great theater exists only as it concerns itself with three basic areas of living conflict—politics, religion, and sex. . . . The theater has always been, and is still, a meeting place for the rebellious spirit and the rebellious mind. Aristophanes delighted huge audiences just because he tore to shreds the moral, political, and military codes of his time. The best of theater . . . feeds on the false values most firmly advocated by the Pharisees of every age. Its favorite butt is the complacent palace guard set up to protect some inviolate half-truth—be it moral, political, military, or religious. In order to delight its audience, to win allegiance and applause, it must shock, awaken, and disturb. . . ."

Since such programming will not promote guaranteed consumership, it is all but nonexistent. "One of the things that killed original drama," said David Davidson, who wrote fine plays during television's briefly fertile period, "is the fear of the sponsor to deal with an unknown quantity—with the world around us today."

5 THE FIRST SEDUCTION

"The idea is to bring music into the home by wireless."—David Sarnoff, in 1916.

Colonel Lemuel Q. Stoopnagle, that rollicking spoofer from the days of radio, once perfected a strange invention—a watering can for people who didn't want to water flowers. For those who were only mildly opposed to flowers, he had a can without twenty-five holes. For those who were violently hostile to flowers, he had a can without fifty holes. Colonel Stoopnagle found it difficult to convince his partner in nonsense, Mr. Budd, that there was a meaningful difference between his two watering cans.

The Colonel would have had far less trouble describing the difference between today's television programming and that which emanated from radio for so many years. "Radio," he might have said, "was for advertisers who didn't want us to hear what they didn't like. Television is for advertisers who don't want us to hear *or see* what they don't like."

A difference without a distinction, which explains why radio and television, so different on the surface, are strikingly similar in behavior and history. Both hurtled through four phases of life: (1)Bumptious, unpredictable youth, (2) fleeting, often fruitful adolescence, (3) eventual seduction by the neighborhood dope peddler, and (4) degeneration before the age of consent.

This encore for disaster was probably unavoidable. If an orchestra manager turned over responsibility for the selection of his musicians' repertoire to a popcorn vendor, in return for money, it is likely that if he then became manager of an opera company, he would look up the popcorn vendor again. That is the story of David Sarnoff and William S. Paley, founders of the National Broadcasting Company and the Columbia Broadcasting System.

These were the men who, during the 1950's, approved the fateful decision to turn television over to the unerring sponsor-pleasers of Hollywood; during the 1930's, the same men turned radio over to the popcorn vendors of Madison Avenue. This clears up the mystery of why radio and television are so fundamentally alike. One does not have twenty-five holes, the other does not have fifty.

There is enough contentiousness in the world without reviving the dispute over whether America's first professional radio broadcast was made by KDKA, Pittsburgh, or by other contenders for the honor. However, because a current defense of television holds that it is young and understandably erratic, it is pertinent to note that in November, 1920, KDKA broadcast the returns of Warren G. Harding's landslide victory over James M. Cox. Practical broadcasting is therefore at least forty years old, or old enough to know better.

Radio's mere existence was miracle enough for listeners with crystal sets and other rudimentary receivers; they were unconcerned at first with the chaos that quickly developed. Commercial broadcasting opened in 1922 (Procter & Gamble sponsored its first program, a recipe recitation, in 1923), and stations sprang up across the country. The American Telephone and Telegraph Company, which operated a station in

New York, claimed the exclusive right to sell air time to advertisers, but others sold time anyway in a lusty, frontiersmen's retort to monopoly. The U.S. Commerce Department, under Secretary Herbert Hoover, eventually assigned broadcast frequencies to over seven hundred entrepreneurs, but the ultra-enterprising operated on any frequency and with whatever power they desired and blasted away at self-assigned hours with more impunity than less. It was not long before interference became a major irritant to listeners; some broadcasters sought more effective federal regulation, but Congress was indifferent. Finally, in 1926, Eugene F. McDonald, of the Zenith Radio Corporation, forced the issue by jumping a wave length with his Chicago station and challenging Hoover to stop him. When the case reached the courts, the Commerce Department was held to be without authority, and it was only then that Congress enacted the Radio Act of 1927, which established the Federal Radio Commission and tamed the wild bulls of the air waves. (The Federal Communications Commission superseded the FRC in 1934.)

It is sometimes said that networks, which were clearly to become the heart of broadcasting, were made possible by this pacification; actually, they could have been operated sooner. In 1924, AT&T began to wire twenty-three stations together from coast to coast—for which it was soon selling $750,000 worth of air time a year. And a year later, AT&T and the Radio Corporation of America brought Calvin Coolidge's monotone to an estimated 20,000,000 listeners living in twenty-six cities. Although this was sporadic networking, its practicality was established; its initiation was delayed by one of the most vicious financial struggles in the history of American industry.

Inventions that were necessary to each other in the radio transmitter and receiver field were controlled by AT&T, RCA, General Electric, and Westinghouse; in addition, AT&T owned the telephone lines, which provided the best method of sending programs from station to station. To make possible the national radio service that was needed, these firms would have had to subordinate property rights to pressing public rights. This they would not do, and the hands-off-business attitude of the Harding and Coolidge administrations did nothing to foster a more civilized climate. All during the 1920's, manufacturers of transmitting and receiving equipment maneuvered for position while violating patents; it was all but impossible to make radio equipment without infringing on someone's paper rights. And no one would enter full-scale network broadcasting until he could gain a legally unassailable patent position. RCA's control was strongest, but not foolproof; thus, a grand stalemate.

The solution brought happiness to all parties concerned. The first step was taken in 1926, when AT&T sold its network to RCA for $1,000,000 and became the supplier of telephone lines for the transmission of network programs. Since AT&T held a virtual monopoly in the telephone-line field, it would make out handsomely. RCA abandoned its hopeless fight to prevent receiver manufacturers from violating what it considered to be its patent position; it licensed many manufacturers and began to collect fat royalties. The final solution was accomplished by backscratching. In September, 1926, RCA formed the National Broadcasting Company but emerged owning only half of it; 30 per cent went to General Electric, 20 per cent to Westinghouse. (Three years later, GE and Westinghouse sold their stock back at a pleasant profit.)

With the financial amenities concluded, the last group at the trough, the public, could then have its network service. And there to provide it was the extraordinary David Sarnoff, a man who looked forward to broadcasting as a glorious national service and now can look back on it as something less.

If Sarnoff has been lucky, as some of his critics like to say, he has at least made luck work for him. Born near Minsk, Russia, in 1891, he was brought to the United States in 1900, when the wireless business was barely existent. At age fifteen, he started at the bottom as a messenger for the Commercial

Cable Company, in New York, but soon moved to a competitor that was to become powerful, the British-controlled Marconi Wireless Telegraph Company of America. Beginning with Marconi as an office boy, Sarnoff moved rapidly through several jobs, and it was he who dispatched distress signals—for forty-eight hours without relief, it was said—when the *Titanic* struck an iceberg in 1912. His signal was the one picked up by a rescue ship that steamed to the sinking liner and picked up several hundred passengers.

Although Sarnoff's company was primarily concerned with the transmission of coded commercial messages, those with foresight understood that radio was only a matter of time. Experimental broadcasts had been taking place, and Dr. Lee De Forest's invention of the audion (tube) had provided tremendous impetus for voice broadcasting. In 1916, with an eye for the future that has served him well, Sarnoff wrote a now famous memorandum in which he proposed "a plan of development which would make radio a household utility." He likened radio to the piano and the more recent phonograph. "The idea," he said, "is to bring music into the home by wireless."

When David Sarnoff spoke in those days, no one had to listen, and his superiors didn't.

But history, luck, and perseverance were now merging for the immigrant youth. In 1919, when he was the Marconi company's commercial manager, Washington became jittery about the firm, which, as the dominant wireless operator in the nation, was still under British financial control. The Navy Department pressured British investors to sell out, and the result was the formation of the Radio Corporation of America (80 per cent of whose stock, an RCA official said later, "would at all times be in the hands of loyal Americans"). RCA acquired, together with a fabulous collection of patents, a number of Marconi radio stations, which formed the core of the NBC network in 1926. It also acquired Sarnoff, who became a leading RCA vice-president and then assumed control of both it and NBC, which he promised would be "a great force for the cultural improvement of the American people."

The Columbia Broadcasting System has been NBC's principal competitor over the years, although the competition has largely centered around supremacy in profit-making rather than in quality of programming. CBS has made the grade handily, having traveled a long way from a shaky start in the hands of some ragged individualists.

According to well-entrenched legend, which seems accurate enough to be serviceable, the CBS idea was born in 1926 at New York's Astor Hotel, where angry broadcasters were gathered to discuss the frequency pirates—station operators who scrambled the air waves by broadcasting whenever and wherever the most money could be made. In the Astor lobby, a promoter and salesman, George A. Coats, overheard much grumbling and concluded that anything worth that much heat was bound to be profitable. Coats decided to go into radio, and he was soon meeting with Arthur Judson, who was successful at managing the leading concert stars but unsuccessful at placing his clients on the NBC network. Judson added a third conferee, Andrew J. White, an enterprising reporter, publisher, and radio enthusiast. White was dynamic and dignified—an old-school man, complete with pince-nez and black ribbon. In early 1927, this trio organized a new network, United Independent Broadcasters, Inc., with far less capital than courage, and leased a Newark radio station as their flagship outlet.

The task of arranging for affiliated outlets fell to Coats, who botched it. He signed up sixteen stations with contracts that would have cost United $35,000 a month in payments to affiliates; the company might have afforded half that. White, hearing that the Victor Talking Machine Company was about to join RCA, quickly suggested to its worried rival, the Columbia Phonograph Company, that it, too, get into broadcasting;

all Columbia had to do was buy up United's operating rights. Columbia did, forming the Columbia Phonograph Broadcasting Company. One year after NBC's debut, it put the competing network on the air with *The King's Henchman,* an opera by Deems Taylor and Edna St. Vincent Millay.

The operation was a rousing success for UIB, but Columbia Phonograph lost blood; it ran the network at the same tremendous deficit that would have been United's; three months later it sold the failing enterprise back to its shoestring originators for $10,000 cash and a credit of eighteen hundred minutes' worth of commercials. White, a man of inexhaustible resourcefulness, then looked up a well-to-do Philadelphian, Leon Levy, who had forsaken dentistry for broadcasting, and soon had not only Levy's investment but $150,000 from one of Levy's friends, millionaire Jerome H. Louchheim. White then hastened to the hustings, where he successfully renegotiated the costly contracts with his sixteen affiliates.

These new infusions of cash might still have gone the way of earlier speculations had it not been for a timely demonstration of radio's tremendous selling power. One of the troubled network's sponsors was La Palina Cigars, made by Samuel Paley, originally of Kiev, Russia, later of Chicago, and at that time of Philadelphia. (Paley was also Leon Levy's father-in-law, but that seems to have been mere coincidence in the events that followed.) Both the cigar-maker and his son, William, were disturbed by the growing popularity of cigarettes, which had reduced their cigar sales from 600,000 a day to 400,000. Deciding to try a radio advertising campaign, they sponsored *The La Palina Smoker,* in which a presumably fortunate woman, La Palina, sat each evening among a group of men who told tales of exotic adventure. When the program increased cigar sales to 1,000,000 a day, the younger Paley, La Palina's hard-driving sales manager, became fascinated by the possibilities of radio. Although his heart was still in tobacco, he prevailed upon Jerome Louchheim and brother-in-law Leon Levy to sell him their shares in United Broadcasters. In September, 1928, two days before his twenty-seventh birthday, William S. Paley became president of the firm which he shortly renamed the Columbia Broadcasting System. It was as if the tall, handsome, wealthy youth had noticed a city and, liking it, simply bought the whole state.

Paley originally regarded CBS as an enjoyable hobby to which he would devote part of his time, but he quickly abandoned that frivolous concept and brought to the network a full ration of energy and determination. His goal was to overtake NBC; to do so, he needed stations, and for help in getting them, he reached into the Federal Radio Commission itself and hired Commissioner Sam Pickard. As a CBS vice-president, Pickard's knowledgeability on Commission matters made him attractive to station operators. CBS's affiliates soon grew from sixteen to sixty-nine. (Later Paley hired a former member of the FRC, Henry Adams Bellows, and installed him in Washington as head of CBS's capital radio station.) Altogether, Paley demonstrated that, as far as he was concerned, broadcasting had grown up and was mature enough to begin pleasing its stockholders.

Although the super-energetic Paley had CBS's earnings moving at a stylish sprint by the mid-1930's, no one has ever contended that the network has not run faster and even more nimbly since it hired the man who is now its president. Frank Stanton, natty, trim, and youthful at the age of fifty-four, came to CBS in 1935 on a beeline from Dayton, Ohio, where he spent his formative years and grasped the value of being industrious and indispensable. According to Robert Lewis Taylor in *The New Yorker,* Stanton went to work for a clothing store while very young and quickly dazzled his employers by learning everything worth knowing about the establishment. During a premedical course at Ohio Wesleyan University, however, he and the faculty discovered that he was not learning everything worth knowing about medicine. This was broadcasting's gain, so to speak, for Stanton turned to radio and psychology, and became interested in what made people listen to what they listened to. Displaying a flair for gadgetry, he constructed a contraption that would fit into a radio and record the tuning behavior of the owner. This, basically, is what the Nielsen rating gadget does for television-tuning measurement today, and thus Stanton may be the secret father of ratings in addition to his recognized distinctions.

Whatever faults may be found in the CBS president, one is not impetuousness; he has a reputation for scanning the horizon carefully before taking off. Thinking ahead is what landed Stanton on the CBS payroll in the first place, back when good jobs were scarce. After finding "representative" families, he installed his tuning-measurement device in their radios and later interviewed them to discover their programming likes and dislikes. The results went into a series of monographs that helped him compose his Ph.D. thesis, "A Critique of Present Methods and a New Plan for Studying Radio Listening Behavior." He sent copies of the monographs to CBS officials, who must have been impressed, because he was offered a job in the network's research department. In 1935 he arrived in New York in a Model-A Ford, and in 1946 he arrived at the CBS summit, where he has since had to roll with both praises and punches. The *Saturday Review* has found it possible to consider him "Businessman of the Year," and Edward R. Murrow has found it possible to accuse him of being ignorant of the problems of handling news. Stanton stands, imperturbably, on an imposing record of Nielsen rating triumphs, convinced that CBS television is the tastiest ingredient of a people's stew.

Sarnoff, Paley, and later, Stanton, pleased the public by providing instant home entertainment—music and laughter—to supplement the piano and the crank-up phonograph. From this packaged convenience grew a durable myth, the notion that what is broadcast is free and must therefore be accepted with humility. Myths spring from awe, and what could better describe the emotion of the millions who happily tuned the

Zenith, the Majestic, or the Atwater Kent on whose gray steel cabinet sat the wired antenna that resembled a kite? At the turn of a knob there was Lowell Thomas, and George Hicks reporting on Lindbergh; *Amos 'n' Andy* and *The Collier Hour* of variety; Rudy Vallee; the A&P Gypsies; Singin' Sam, the Barbasol Man; and the Mills Brothers. For many there was also an introduction to what was called "serious" music, ranging from symphony and opera to the finest voices in the land. Noisy mavericks, too: the Midwest had John R. Brinkley, who used radio to promote his goat-gland rejuvenation parlors; the South had Colonel Henderson, who said, "I operate my station for the greater glory of God and the damnation of chain stores." Later the entire nation could hear a rough but compelling voice declare, "Hello, folks, this is Huey Long speaking." But meanwhile, there was depression-time diversion from Jack Benny, Fred Allen, Eddie Cantor, Fibber McGee and Molly, and, to be sure, Major Bowes and his gong. Hope came from Franklin Roosevelt's fireside chats, and radio news revolutionized communications—so much so that newspapers and press associations declared war on this fleet competitor, tried to shut off its sources, and succeeded eventually in forcing the networks to establish their own news-gathering organizations.

There seemed to be something for everybody on radio.

But the seeds of disintegration were there, too, in the form of the commercial, which began as an unobtrusive message from a sponsor and went on to dominate the medium altogether. The interesting thing about commercials is that there has rarely been a time when they did not worry even the most dedicated of free-enterprisers. David Sarnoff, for example, did not contemplate the din of the pitchmen; he thought radio would be more sensibly supported by a tax on receiver manufacturers. And as early as 1924, Secretary Hoover spoke forebodingly: "It is inconceivable that we should allow so great a possibility . . . to be drowned in advertising chatter."

The commercial was in such poor odor by 1930 that Merlin

Aylesworth, then president of NBC, was moved to explain why he had not allowed college football games to be sponsored. "With all these youngsters," he said, "I just did not quite like to see the Yale-Harvard game announced 'through the courtesy of so-and-so.'"

A year later, the blare of commercialized radio had become so obnoxious that the United States Senate took the extraordinary step of challenging the private-enterprise basis of broadcasting. Referring to "growing dissatisfaction with the present use of radio facilities for purposes of commercial advertising," the Senate asked the Federal Radio Commission to supply data on twelve questions, two of which are pertinent here:

"What information there is available on the feasibility of government ownership and operation of broadcasting facilities. . . . Whether it would be practicable and satisfactory to permit only the announcement of sponsorship of programs by persons or corporations."

The Radio Commission disposed of these questions without difficulty. To the first, it replied, "None," and dropped the matter. It responded to the second question in a way that commands admiration: it asked the opinions of advertising agencies. The agencies objected unanimously, many declaring that if sponsors were restricted to mere mention of their names, they would desert radio forthwith, with disastrous economic consequences. H. K. McCann, a founder of the huge McCann-Erickson ad firm, said he would regret this action because it would add thousands to the ranks of the unemployed, and to this solicitousness he added a thought that network executives have found useful ever since: "In any case, every radio set has a switch on it—the owner has only to reach out a hand and tune out the program that displeases him . . ." Here was the first documented suggestion that if an audience did not like the service it was getting over its own air waves, it could do without service altogether.

In any event, the Senate managed to repress its dismay

and move on to other affairs. Radio moved on to the cacophony of jingles. Inexorably, standards were lowered until, by 1940, news programs were being interrupted for commercials. In our numbed state, it seems surprising that a time existed when news programs were *not* shot through with commercials, which in those days were often called "plug-uglies." Commentator Raymond Swing generated a broadcasting crisis in 1940 when he declared that his report on the German invasion of France was not to be interrupted. The matter reached such a pitch that Justin Miller, president of the National Association of Broadcasters, commented: "There is no more reason why a newscast should be interrupted for a plug-ugly than that such ads should be inserted in the middle of news stories or editorials in a newspaper."

By 1944, this old-fashioned delicacy had been dismissed and advertisers were being allowed to use World War II itself as a selling device. "As every one of you well knows," related a commercial, "the United States is face to face with a great challenge. People everywhere are seriously concerned about the nation's all-out effort. Regardless of how or where you serve, your first duty is to keep well. . . . When a simple headache develops, or the pain of neuralgia strikes, try a BC Headache Powder. The quick-acting, prescription-type ingredients in the BC formula . . ." Lewis Gannett, the thoughtful book critic of the New York *Herald-Tribune,* came home from the fighting fronts and remarked, "The aspect of home-front life which most disgusted me on return was the radio . . . a sick parade of sicknesses, and if they haven't yet made us a sick nation, I wonder why."

NBC and CBS had been seduced by cash. Their advertising receipts had risen from less than $4,000,000 in 1927 to $10,000,000 in 1928 and $19,000,000 in 1929. Profits, NBC had said in 1926, would be plowed back into improved programming, but generosity before tabulation is an old human weakness. As advertising income increased, so did raucousness. The networks made public pledges of dignity and private deals that doomed dignity. Hawking of prices was prohibited during evening hours, but cigar manufacturers were allowed to state that their product cost "the smallest silver coin in circulation," and clothing establishments were not banned from advertising that "men who pay $45 for their suits can now get them for half that." By 1934, radio had become a noisy barker for package goods; three-fourths of its advertisers were drug and toiletry manufacturers, food, beverage, and tobacco firms, and the auto makers.

But this was not utter capitulation, and advertising would not settle for a seduction less than complete. So radio was asked to give up its soul, too, and she obliged. A new idea was born—instead of the networks deciding what to broadcast, the advertisers themselves would become the arbiters of culture. Steadily and quietly, the ad agencies took over the programming function, with the consent of Sarnoff and Paley, until the transformation had been accomplished with few outsiders the wiser. Programs then had to survive or die on the basis of Hooper ratings, not quality, and Fred Allen concluded that radio had simply become a by-product of advertising. NBC vice-presidents censored Allen's humor—he couldn't do a sketch in which a woman's home blew up because she left the gas on; gas companies didn't like jokes about gas explosions. And programming balance gave way to time blocs. The hour before dinner was turned over to the food men, who dispatched *Dick Tracy, Little Orphan Annie,* and *Jack Armstrong,* through which children learned to decode secret messages and send in box tops so they could be the first on their block to own something. The hours after dinner were captured by *Gangbusters, Mr. District Attorney, Fu Manchu, The Green Lantern,* and other drug, drink, and inhale shows that exposed crime by dramatizing it for hours on end.

The conditioning technique was applied most thoroughly to daytime radio; it was justified by the expedient of developing a convenient hypothesis and then representing it as certified fact. This process of reasoning was a tool of market research, one of the early and assiduous users of which was Procter & Gamble. P&G used radio to push its Chipso, Oxydol, Ivory, Camay, Crisco, and other goodies among the women of the populace, and these women have never been regarded very highly by advertisers. A recent history of P&G explains, with skin-caressing blandness: "Another job done by market research uncovered the fact that many housewives wanted to be entertained, not instructed." Here was the Soap God again, declaiming that all the American woman had advanced through during the previous century was twelve hundred menstrual periods. P&G spoke with authority that counted, since it was already spending heavily in broadcasting, and since it was already creating, for want of a more accurate word, the scripts of its shows. This attitude and others of its kind made it possible for radio to foreclose on risky experimental, imaginative, or simply intelligent programming. More important, here was the skillfully prepared rationale for radio's most persistent art form, the weeping, seeping, dripping soap opera, courtesy of P&G, Lever Brothers, General Mills, General Foods, and other companies in the manipulation business.

These companies were aware, during the early days of the Great Depression, that the American woman was burdened with several problems of great moment. There was, first, her skin, which, with the advancing years, tended to lose its soft, youthful, creamy luster. Her skin was what she had won her husband with, and its debilitation imperiled his affection to the point that many marriages were going on the rocks. There was, too, the problem of the woman's hands, which, as a consequence of dishwashing, became rough, red, and chapped. She had to hide them at cocktail parties, and this made her clumsy at the hors d'oeuvres boards. As a result, she became tense and intermittently undernourished. And of course there was the depressing problem of the woman's weekly wash, which betrayed a tattle-tale gray as it hung on the clothesline. This caused her neighbors to talk about her, and not pleasantly. The woman's cakes were another problem, since they cost her husband promotions and raises; his boss was ill impressed by the flat pastry he was fed as a dinner guest. And finally, there was the problem of the woman's emotional life, which resembled hash. It may well be that this was the most serious problem of all. Suffering from feelings of inferiority and drabness, she was jealous of her husband's secretary and constantly wondered if her own magic had gone over the hill. Chained to her washboard, stove, mop, broom, and Pablum spoon, her future loomed as a lackluster dead end.

It was for this scrambled creature that the soap opera was manufactured. In its perfected, aired form, the soaper may not have done more to degrade the woman than concubinage, but at least it tried. It performed a tranquilizing function during an unsettled period in American life—an era in which many unfashionable women even strolled on picket lines. (Few people in broadcasting recall the social ferment of the early and middle 1930's, but it can be found in musty old books.) The daytime serial, through thin-lipped glorification of unending travail, taught the listener to reach for an emotional bath instead of a thought. It propounded an uncomplicated syllogism: (A) good people suffer, wash clothes, mind their own business, and submerge sexual desire, while bad people debauch themselves with sex, cigarettes, politics, and laughter; (B) Mrs. Listener is the long-suffering type; therefore (C) Mrs. Listener is virtuous. This Billy Sunday morality, according to some sociologists who took money from the networks, gave housewives fortitude with which to endure runny noses and dirty dishes; if a crabby critic pointed out that such applesauce also dissuaded women from expanding their horizons beyond *kinder* and kitchen, a merchandiser-sociologist would explain, with suffocating condescension, that women preferred entertainment over instruction, anyway. The networks could then add that they were merely giving the people what they wanted. (No one has ever won an argument with a network, anywhere, on any subject; it is company policy to triumph over threats to income.)

The soap operas also legislated a number of interpretive dogmas to help women contend with the complexities of modern life. Some of these fundamentalist dicta dealt with problems that are likely to engage the concern of interested parties for decades to come, but serial carpenters solved them regularly, between commercials. There was, for example, the problem of the role of the husband and father in the family. In soap operas, he was perennially confused and gutless while mother was invariably heroic. (In television situation comedies, father is not gutless; he is merely idiotic while mother is cool, clear, and sensible. The world does move.) The listening housewife, whose family was in debt, whose children needed new clothes, and who could not often enjoy the graces of life, could thus identify her own husband with the soapsud eunuchs and feed ecstatically on his failures. But there was always the underlying salvation: *everyone's* husband was a fool; we will suffer together in silence and thus find joy. Emotional mildew? That's the way the architect of one serial described his product.

The soap woman, or at least many of them, also used the caricature of the castrated male as a blind behind which she could toy with what, presumably, the repressed Mrs. Listener wanted to toy with—illicit love. Helen Trent, for example, set out to prove, in 1933, "what so many women want to prove—that she can capture romance at thirty-five and even beyond." Helen bounced around among thirty men—some of them already married, but unhappily—during a quarter-century search for permanent love on radio, and not one Walter got her to an altar. But there was redemption in this sadness; the listening housewife could understand the suggestiveness of it all and engage in a daydream in which *she* was bringing out the man in those handsome weaklings. It will probably never be known how many mildly discontented women found full-blown neurosis through addiction to these titillations.

When critics discovered, after years of debate, that they could not dislodge the weepers from their pedestal, some of them concluded that because the female suicide rate had not risen alarmingly, the programs must be less deleterious than had been imagined. Actually, their effect was never acute (although Ma Perkins was once called to account by the National Tuberculosis Association for disseminating alarming medical misinformation). The soapers simply added to and multiplied a number of fictions about life in the United States. Characters who lived in Crisco Corners or some other sterile hamlet were automatically deep-down fine and honest; big-city residents were wicked and slothful. Women who smoked were low, as were those who nipped. Common sense was better than book learning. These were the shorthand clues to the solution of all problems; they all led up to the major moral: dote on your own life and leave inflation, atomic bombs, and school-bond issues to the experts.

This P&G-Lever view of the ideal life was appealing to the radio networks; it enriched their outlook by millions of dollars each year. By 1940, the average network station was devoting five hours a day, in fifteen-minute program segments, to soaps, and in some years the advertisers spent approximately $100,000,000 in time and talent charges to present them. This all helped CBS and NBC ring up $75,000,000 in profits after taxes by 1940—a lusty sum for two teen-agers. The shows persisted, although with declining vigor, until 1960, when the old tub Soap Opera sank in the murky waters of CBS Radio. As Julie Stevens, the actress who played Helen Trent, made her way from the studio, she surveyed the wreckage with an understandable absence of dampness. "It's no great tragedy," she said.

Network radio itself is in wreckage. It is, in fact, all but dead. But was it really murdered by television, as it likes to maintain, or did it take poison before television arrived and merely linger to attend its own rites? It is difficult to tell; perhaps radio would have abandoned the network system even without the carnage wrought by television. Local stations had been itching for years to turn themselves into commercial juke boxes. But the networks' death rattles were, in a moldy way, interesting to watch. They backslapped one another like auto salesman during a recession; NBC, as an example, exhibited clinically fascinating symptoms when it sought to sell time on the premise that radio provided "imagery transfer." That meant, as any fool would know, that television sponsors should buy time on radio, too, because the pictures on their commercials "carried over" in the listener's mind when he heard the message on radio. See?

It is interesting, too, to note that network radio became somewhat revitalized once its expensive toys were taken away. NBC's weekend *Monitor* has provided service, diversion, and intelligence, and so has the potpourri of interviews, news, and civilized music that emanates from CBS's owned stations.

But it all came too late. Miracles have to act like miracles.

6 INEVITABLE RAPE

"We can't go off the air with a dead man. How are we going to put our commercial in there?" —An advertising man.

If the early promise and swift degeneration of television could be chronicled in a few telling remarks, these selected samples would do better than most:

> The family watching NBC television will know more about things, be interested in more people, more places, more everything. —Sylvester L. Weaver, Jr., 1949.

> We're programming for the younger, larger families—the ones with more teeth to brush, more bodies to bathe, more hair to shampoo. —Oliver Treyz, 1961.

> The junk around us! The sea of junk! And after all the scandals it's worse than ever. —David Susskind, 1961.

As head of the NBC television network, Pat (Henry Clay) Weaver tried to arrange a compromise under which the mutually antagonistic peddlers and creative artists could co-exist in the house of television. The peddlers won and he left.

Oliver Treyz, the deposed president of ABC television, is a salesman, advertising man, and "researcher" who re-proved a maxim that hadn't needed new research in several hundred years—there's much cash in trash. When Treyz's name is mentioned among television's leaders, it frequently evokes a reaction that tells its own story: "I don't like what Ollie has done, but I've got to admire him for his guts." ABC's programs are chock-full of guts, as most viewers know.

David Susskind, who has been said to confuse himself with God, at least equals Moses on occasion. He makes the sea of junk part, whereupon he dashes through the gap with a good piece of drama. He is one of television's last angry men and, in this role, unquenchably defies highly placed people who suggest that he shut up about the wasteland. Susskind, president of Talent Associates, Ltd., an independent production organization, is accused of egocentricity, and of having taste and talent; he would have difficulty defending himself against either charge.

In these three men's successes and failures, much of television's brief, disastrous history can be read.

When Pat Weaver joined NBC in 1949, a quarter of a century had passed since Vladimir Zworykin of RCA developed the iconoscope, the heart of the electronic camera. Zworykin had studied the problem of picture transmission since 1910, but evidently without contemplating pictures of "Rivak the Barbarian" that NBC would one day transmit. "From the beginning," he once explained, "we thought of television as an extension of human sight, with applications as broad as this idea implies." Experimental broadcasts were made by 1925, and a mere six years later—talk about miracles!—Kate Smith stood before a camera singing "When the Moon Comes Over the Mountain." In 1932, CBS televised the Presidential election returns, and in 1939, Franklin Roosevelt was shown opening the New York World's Fair. Gertrude Lawrence appeared in scenes from *Susan and God,* and there were presentations of *Mamba's Daughters, Stage Door, Happy Journey,* and *Three Men on a Horse.* Then came the interruption of World War II, whose conclusion NBC illustrated with films of the Japanese surrender aboard the U.S.S. *Missouri.*

Remarkably, the television that developed from this beginning—the crude, infant television of the late 1940's and early 1950's—*was a better medium than we have today*. It is amusing to reminisce over the plunging-neckline era, when a viewer was never sure what would be shown next, and to recall the stagehands who bobbed into the pictures, but it is more significant to note that there was programming for widely disparate tastes *during the evening hours.* Interest in television was not simply a matter of "new excitement," as broadcasting executives claim today when they are not advancing some other excuse for their failure.

Situation comedy? William Bendix in *The Life of Riley* and Eve Arden in *Our Miss Brooks.* Variety? Ed Sullivan. Quiz and panel shows? *What's My Line?* and Garry Moore. Sports? Boxing, baseball, football, Gorgeous George, and fantastic women on roller skates. Humor? Uncle Miltie and Jimmy Durante. Admirable girls? Faye Emerson, Arlene Francis, Eloise McElhone, and more, more, more. Handkerchiefs and heartaches? *This Is Your Life.* Reality? A blue-baby operation at Johns Hopkins; the Kefauver Crime hearings. Music? *The Voice of Firestone.* Drama? *Studio One, Philco-Goodyear Playhouse, Kraft Theater, Robert Montgomery Presents.* The issues of the day? *See It Now,* with Edward R. Murrow. And Garroway, Godfrey, and Caesar and Coca, and viewers opening conversations with, "Did you see . . . ?"

What they saw was a groping, self-conscious medium with the power to expand knowledge, multiply experience, and make tired feet feel better. Early television, for all its imperfection, achieved a semblance of balance, which means some of this, some of that, and two cups of miscellaneous.

When Pat Weaver assumed control in those early years at NBC, he described his own background succinctly. "Before I got into this racket," he said, "and since, and during, I have been an advertising man." Weaver entered radio around 1930. ("We in the ad agencies ran radio programming," he recalled recently.) Weaver produced the Fred Allen show for the

Young & Rubicam agency, one of his first acts being to ask Lee Bristol, president of the sponsoring Bristol-Myers Company, to leave an NBC control room in New York. He rose in the ranks of Y&R but then left to direct advertising for the American Tobacco Company, which was then being ruled by the ogrous George Washington Hill. On Hill's death, he returned to Y&R and, in 1949, took over at NBC.

At that point, Weaver enunciated a number of policies designed to keep the medium balanced—to strike a compromise between selling and enlightening. His views were no secret because, like David Susskind, Weaver is rarely reticent. His weapon is the Olympian memo; he can conceive a 10,000-word epic on the state of civilization during a shower and breakfast. In true Madison Avenue style, he is also a minter of grand phrases and epigrams. ("Let us dare to think and let us think with daring.") Moreover, Weaver's sense of mission has led him to preserve his NBC state papers; they repose today in bound volumes under a quietly lofty title: "Concepts and Policies." The contents tell of many frustrated ambitions, such as plans for "telementaries" (documentaries, that is), and "Operation Frontal Lobes" (a campaign of "enlightenment through exposure" to "brain-electrifying stuff"). These memos constitute a rambling manifesto on the proper use of television—*as a stage for entertainment, with information and intelligence artfully interwoven.* A brief rummage through the collected works of Weaver indicates some of what might have been.

"Television is the greatest communications invention since man learned to speak," reads the noncontroversial opening sentence. "Television is the medium of reality, not the merchant of dreams." Another document reveals the difficulty of reconciling the clashing interests in the house of television. Major sponsors, Weaver said, "want to put on entertainment that will be inoffensive to everyone. They have no real interest in public service. They have no real interest, in most cases, in giving the public anything but escape, and selling them their products." But he noted, on the other hand, that "we are first of all engaged in a capitalistic enterprise, which means that we must make money." Then, having established his responsibility to the stockholders, he ruminated on television's responsibility to American *life*holders.

Weaver suggested that NBC deal with "the conflicting opinions about the relative possibilities of war or coexistence with communism." He envisioned programs dealing with "the great issues," in co-operation with Dartmouth College (from which he had graduated *magna cum laude*). He was interested in a book by Bertrand Russell, *Authority and the Individual*—"spotlighting the great issue of our time, between the necessity of the society's limitations on the individual freedom of our people and the necessity of the individual in fully developing the potentiality latent in him."

In one memo, Weaver revealed that his subordinates were sometimes neither perceptive nor sympathetic. He explained why he had "made a fuss" over NBC's failure to develop a program out of a 1952 speech by the eminent Judge Learned Hand, who had condemned vigilante-type actions at the height of the McCarthy period. Judge Hand had said: "Risk for risk, for myself I had rather take my chance that some traitors will escape detection than spread abroad a spirit of general suspicion and distrust which accepts rumor and gossip in place of undismayed and unintimidated inquiry."

"My point," Weaver patiently noted, "was that we were not coming to grips with our responsibilities as a communications medium. . . . It is only by pursuing this responsibility of *ours* that we will force a new and positive approach by the men of wisdom to *their* responsibility of conveying to the people the alternatives that face them in these critical times."

Since such words contrast sharply with the usual emanations from the NBC high command, it should be remembered that Pat Weaver also had his eye on the cash register. Combining twin passions for profits and innovation, he established the *Tonight* show with Steve Allen, the *Comedy Hour*, the *All Star Revue*, *The Home Show*, and *Wide Wide World* (as well as a dripping soap opera derivative called *Matinee Theater*). It should also be said that while many of Weaver's proposals for thoughtful programs never made the leap from memo to home screen, this was not due to hypocrisy but to a silent mutiny by much of the crew. NBC was loaded to the scuppers with radio men who thought television shows should be produced as radio programs were—in the advertising agencies. Loyal to the precepts of the great teacher, David Sarnoff, they envisioned the network as "a plumber's pipe."

So it was that Pat Weaver found himself increasingly isolated, more and more frustrated. Where he wanted to create a feeling of spontaneity by interrupting routine programming with specials, spectaculars, or other stylistically named one-time programs (only some of which were good), the trend was inexorably toward total surrender to the deadly series form, produced on film, delivered in cans, and guaranteed to offend no one but the intelligent. Weaver's eventual successor, Robert Kinter, explained: "The regular presentation of half-hour programs on radio and television are the basic ingredients of our business that entertains millions of people each week . . . the great bulk of our watchers desire to see and hear familiar faces and familiar voices. I see nothing wrong with catering to this basic public taste."

As the crusade against innovation progressed, Weaver's authority diminished. Eventually he was kicked upstairs to chairman of the board and David Sarnoff's son, Robert, was installed as NBC president at the age of thirty-six. In December, 1956, Weaver was through. On his way out, he accused the networks of "mesmoronizing" huge audiences and intimated that he might compete with them as an independent program supplier. This threat must have been made in a burst of anger because Weaver would never have been able to break into prime time through the three-network monopoly on station affiliations. In any event, he abandoned the idea and settled back into the advertising business at McCann-Erickson, Inc., from where he occasionally fired a verbal shot at the pap dispensers. In 1960 he told John Crosby: "Television has gone from about a dozen forms to just two—news stories and the Hollywood stories. The blame lies on the management of NBC, CBS, and ABC. Management doesn't give the people what they deserve. I don't see any hope for the system as it is."

A year later, when he assumed control of McCann-Erickson's television department, *Variety* suggested that Weaver might force some reform on behalf of powerful clients who were concerned over the medium's drabness, but that seemed to be stretching optimism beyond all permissible limits.

When Pat Weaver left NBC, that network and CBS had already begun their decline. A year later they were careening wildly downhill (in programming quality if not in profits). Since they will not admit, however, that their direction has been anything but heavenward, neither will they concede that the final shove toward disaster came from a tough, adolescent competitor, the ABC television network. ABC was directed by the super-energetic Oliver Treyz, a man who displays many traits of, and on occasion faintly resembles, a healthy young bulldog quivering before a tray of beef. While at ABC, Treyz was a man of distinction; he made only $100,000 a year, but he did more to lower the standards of television than some higher-paid television executives.

Ollie Treyz's drive and blinkered purposefulness insulated him from detractors more effectively than would an electrified fence. Moreover, his ability to balance the truth on its head was of championship caliber. He refused to let facts buffalo him, and in the *Hawaiian Eye–Surfside Six* business, such imperviousness is money in the bank. Treyz demonstrated this attribute many times, but his Emmy-qualifying performance took place in 1961, when a Senate subcommittee was annoying him over ABC's infatuation with guns and gore. Whenever possible while testifying, Treyz doted on the future, a period in which ABC was invariably made to resemble a network of contraltos, Shakespeareans, ballerinas, and news analysts, but on this occasion the subcommittee's counsel preferred to linger with the crooks and cowboys of the murky present. He suggested that ABC was overloaded with westerns and action-adventure (bang-bang, you're dead) shows. Treyz, all the while dissenting from this characterization, was led into the following colloquy when asked to categorize some samples from his evening fare:

Q. *Adventures In Paradise.*
A. Action-adventure.
Q. *Ben Casey.*
A. I think it would be . . . general drama. It is not action-adventure.
Q. *Naked City.*
A. That is action-adventure.
Q. *The Untouchables.*
A. *The Untouchables* is action-adventure.
Q. *The Corrupters.*
A. *The Corrupters* is action-adventure.
Q. *77 Sunset Strip.*
A. *77 Sunset Strip* is action-adventure.
Q. *Hawaiian Eye.*
A. The same category.
Q. *The New Breed.*
A. Same category.
Q. *Surfside Six.*
A. That is an action-adventure program.
Q. *Bus Stop.*
A. *Bus Stop* is general drama.
Q. *Lawman.*
A. *Lawman* is a western.
Q. *Rifleman.*
A. Same thing.
Q. *The Roaring Twenties.*
A. *The Roaring Twenties* is action-adventure.
Q. *The Racer.*
A. *The Racer* is in the adventure category.
Q. The *Cheyenne* show.
A. Western.

Some people say that ABC became a showcase for slaughtering techniques because of economics. The network began life with audiences too small to excite advertisers, set out to make them huge, and then bought them with the unconscionable but business-is-business device of pandering to the most primitive impulses of the population. This course required neither genius nor aberration, but amoral single-mindedness; Treyz and his associates have that. As an advertising man told the trade magazine *Sponsor:* "You've got to hand it to those ABC guys. They've got a clear-cut point of view. They think in a straight line. Maybe you don't always agree with them, but at least they're not fumbling around."

This straight-line operation had its origins in the Blue Network, which the government forced NBC to sell off in 1943. Eight years later, as the American Broadcasting Company, it attracted the attention of Leonard H. Goldenson, president of United Paramount Theatres, Inc., a chain of movie houses that had been split away from Paramount Pictures by antitrust action. Goldenson bought ABC with television in mind and immediately merged the two firms to consolidate his working capital. But the Federal Communications Commission, proceeding under its traditional rule of maddening procrastination, did not approve the merger until 1953. During this critical delay, CBS and NBC busily signed up affiliates among television stations around the country. When American Broadcasting–Paramount Theatres opened shop as a network, it had thirteen basic affiliates, as compared with many times that number for each of its competitors. CBS and NBC were on their way to blanketing the nation, but ABC's programs (which were horrendous even then) were inaccessible to almost two-thirds of the viewers.

The cure for this seedy condition, which discouraged advertising revenue, came from jovial Robert E. Kintner, who was then ABC's president, having previously been a public relations man and a column-writing partner of Joseph Alsop. Kintner decided to entice stations, and thus get exposure for advertisers, with a shock treatment—guns, fists, and fury, made in Hollywood. Although he has since found it desirable to say that if he were still at ABC, "I wouldn't have carried the pattern that far," corporate boss Goldenson is hardly as reticent. ABC, he once explained to the FCC, was determined to supply the American people with a scarce cultural commodity, i.e., blood and thunder. "It was our judgment," he said, "that the public was being deprived of a very significant form of programming due to the rather limited exposure of the action-adventure form of entertainment." When, in 1960, Goldenson recounted the wholesale subjugation of ABC's program schedule to the Hollywood massacre merchants, he displayed a flair for ingenious interpretation at least as artful as Oliver Treyz's. "It is not difficult now to assess the great benefits that have been derived by our industry from . . . this outstanding program source," he said. "Can any history or evaluation of television in its first decade overlook *Disneyland, Mickey Mouse Club, Cheyenne, Maverick, 77 Sunset Strip,* and *Adventures in Paradise*—to mention just a few? Can it be questioned that these programs enriched the public's enjoyment and choice and helped to further the art and science of television?"

Three weeks after giving this testimony, Goldenson announced in *Variety* that ABC, having achieved large audiences, was finally prepared to schedule informational programs (which had been almost nonexistent). No man to quit while he was ahead, though, he added: "But what of *Wyatt Earp* and *The Untouchables?* These two, at first glance pure escapist action-adventure shows, have important truths to impart about two epochs in our history and about real people who helped shape that history."

Goldenson also speaks of "totalitarianism and the subjugation of man" when he is fending off criticism by federal regulatory agencies, but his remarks betray a certain amateurish caste. Censor-flogging requires experts, such as those who operate at CBS and NBC.

When Goldenson and Kintner quarreled, and Kintner went to NBC (where he was soon extinguishing *Omnibus, Wide Wide World,* and live drama), the head man turned to Treyz, who was also known as "The Bromo-Seltzer Kid." Treyz could do anything Kintner could do; moreover, he could get along with Goldenson. The Bromo-Seltzer Kid had joined ABC in 1948 after selling, conducting a radio quiz show, and holding jobs in advertising agencies. One writer, Martin Mayer, observed him and found none of the attributes of a showman and all the instincts of a businessman. Mayer explained that when Treyz "likes something he sees in an ABC show, he does not say, 'Good, good,' the way most people in the entertainment business would; he says, 'Smart, smart.' "

As Leonard Goldenson's battering ram, Ollie Treyz made ABC a profitable operation that now collects approximately a fourth of the three networks' revenues. It still does not have as many outlets as its competitors, but it has some they *used* to have; station managers are not oblivious to the drawing power of gook. Shortly after a Pennsylvania station switched its affiliation from NBC to ABC, its sales manager told the *Wall Street Journal:* "Folks have their problems during the day, and when they come to television at night they want to escape. ABC is programming so people can escape from everyday life." When a CBS affiliate switched, its owner implied that CBS's news department was in the pocket of the left-wingers, but that is recognized as a shorthand method of talking about money money money.

ABC's audience of escapists, as Treyz made clear so many times, consists largely of members of "young" families who are also, not coincidentally, the most proliferate purchasers of package-goods products, whose manufacturers—no coincidence again—are television's dominant advertisers. That was the meaning of Treyz's references to "people-oriented" ABC, and to viewers "with more teeth to brush, more bodies to bathe, more hair to shampoo." To help these people hide from the disturbing realities of life among the megatons, ABC has employed the slick and sick talents of Warner Brothers and other Hollywood celluloid works and has perfected the hypnotic action-adventure format.

There is something to say for action-adventure, though; its layers of hammering brutality are interleaved with a philosophical message. Action-adventure shows (*Surfside Six, The Roaring Twenties, The Untouchables*) teach that fists provide lasting solutions to problems and that, consequently, nice guys drop to last place unless they keep their dukes up. Adolescents are strongly attracted to action-adventure, and perhaps by 1975 or so, when they will be influential in our political life, we shall see how well they have absorbed their instruction.

But there we go getting away from business affairs. ABC succeeded in making off with many viewers who had previously been wards of CBS and NBC. The reaction in those quarters was predictable: Get 'em back, dead or alive. This involved no special strain on CBS's and NBC's capabilities inasmuch as the NBC network was being directed by Robert Kintner and CBS by James T. Aubrey, Jr., who had been brought over from the ABC stables. Oliver Treyz enjoyed himself on occasion by publicizing examples of how these men imitated ABC. "Our own *77 Sunset Strip* quickly became Friday night's viewing favorite," he once explained. "Whereupon [CBS] promptly scheduled another action-adventure show against it. This second show was strikingly similar in appeal, with two young male leads and other more than coincidental resemblances. In fact, perhaps the basic difference lay in a change of titles and numbers: *Route 66* versus *77 Sunset Strip*."

Both CBS and NBC produced overblown specials, then pointed to their poor ratings as justification for preferring the endless, uninterrupted action series. "The public isn't wild about specials simply because most of the shows just aren't very good," commented Max Liebman, who produced many of Pat Weaver's early spectaculars. NBC turned to such sadistic exercises as *Whispering Smith* and CBS financed a large number of gory clinkers. Soon CBS press releases were describing episodes of *Malibu Run:*

June 14: Laura West dates Larry Lahr and as a result becomes the kidnap hostage of Paul Price, a desperate prison escapee who seeks refuge in a storm-lashed Pacific Coast lighthouse. Lahr and Mike Madison face the fury of the storm to rescue her.

June 21: Jeremiah Wilson, well into middle age, wants the diving team of Larry Lahr and Mike Madison to teach him how to use underwater swimming gear within two days. Larry agrees to do the teaching, unaware that Wilson is a parolee intent on murdering the man he blames for sending him to prison—wealthy newspaper publisher Homer Dean . . .

Was this rot necessary? An icily logical answer has been given by James Aubrey, whose attitudes frighten a number of people. Aubrey is a tall, lean, well-tailored administrator who somehow suggests a creature of the twenty-first century, making automatized decisions independent of their effects. Cool was the word for Aubrey when, in 1961, he condensed the history of television's decline into two sentences during examination by a congressional committee:

Q. . . . do you feel that the trend to or the increase in [action-adventure] programming over the last four or five years has been, let us say, unfortunate?

A. No, I certainly would not use that adjective in describing it.

Q. What adjective would you use?

A. I think to a certain degree that it was inevitable.

Aubrey was right as rain, so long as the rights of viewers do not clutter the analysis. Advertising expenditures over the 1950–1960 period tell the story with precision. While ad money was increasing 258 per cent for all other media during this decade, television's share was rising 1,000 per cent. No medium can survive such pressure in the absence of a fundamental decision to resist rape. Nobody resisted. Money money money.

Nobody resisted, that is, but a few stubborn malcontents, the most loquacious and self-sufficient being David Susskind. To adapt an observation made by Dorothy Parker on an unrelated occasion, the affair between David Susskind and David

Susskind will live as one of the prettiest love stories in all of show business. Here is a man who appreciates his own virtues, eschews false modesty, and can therefore perform admirable works and also be led into such incredible debacles as his mismatch with Nikita Sergeivich Khrushchev, the heavyweight champion from the province of Kursk. Susskind, a heavy bantamweight from Harvard, Hollywood, and elsewhere, proved in that *Open End* encounter that a red-blooded, hot-tongued American cannot be prevented from getting egg on his face in public. Some thought the challenger was under the impression that he had been appointed Secretary of State, but others felt that this sold Susskind short; comedian Jack Carter said Ed Sullivan was casting a religious epic, and that "the role of the Lord is being sought after by Jack Paar, but David Susskind will probably get it."

Now that the trivial nonsense about Susskind's role in television has been attended to, it is time to say that, barring the bout with Khrushchev, his exuberant self-confidence, incessant carping, and nagging persistence are what television desperately needs. His passion may not be fashionable in the age of blandness, but it is preferable to Aubrey's clinical uncreativity, Treyz's open-faced cynicism, and Kintner's cash-register heartiness.

David Howard Susskind, having just turned forty, probably has his best days before him; when pay television becomes a reality, he will undoubtedly walk away from the current form of the medium as speedily as he can manage, and no man would have more reason. He has produced over seven hundred programs and has suffered certainly three times that many indignities at the hands of sponsors, their batmen in the advertising agencies, and network executives. Susskind is the man who was told to produce "happy shows for happy people with happy problems." He is also the man who, having induced Sir Laurence Olivier to play the lead in "The Moon and Sixpence," was asked by an ad man, "Who is Laurence Olivier?" Susskind has a knack for breaking through such barriers: "I explained he was Vivien Leigh's husband at the time." That, however, was the least of the problems he encountered with the story of Gaugin. He was told that the artist in Somerset Maugham's novel was a "kook," like all artists, and "not commercial"—and that in the television version it would be preferable if he stayed home with his family instead of running off to Tahiti. He was also informed that death from leprosy would make a distasteful ending. "I was told you can't have him die: 'We can't go off the air with a dead man. How are we going to put our last commercial in there? And if he's got to die of something, for God's sake let it not be leprosy; that's an ugly way to go. Let him have cancer or heart trouble.' "

This explains why Susskind may live with advertising men without appreciating them. He is accustomed to their literary obliqueness, but he marvels at the ineptitude with which they sometimes handle their clients' best friend, the commercial. He tells, as an example, of an episode of *The Untouchables* in which a woman had squealed on some nefarious characters. "She was lying on a hotel cot in a slip," he recalled, "and the door was kicked in by three men with sawed-off shotguns. They proceeded to kill her, quite dead, and the picture faded. It was obviously the end of the act. And up came a smiling middle-aged woman who said: 'Mothers, for baby's milk you can depend on . . .' I submit this is not the climate in which to purvey goods." There are times, too, when Susskind simply classifies sponsors as part of "the insanity that has gripped our profession." He tells of a spark plug manufacturer who sponsored *The Mark of Zorro* series, which was faithfully viewed by a small boy at the Susskind home on upper Fifth Avenue. "And then the commercials would come on," father Susskind says, "and there would be a rather scientific hard-sell on spark plugs, the super firepower of the plugs. My son would go to the bathroom, go for a Coke, talk to his friends. He didn't know what a spark plug was; he was getting a nickel a week allowance and couldn't buy one if he wanted one. Now . . . despite the rather exciting ratings of the program, it came to the attention of the corporation that they weren't selling a lot of spark plugs. So they engaged a research company to make a thorough scientific study of this enigma. And upon payment of substantial monies, they were advised that their audience consisted of roughly 26,000,000 five-, six-, and seven-year-olds who had very little passion for spark plugs."

All of which is typical—David Susskind with opinions on everything but the art of basket weaving. The man is correct often enough to be impressive, though. While the bright boys have been producing foolish commercials and puffed-up "research" reports for advertisers, he has been producing theater, from the old *Philco Playhouse* to the *Kraft Theater, The Art Carney Show,* the first excellent offerings of *The Play of the Week,* "The Bridge of San Luis Rey" for the du Pont series, and more. His Talent Associates organization has also produced a film version of "Raisin in the Sun." True, Susskind was also responsible for *The Witness,* one of the more spectacular television disasters of recent times, and he has relied rather heavily on safe adaptations of classics. Unfortunately, he does not own his own network and is therefore something less than omnipotent.

Susskind tries, and in today's television that is a cause for applause. The odds against which he labors were indicated by an advertising agency official who explained, on one of his frank days, why television sold out to "the velvet embrace of Hollywood." The film factories, he said, "have lived off imitativeness for forty years, and television has fallen into the same pattern." As a result, he pointed out, "television has ceased to be television, doing what it is uniquely equipped to do, and has become a junior-grade Hollywood, doing what *it* is equipped to do—produce volume against deadlines."

The ad man predicted, of course, that programming would nevertheless soon improve, which it will not.

In February, 1962, television performed spectacularly as it covered John Glenn's orbital flight of the earth. It showed the astronaut's blast-off and held dozens of millions of viewers transfixed as it reported his progress for several hours. Everything that could be done from the ground was done, and models, maps, and other visual devices all but took the viewer into space as well. If the networks had staged the flight instead of the government, this limitation would undoubtedly have been removed; there would have been two space capsules in orbit, one containing cameras to record every second of the event.

Television has created some glorious moments with entertainment, but its most unforgettable hours—stretching sometimes into days—have come from the coverage of news and special events and the illumination of important but dormant problems. It is difficult to forget, for instance, that in 1950 the attention of millions was caught by the agonized features of William O'Dwyer and the twitching hands of Frank Costello, real-life stars of a political drama produced by Senator Estes Kefauver. Jarred from the humdrum, people became part of the actuality around them. The achievement was far beyond the capability of radio; now, every intonation, every human blush and flush, could be heard *and* seen. Thousands rushed to appliance stores, and the following year they heard the effective understatement of Edward R. Murrow as he inaugurated CBS's *See It Now* series with a picture of the Atlantic and Pacific oceans. "We are impressed," Murrow said, "by a medium through which a man sitting in his living room has been able for the first time to look at two oceans at once." Two years later, Murrow and producer Fred W. Friendly dissected Senator Joseph R. McCarthy on *See It Now.* Only 5,000,000 persons watched, the rating services said—but the show drew 49,928 letters; the Senator's rebuttal drew 26,156 more. Then housewives ironed before the television and office sets were turned on as attorney Joseph E. Welch questioned (or answered?) the actions of McCarthy and a couple of lads named Roy Cohn and David Schine. In recent days, Arthur Morse's "The Influential Americans" was awarded a lower-than-average rating as a special on the *General Electric Theatre,* but this study of educational problems brought 10,000 letters from teachers alone.

There lies the inimitable ability of television—to reach and stir huge numbers of people about important issues, instantly. It cannot provide the continuity of a good newspaper, but it can do *its* job in a stunning way. Walter Lippmann recognized this when he abandoned his reluctance to appear on *CBS Reports.* "You've dragged me, kicking and screaming, into the twentieth century," he said. Lippmann provoked thought: he commented that President Kennedy had failed during his first year in office to begin educating the American people in the realities of modern power politics, and he said, "I hate old men who start wars for young men to fight." The amount of agreement with Lippmann is not important; he stimulated thought about the problem of preserving the world.

While controversy does not in itself guarantee public service—Jacqueline Kennedy's tour of the White House was bland but fascinating—the cry of a wounded entrenched interest often indicates someone's heretofore private preserve has been invaded. The unbridgeable gap between men devoted to tough public-affairs programming and those who regard the genre as a pain in the neck lies in an attitude toward flaws in American life. The searching documentary journalist, who is a social critic, considers these flaws the unfinished business of a democracy. Some of the offended feel that only the positive should be accented, while others among them simply like flaws because there is money in them. As a result, studies of automobile-accident causes are more than half safe while treatments of highly charged social issues are not. It is almost axiomatic that a producer's success in arriving at the guts of a truly vital subject is proportionate to the abuse he will suffer afterward.

Examples are numerous. When David Lowe produced "Harvest of Shame," which exposed the feudal conditions under which migratory workers exist, *Variety* called it "a needed indictment of a blight on the American scene." But the American Farm Bureau Federation accused *CBS Reports* of presenting a "rigged documentary," of committing factual errors, and of other dark misdeeds (including a narrated reference to *The Grapes of Wrath*). Congressmen from migratory-farm areas rose in the Capitol to denounce the program as "unfair" and "a great injustice." CBS, which received 2,540 favorable comments from viewers and 160 criticisms, issued a point-by-point rebuttal and emerged with dignity and unblemished integrity. (The only error was narrator Murrow's; when he became head of the U.S. Information Agency, he tried to dissuade the British Broadcasting Corporation from showing the documentary, an action he later described as "foolish and futile.")

When NBC presented a *White Paper* on irritations in Panama toward the United States, a congressman implied treason. ". . . subversive forces control not only many of the great newspapers of the country," he said, "but also the television and radio networks. . . ." When ABC's *Close-Up!* depicted the still unhappy lot of Northern Negroes in its intensely moving "Walk in My Shoes," Southern newspapers attacked the show, one with the headline: "TV Threat to Racial Harmony," and a Shreveport, Louisiana, station donated reply time to the White Citizens' Councils of America. And, not least, when Stephen Fleischman dealt with the commercialism of modern medical care, his powerful *CBS Reports* show, "The Business of Health," inflamed the American Medical Association, which did not, however, reply convincingly to many well-documented revelations.

The grandfather of public affairs programming, if not its most vigorous exponent in recent years, is CBS. With the exception of *Eyewitness,* which usually deals with subjects current in the news, and quite ably, the network's only regular information program in the evening is *CBS Reports.* Although the placement of this show opposite *The Untouchables* on ABC is often regarded as a sacrifice of time that could only be sold at a loss anyway, executive producer Fred Friendly prefers an optimistic view. "We are the 'touchables,'" he says. "We meet the unreality of *The Untouchables* with the reality of the world."

Friendly fights for public affairs exposure and creative freedom with sharp weapons: a keen, serious mind, the intense loyalty of his producers and crews, a superb record, and—perhaps most important—the fact that he *cares.* Without invidiousness, he can be described as the man behind the voice of Ed Murrow; doubtlessly, he was prominent among those Murrow spoke of when he said, "For many years I have received credit for what other people have done." Friendly is given to somber epigrams ("What you don't know can kill you") that make sense. He is an extremist, and a well-advised one, in dealing with sponsors; he does not allow them to confuse their financial support with the right to meddle in program content. He has even refused to permit advertisers to dictate the placement of their commercials, on the theory that thoughtful programs should be interrupted at sensible, appropriate times.

After having been overshadowed by CBS for years, NBC has caught up, largely because of the popularity of newscasters Chet Huntley and David Brinkley. The network's *Project Twenty,* produced by the imaginative Donald Hyatt, is more cultural than informational, but this division is often sketchy. The *JFK* series has been outstanding and so have such *White Papers* as "Angola: Journey to War." NBC's vice-president for public affairs, Irving Gitlin, spent many years perfecting his trade at CBS, and he, too, cares. Gitlin has said that ". . . those who deal in ideas: those writers and producers and directors and cameramen and stars and extras and all the rest—know in their bones that national disasters come from not tapping the deepest and most truthful responses of its people." Gitlin also feels that if "an upsetting idea can't get through, then we are cooked indeed. Because we may as well face it, we are in for a time, measured in generations, of upsetting ideas.

Run for cover if you will, but there is no longer any place to run to."

ABC ran from reality for years and is now involved in a panting attempt to make a showing in public affairs. But it is having difficulty learning that this service does not have to be merchandised as a great train robbery. The original producer of its *Winston Churchill: The Valiant Years* would not rest his case on one of the most colorful men in history; he had to call the series "a historical-political western." The story, he said, "contains all of the basic elements of the western. . . . Winston Churchill is the hero, Adolf Hitler is the villain, and the chase is the greatest war man has ever waged."

If James C. Hagerty was abashed to proceed from the White House to the network that interrupted coverage of the 1960 Presidential election returns to present *Bugs Bunny* and *The Rifleman,* his discomfiture was understandable. He immediately issued a pledge to build a competitive news and public affairs department for ABC. One of Hagerty's accomplishments can be seen in the network's final news broadcast each weekday night. Reporters who have covered their own stories appear and consistently form a program that is outstanding among network news shows. Hagerty has acquired William H. Lawrence from the *New York Times,* Howard K. Smith from CBS, and other veterans. It is not unkind, however—merely realistic—to say that any improvement at ABC will take on a special luster in view of the network's history; Hagerty's monumental successes lie before him.

Networks have more money but are not alone in the ability to put together unclichéd programs when they are so moved. Some local stations have presented fresh ideas, although network affiliates do not usually interrupt the prime-time produce from New York and Hollywood; their own efforts are most frequently seen in off-peak hours. Given these limitations, Chicago's WBBM-TV has achieved great popularity with Irv Kupcinet's late-night show, a high-caliber, often controversial, usually stimulating talkathon. Kupcinet, a columnist for the

Chicago *Sun-Times,* tries to select guests who have something to say and aren't afraid to say it. David Susskind's *Open End* provides mental refreshment when its topic is worthy, and the Westinghouse Broadcasting Company's *PM* show, with Mike Wallace, showcases excellent young performers, provides intimate glimpses of established personalities, and features thoughtful guests who talk about vital things.

In the case of *network* public affairs shows, good efforts are often as effective as shouting down a rainspout. Large numbers of affiliates turn on the network switch when vapid entertainment programming is scheduled but turn it off when an informational show is coming over. In its place, they present Hollywood films in which one man chases another up a hill, down a highway, or through the air, and which a local merchant sponsors. In 1957, CBS arranged an interview with Premier Khrushchev that made world-wide news, but the number of Americans permitted to see and hear it on television may be gauged from the fact that only half of CBS's affiliates considered the interview attractive enough to carry; later the same day, they all carried *The Ed Sullivan Show.* When ABC originally offered a young people's series, *Discovery,* and 40 per cent of the affiliates refused it, sponsors said their commercials would not appear in enough "markets"; the show would have been available only to an estimated 14,000,000 children. NBC has had similar difficulties; affiliates ignore roughly half of all public affairs shows.

Newton Minow once suggested that stations be required to reveal their acceptances and, in the case of rejections, to report what shows they carried instead. "The public should know which licensees consistently reject network public affairs programs and whether they were rejected for [valid] reasons or for other reasons having to do with ratings and dollars," the FCC chairman said. His six colleagues solidly voted him down.

This profitable abdication of responsibility explains why, when the networks cut away to the United Nations in the fall of 1960 to cover the activities of President Eisenhower, Prime Minister Macmillan, and Premier Khrushchev, a large number of viewers protested the cancellation of their soap operas and game shows. Television had done its best to lure them into a world of fantasies, and they resented the interruption.

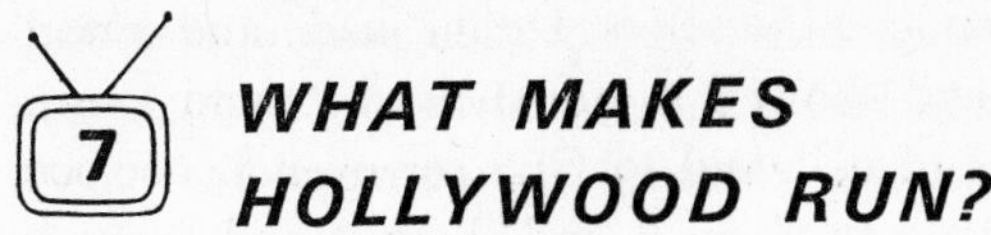

7 WHAT MAKES HOLLYWOOD RUN?

> *"People still think this is an art. It's a business. We make shows for sponsors."* *—Dick Powell, president, Four Star Television.*

All in one lifetime, Desi Arnaz has been many things—son of a deposed Cuban mayor, leader of the only known five-man septet, singer, soldier, actor, producer, and husband of Lucille Ball. Currently, Arnaz is president of a bustling Hollywood factory, Desilu Productions, Inc., that manufactures television entertainment. As such, he is not interested in making products that will please "the off-Broadway crowd," which is his slightly complimentary term for eggheads. "I want to do shows," he explains when pressed, "for the folks that live in Omaha, Nebraska. Sometimes people forget that between Hollywood and New York there are 160,000,000 American people."

Demonstrating Arnaz's concern for the 160,000,000 residents of Omaha, Desilu filmed, during the decade that ended with 1961, over six hundred episodes of such series as *I Love Lucy, The Ann Sothern Show, The Texan, Whirlybirds, Harrigan & Son, Guestward Ho!,* and *The Untouchables.*

As even the haughty off-Broadway crowd is aware, *Lucy*

was a phenomenal crowd pleaser from the moment Miss Ball displayed her saucer eyes and Arnaz his practiced mispronunciations. CBS financed the series, Desilu made and owned it, CBS showed it, and showed it and showed it, and Desilu finally sold the cans of celluloid to CBS for over $4,000,000, so CBS could continue to show it and show it and show it. At last report there was no one left in the United States who had not seen at least one of Lucy's escapades, and arrangements may shortly be made to exhibit them to the newborn as soon as they can see. This success has caused Arnaz to believe that *Lucy* is what killed live television and brought about the triumph of the Hollywood film men; the supposition is not accurate but it is useful to Desi, who relates it to his stockholders.

Since Arnaz embarked on his mission to amuse people—"to make them pass their time a little better," as he puts it—he has become an important figure in entertainment manufacturing. He owes and is owed millions of dollars. He holds the deeds to three Hollywood studios, at which Desilu has filmed shows for other manufacturers, including those of *Miami Undercover, The Real McCoys, Wyatt Earp,* and *The Danny Thomas Show.* Arnaz financed the Broadway musical, *Wildcat,* in which Miss Ball, to whom he is no longer married, starred. And he even has a Remington Rand Univac.

Yes, the leader of the five-man septet now has a Univac computer to help him; he uses it to reduce guesswork and bring "the scientific approach" to show business. In the fall of 1960, with his thinking machine and his mortal colleagues at Desilu, Arnaz set out to demonstrate that Hollywood, which practically invented copycatting, wasn't being *scientifically* imitative. He was led to this belief while pondering the entertainment manufacturer's most pressing problem—that of the pilot, a sample film of a projected series. Gambling on pilots represents one of the few forms of high-stakes wagering that are left in Hollywood; the extrusion of a half-hour pilot normally costs from $60,000 to $100,000, an hour product from $100,000 to $200,000. When the cost of machining these bangles was lower, they were produced with a saturation bombing approach: make a dozen, dump them on networks and advertising agencies with high-altitude runs, and hope to hit with four or five. As prices rose, the precision technique was substituted: determine sponsors' desires, make only four or five pilots, and try to drop them all on the target with well-planned sorties over the Madison Avenue lines.

Having been stuck with some of his own bombs despite precision warfare, and despite the success of his educational series on machine-gun usage, *The Untouchables,* Arnaz felt that casualties had to be reduced still further. The way to make each pilot a winner, he reasoned, was by casting new hopefuls in the image of old hopefuls that had won the rating battles. He decided to make pilots only "after a careful analysis of the types of shows that are winning the best audiences." This would leave no room for programming that was refreshingly different, but that was not Desi Arnaz's problem. He pulled a chair up to his Univac, and employing a method that has not been revealed, found out what the American people—those living between Hollywood and New York, at least—wanted to see on television.

It was an effervescent event at Desilu's executive offices on Gower Street when Univac tapped out its answer. The message was fairly puzzling—"CIC," it said—but Arnaz decoded it and was thus prepared for a series idea called *Counter-Intelligence Corps,* which soon presented itself. The show, later retitled *The Silent Ones,* dealt with the exploits of U.S. government private eyes. Inspired by the novelty of the creation, Desilu executives shared the secret of their impending success with the McCann-Erickson advertising agency, whose executives also knew a good thing when they saw it; they pledged $175,000 toward the production of the series.

Lights! Camera! Action! *The Silent Ones* was cast, scripts for a two-hour, two-part pilot were written, and publicity was released: "The world is the stage for this powerful, action-filled series, which for the first time will dramatize the hitherto untold, often unbelievable but startlingly true exploits of the men of the U.S. Counter-Intelligence Corps. . . . *The Silent Ones* re-creates the history-making headlines covering the period shortly before World War II and immediately following the Korean conflict. The initial show, 'Teheran,' a two-part teleplay . . . unfolds the suspenseful and compelling story of CIC activity behind the famed Big Three (Roosevelt, Churchill and Stalin) meeting at Teheran in 1943. . . . *The Silent Ones* is narrated by Westbrook Van Voorhis, known to millions for his former role as the voice of *The March of Time*."

On a day that will not soon be forgotten at Desilu, the film was shown to executives of the ABC television network, who, Arnaz was confident, would clutch *The Silent Ones* as fervently as they had *The Untouchables*. But it was a turkey—one of the most odorous birds Hollywood had seen in a long while. Arnaz had spent well over a half-million dollars on the venture, and all that it lacked was basic artistic honesty. Other television shows lack this ingredient and go on to glory, true, but they are not often so pretentious. The pilot of *The Silent Ones* masqueraded as "startlingly true," based as it was, Arnaz said, on an international political murder intrigue that was supposed to have threatened the Big Three. But the treatment of the alleged episode was so clumsy and lackluster that fact and fiction could not be differentiated. Actually, "Assassination at Teheran" was a classic Hollywood version of history—just good, dramatic, reckless fun.

Apart from its appeal as a vaguely reassuring failure story in a land of grotesque success, there is good reason for recounting this tale: It helps to explain the modern Hollywood factory, which differs from the old plant in that the opportunities for cranking out inferior entertainment have been multiplied. The production of motion pictures was always limited by finite factors, such as the number of theaters available and the frequency with which managers would change their schedules. This provided more than enough work to keep the major producers, a few independents, and a husky number of actors, directors, and technicians fat and happy, but the limit was ever present. Television, after giving Hollywood a brief case of financial heebie-jeebies, has lifted the limit and made possible an even longer and faster assembly line. The film-grinders now make their product for a huge portion of an eighteen-hour television day—a day which by grace of the solar arrangement begins anew every morning and occurs three hundred and sixty-five times each year. Moreover, they manufacture film for networks, which stuff affiliates with it; film for affiliates to use during the hours they are not being force-fed by the networks, and film for independent stations that do not have access to network culture.

It is not difficult to understand, in view of this, why Hollywood is the site of a certain amount of anarchy. Warner Brothers, Metro-Goldwyn-Mayer, 20th Century-Fox, and the other legendary lords of the fiefdom are still in command, of course (their television production overshadows their feature-film work), but the new market is so vast and lucrative that lesser knights have been tempted to invade the domain. Some of these bumptious fellows have been highly successful, while others are living in quicksand and still more are merely trying to get into the quicksand. In short, there is a lot of loot to scramble for; the grand shake-out is yet to come.

This is the kind of frenetic activity that is supposed to induce healthy competition: Studio X vows to turn out higher-quality products than Studio Y and thus win fame, fan mail, and fortune. For quality competition to take place, however, there must be a demand for quality. This is elementary. But since the competitors are working for television, which is simply not interested in quality, almost none emerges. Television is a market for B-pictures.

The depressing result is that the industrial complex called Hollywood—from Burbank to Culver City and from Gower

Street to Fox Hills—is a place where the incredible has become routine. It is a place where Budd Schulberg (*What Makes Sammy Run?*) can sign his name to a literary insult known as *Everglades,* and where a *Lassie* editor can turn down a plot in which a boy helps a woman enter a flower show, then discovers that his own mother is a contestant. "It's a story about a conflict of loyalties," the writer explained. The editor frowned. "We don't want to get into conflicts of loyalty," the editor said. "We want wholesome stories."

The new Hollywood is the old Hollywood, but now there is more of it, and it is richer, and more insufferable.

Hollywood first greeted television with all the warmth and understanding of a hysteric. The world headquarters of escapism was seized by nervous panic—as in a bout of shingles—when the electronic monster began to invade homes and hypnotize the American people, whom the studio bosses had come to think of as *their* property. The more egocentric filmmasters took television as a personal affront, while others blamed it on everything but the Russians. (Zworykin, David Sarnoff, William Paley's father: maybe they overlooked a possibility.) The men of the movie industry have never betrayed a strong sense of history; they were confused by the sudden silence on their sound stages. Their peace of mind was not promoted, either, by the frightened questions of their baffled and never trusting allies, the owners of the nation's movie theaters. (Over 6,000 movie houses went out of business before the hurricane spent itself.)

As in all industries, though, motion pictures contained a few men of wisdom, and among them was Sam Goldwyn, who never felt a strong need to think the way everyone else did. Goldwyn could be heard, as far back as 1948, quietly predicting that everything in time would be rendered unto the gods, by which he meant Goldwyn, Schenck, Skouras, Mayer, Wall Street, and company.

After a fadeout denoting the passage of time, we come up

again on the Hollywood scene. It is 1961 and there on Beachwood Drive is the Columbia Pictures' lot, most of which is now operated by a subsidiary, Screen Gems. The sound stages are bustling. *Dennis the Menace* is being shot, day in and day out, and so is *The Donna Reed Show,* day in and day out, and the *Flintstones,* and *Hazel,* and *The Hathaways.* At Warner Brothers there is *Maverick, Cheyenne, Lawman, Surfside Six, Hawaiian Eye, 77 Sunset Strip,* and *The Roaring Twenties.* The scene is the same elsewhere, with television production outstripping movie-making by ten to one, so that Hollywood can fill almost 90 per cent of the networks' nighttime schedules. Almost 3,000 television films are being ground out each year, and the studios' employment rolls are at their highest in a dozen years. "The principal source of amusement and entertainment for all of us is at the very peak of its prominence and influence," announces the Alliance of Television Film Producers.

And the return on the investment is a joy to calculate; profits of the old-line studios are approaching those of the lush immediate postwar years. They sell stock in their enterprises, and so do the more recent contenders. The stock goes well because the studios look after the stockholders, if not the viewers. Some studios are now involved in the production of commercials, too. They are wedging their way into the live-show field, preparing "new" versions of game shows, and are buying into television stations. In addition to all this is the world market; Hollywood exported $40,000,000 worth of television films in 1960. Through this hands-across-the-sea effort, foreigners were able to gain a better understanding of the American family, comprised as it is of Dodo the Father, his derisive children, and his wife, Myrt the Stouthearted. They have also learned that there is no more crime or shooting in America; they have seen all the criminals shot, every week. (When someone suggested that the outside world might be getting a distorted idea of our existence, the president of the industry's export organization retorted that such irresponsible comments could adversely affect the U.S.'s balance of payments position and cause a crippling drain on our gold reserves.)

But the most deep-down satisfying source of the film industry's revitalized income has been its vaults, in which movies were thoughtfully preserved from ancient times. Invoking a form of Montezuma's revenge, Hollywood has stuffed the television intruder with over $1,000,000,000 worth of "feature films," from *The Sheik* to *King Kong* to King Gable. These are the "pre-48's," the year referring to the studios' original refusal to share with actors and technicians the proceeds of films made after that date. When this difference was adjusted, "post-48's" were also released to the home screen; NBC even presents them in prime time, as a sort of substitute for television. They are immensely valuable. For example, Columbia Pictures, having disposed of its older features for $25,000,000, expects to receive three times that amount for its post-48's.

So it has been with only fleeting melancholia that Hollywood has readjusted by drastically reducing the number of movies it makes—from an annual average of four hundred-odd during the 1940's to one hundred and sixty-five during 1960. For theaters, profitable wide-screen, special-effect extravaganzas: *Around the World in 80 Days, Ben-Hur, King of Kings.* For television: profitable sausage links of *Adventures in Paradise, Bonanza, The Corrupters,* and other products of hasty carpentering.

The key to Hollywood's second success was cost-cutting, a phrase that dominates every thought and action on the studio assembly lines. The networks usually describe the expense of buying television shows in a way designed to induce awe. It is pointed out that the cost of producing each segment of a one-hour series is approximately $100,000. Since hour-long series are usually contracted for with a network guarantee of at least twenty-six shows, the total cost comes to about $2,500,000. Feature films, on the other hand—with the exception of the furbelowed extravaganzas—are generally made for something between $1,000,000 and $3,000,000. Therefore, even if a television series is compared with a low-budget feature, it can be seen that the networks' jot-and-tittle men are shopping in a bargain basement. For $2,500,000 they get enough footage to kill not an hour and a half, but *twenty-six hours* of commercial-laden television time. They can buy thirty-three segments of a half-hour series (and re-run six of them) to produce almost twenty hours of programming for $1,500,000.

Perhaps awe is indicated, but not over high costs. Awe is again for The System, under which a network can *lose* this money because programming is so terrible that not even tasteless sponsors will support it with their commercials. About half of all Hollywood-produced series now collapse within a year of origination; initiated on wildly implausible premises, prolonged beyond all excuse, peopled by dispirited actors and energetic non-actors, they simply die because they bore *everybody*. To the public, they are apparently faceless; a television industry survey made during September, 1961, reported that almost no one could identify the new shows of the 1961-62 season, although by mid-month they had been accorded extensive publicity. It is also a cause for wonder that the networks' instinctive response to the demise of one of these anonymous turkeys is a return to the scene of the abomination, where a deal is quickly made for the purchase of another gamey bird. Or, if the network executive is inspired, he may develop an idea for a "spin-off." *Gunslinger* was spun off *Gunsmoke, Pete and Gladys* off *December Bride, Always April* off *The Ann Sothern Show,* and so on and on and on. Conferences at which such inspirations are discussed produce what is referred to as the incredible emotional strain of creativity.

There is also in currency, however, a view that the networks' appetite for Hollywood turkeys is explainable on grounds other than foolishness. Holders of this view note

NBC, CBS, and ABC own various "rights" in from half to three-quarters of the filmed series they present during evening hours. This gives them what, if this were a muscle-in by a mob, would be called a cut of the swag. Those who would not refer to network executives as mobsters nevertheless point with suspicion to the facts that (1) prime time is limited and therefore precious, and (2) financial "participation" by a network seems to help a show find an evening time slot. Observers who wonder if the Sherman Act is being trespassed may gain some understanding from a pointed explanation in *Variety:* "Where once the producers . . . abhorred such practice as an invitation to anti-trust probing, now that they're partnered in a crap game it isn't likely they'll go squealing to the cops."

Interestingly, or depressingly, this situation is particularly destructive to the bottom man on the totem pole, the viewer. A producer with a sensational program need not submit to a network's desire to have a piece of the action; the network knows that if it doesn't take the show, another network might. Conversely, a producer with a product from the garbage can is more than willing to let a network finance his pilot, or his series production, in return for a time slot. The bad drives out the good.

In practical terms, it is illuminating to look at some prime-time shows in which networks have had a financial interest. NBC had such an interest in *Michael Shayne,* a series so ineptly done that Brett Halliday, the private eye's creator, denounced it publicly while the nonsense was still on the air. CBS had money in *Gunslinger,* a clunking imitation of *Gunsmoke* that could not withstand viewer disinterest more than one season. ABC was receiving a percentage of the proceeds of *Hong Kong,* a positively abysmal action-adventure show. What is this—television, or an investment house?

A frank reply—it's an investment house—can be had almost for the asking in Hollywood, where practitioners of the trade are considerably more frank than their network counterparts in New York. There is, for instance, a flamboyant, outspoken gentleman named Don McGuire, who manufactured *Hennesey,* a harmless exercise for Jackie Cooper. McGuire and other members of the Television Academy of Arts and Sciences once gathered to ponder the question: "Is television indeed a wasteland?" Inasmuch as television was represented by the producer of *Lassie,* by an actress who consorts with chimpanzees in *The Hathaways,* and by the television directors of the Screen Gems, 20th Century-Fox, and MGM studios, Newton Minow's description was probably verified before the meeting began. But that is another matter. After a desultory discussion, Lassie's proprietor ventured the airy observation that "we have a moral responsibility to the viewing public"; McGuire corrected her sharply: "Our real responsibility," he said, "is to the bank." The man from Screen Gems, William Dozier, was no less candid. "In our business," he said, "the shows are paid for by people with products to sell, and they're going to buy the programs that will sell their products to the most people."

Even actors, notorious (among producers) for their lack of business sense, have become practical. Perry Como, for example, has discovered that the success of his show puts NBC in the mood to buy other shows, such as the dreadful *Happy,* from the singer's company, Roncom Productions. Robert Stack, the Eliot Ness of Culver City, has a 25 per cent interest in Desilu's *The Untouchables* and tries to defend his slaughterhouse show against critics. During the filming of one of his machine-gun operas, the director provides a gangster with a foaming alkalizer for his hangover; this inspires a discussion of whether the potion might be identified as a particular product. "That's a dangerous area," observes actor-businessman Stack. A telephone call is made to an advertising agency arbiter, a decision is handed down, sugared, non-foaming water is used, and the pursuit of culture resumes.

Perhaps the most practical of all actors in Hollywood is

Dick Powell, president of Four Star Television, Inc. Genial and hospitable in his offices at the old Republic Studios in North Hollywood, he eschews pretentiousness. "People still think this is an art," he says. "It's not. It's a business. We make shows for sponsors." Powell's show-business career began in vaudeville and radio; he saw television demonstrated by KDKA in Pittsburgh as early as 1928. But when television became a reality almost a quarter of a century later, he has explained, "all we old motion picture actors did not know which side of the river to walk on." It was not long before he solved this dilemma. With Charles Boyer, Rosalind Russell, and Joel McCrea, he organized the first Four Star venture, on the business side of the river. When Miss Russell dropped out, and McCrea, after a brief look at television, elected to go into cattle-raising, David Niven joined the firm. Today, in his mellow fifties, Powell and television have settled into middle-age together. With the assistance of a former advertising agency vice-president, he produces action-crime, western, and situation comedy programs, is addicted to the word "quality" in describing them, avoids the temptation to "show any minority problems, or take sides in any controversial matter," and sells stock in Four Star Television, Inc., to the public. Dashing Dick Powell has become Richard E. Powell, and acting has become a time-consuming chore, occasionally required in the business of making shows for sponsors.

All things being relative, however, the above-named gentlemen are mere amateurs when compared to The Octopus. In Hollywood, octopus is spelled MCA, for Music Corporation of America. In television, MCA means *Wagon Train, State Trooper, M Squad, Shotgun Slade, Whispering Smith, The Deputy, General Electric Theater, Riverboat, Bachelor Father, Laramie, The Millionaire, Markham, Leave It to Beaver, Checkmate, Tales of Wells Fargo, My Three Sons,* and, yes, many more shows which it has either produced, co-produced, or collected commissions on as sales agent. MCA also means

Phil Silvers, Ozzie, Harriet, Rick, and David Nelson, Alfred Hitchcock, Ronald Reagan, Robert Cummings, Nanette Fabray, Danny Kaye, Dean Martin, Fred MacMurray, Art Linkletter, William Bendix, George Burns, Boris Karloff, Ingrid Bergman, George Gobel, Ralph Edwards, Jack Paar, Ed Sullivan, and many more performers on whose earnings it collects commissions.

MCA is the biggest talent agent in television—in all of show business, for that matter. It is also, and not coincidentally, its critics say, the biggest producer and distributor of television programs; the twain often meet. MCA is closing out a decade in which it has spectacularly performed the balancing act of the ages: As Revue Productions, it made shows whose financial success was closely dependent on how little money they could be made for; as MCA Artists, it cast many of those shows with its stars, whose financial success was closely dependent on how *much* money they could get out of the producer. Conflict of interest? Few of the major stars would say so; they have made a mint. Others contend that they have been observing the most super-colossal ethical conflict since Judas pondered whether to take the money. These are people who have felt various forms of pain which they ascribe to MCA's tentacles and sharp teeth.

A tourist in Hollywood would be unimpressed by a visit to The Octopus's retreat in Beverly Hills. An old, sprawling, white brick building, it is guarded by double green doors over which is inscribed a spare legend: MCA. If business had time for puns, the cryptic designation might well read: SPQR, for inside sits Emperor Jules Caesar Stein, the happy, hearty millionaire who founded the dynasty. As a young man, Stein got into the wrong business—tending to the sick. While pursuing a hobby as a violinist and a career as a resident at Chicago's Cook County Hospital, he organized a band. One night, finding himself scheduled to appear in two places at once, he booked another group into one of the spots. After a while, Stein was booking a number of bands, for a fee. As this sideline progressed, he teamed up with piano-player William R. Goodheart, Jr., in 1924, to form MCA, and as it became particularly lucrative, he progressed out of medicine altogether. The partners, after discovering several hard-fisted ways to gain supremacy in the band-booking field, expanded into Hollywood and the representation of movie and radio stars. In 1936, they hired Lew Wasserman, a movie-house publicist who was twenty-three years old, to supervise the drum-beating for MCA's stars. Ten years later, after Goodheart's retirement, "the student surpassed the teacher," in Stein's words. Wasserman became president. The expansive, cheerful Stein now lurks in the background as MCA's chairman, while tough, single-minded, rarely smiling Lew Wasserman operates out front. Between them, their non-admirers say, they have arranged for MCA to make off with a buccaneer's share of television's treasures.

If the take has been impressive, the manner in which it has been garnered has been significant. In 1954, for example, MCA took in approximately $6,000,000 from commissions on its talent contracts and $9,000,000 from Revue Productions, its series-grinding subsidiary. In 1961, the Revue mill earned over $70,000,000, or 80 per cent of MCA's revenue. Revue has rung up a quarter-billion dollars in sales of television properties which it has produced, co-produced, or acted as agent for; their quality has been no poorer than any other factory's sausage.

Admirable? Revolting, say the dissenters. It's all done with leverage. CBS, they point out, felt the strength of this leverage when it sat down with MCA representatives to discuss the renewal of Jack Benny's contract. MCA simultaneously had an idea for a show—no pilot, no scripts, just an idea. With NBC and ABC hovering in the wings, eager to sign up MCA client Benny, CBS developed a craving for MCA's show, which was an undistinguished regurgitation of the private-eye theme.

MCA leverage stories are many and complex. One has appeared in *Fortune* Magazine:

> A Hollywood saying has it that "If MCA isn't God, nobody in the company knows it." It would be hard to blame MCA executives for playing God occasionally, for that's how many important entertainment-industry executives treat them. Consider President Robert Kintner of NBC. One spring night in 1957, Kintner and Chairman Robert Sarnoff called a meeting of the network's programming executives. After they had assembled, the door opened and in walked MCA Vice President David A. (Sonny) Werblin. Without any preliminaries, Kintner said to him, "Sonny, look at the schedule for next season; here are the empty spots, you fill them." The rest of the evening the NBC executives meekly watched Werblin rearrange their schedule and insert new shows. When finished, the schedule showed fourteen series . . . in prime time that MCA either had produced or sold. And that was the way it remained.

When asked to explain this at an FCC hearing, Sarnoff denied that the meeting as described had been held.

After many years of prosperity, MCA is now faced with the loss of some of its valuable tentacles. The Octopus owes the opportunity for its success to the Screen Actors Guild, which in 1952 first allowed it to engage in the delicate practice of employing the very performers it represented. The actors' union permitted this duality in order to promote the rapid formation of a television film industry—a dubious endeavor if one ignores the problem of employment for Hollywood actors. But now that the West Coast organ grinders are as gouty-rich as their patrons, the Eastern networks, MCA's special dispensation has been canceled. Faced with the necessity of quitting one business or the other, it will give up talent representation in favor of program production; thus, the tail that began to wag the dog will replace the dog altogether, although this is not to suggest that dogs will no longer be exhibited to the public.

While competing agents—William Morris, Famous Artists, Frank Cooper, General Artists, and others—scramble for MCA's clients, the future financial happiness of Jules Stein and Lew Wasserman will rest on television's continued hunger for the product of the Hollywood sausage factories. The monumental enterprisers do not appear concerned.

Behind the high finance and hot blood of the network-oriented Hollywood factories lies a drab quarter of the entertainment business known as syndication. Successful syndicators make a lot of money, but they also call to mind the story of the old circus man who told a drinking companion that he was being forced to retire.

"Imagine me leaving show business," he complained. "Why, I've never been in anything else."

"I didn't know you were in show business," his companion replied. "What do you do?"

"I've been cleaning out the elephant's cages for thirty-five years," the man explained.

Similarly, syndicators inhabit and operate in the unglamorous quarter of television. They tirelessly travel the dusty rural roads, selling their wares to non-network-affiliated local stations, and to affiliates for use during the daytime and early evening non-network hours. Their merchandise is of two types —series that have tired themselves out on networks, and series made specifically for syndication, which are often tired before they begin. For a reason whose logic is elusive, syndicated shows are usually manufactured with an extra ration of corner-cutting; the difference between the budgets of a network and syndication half-hour series is usually $10,000 to $15,000 a show.

"A syndicator is to sell, not win Emmys," *Broadcasting* Magazine once said. The object of its non-moralizing realism was Henry Saperstein, president of Television Personalities, a Hollywood syndication firm. Saperstein had provided the motif himself when he said: "We aren't in business to win Emmys. And I'm just as happy to have it that way. Win an Emmy and there's only one way to go—down. But with our bread-and-butter, grassroots kind of shows, we can go on and on and on. They're the backbone of television." Among Saperstein's vertebrae have been *Championship Bowling, All-Star Golf, Mister Magoo,* and *Dick Tracy.* He sells them over and over on the theory that the familiar is good, and the more familiar the better. This is a premise whose worthiness was conveyed to him during an early career peddling home movies to rental stores. "I had a bunch of Mickey Mouse and Donald Duck cartoons," he notes, "and I never had to waste any time telling the dealer what they were. The principle holds for television just as well."

Syndicators are particularly devout believers in the Desi Arnaz notion that residents of metropolises are somewhat foreign and fruity, while true, red-blooded, unpretentious America is represented in such precincts as Raleigh, Peoria, and, indubitably, Omaha. For these people, Saperstein has syndicated *The Lone Ranger, Lassie, Wyatt Earp, The Three Stooges, The Gale Storm Show,* and similar extracts from the annals of Americana. In the same vein, a producer at Ziv-United Artists, the largest syndication factory in Hollywood, explained that his firm programs with a handful of fingers on the pulse of America. "We have the greatest sales force in the business," he sad. "Our men hit every small town in the country and report back on what people want and don't want. So we find out, for instance, that while a lot of people on the coasts like high-flown drama, the Midwest and the South like motion, not emotion. We make programs for the people between the two great mountain chains."

In the socio-economic development of syndication may lie the answer to the peculiar puzzle of why, as a generalization, station-by-station shows are more vacuous than network shows, which are so vacuous. While syndication was originally designed to fill the schedules of non-affiliated stations, and even to compete with networks, the business soon raced off on what became known as the beer-and-oil run. Makers of these products usually sell in regions, rather than nationally, and have little desire to bring fine, or any other kind of, entertainment to people who do not live where their goods are sold. Since networks provide a national service, beer and oil set up their own regional networks, whose stations were strung together by cans of film rather than electric wire. And since syndicated shows were then being made for a specific type of sponsor, their contents became specifically tailored. Because beer men were primarily interested in the male viewer, action shows were indicated. (Tough day, can of beer, feet on the television, and all that.) Because gasoline and oil men were also primarily interested in the male viewer, automobiles, speed, and the screeching brakes of highway patrol cars were *de rigueur*. Because there was then so much motion and so little emotion, corner-cutting could be accomplished in numerous ways. Scripts did not require thoughtful plots or sensible dialogue; they could be written cheaply by third- or fourth-raters: "You cover me, I'll flush him out from behind that rock." "O.K., Jim. Good luck." "If I don't come out of this alive, take care of Sarah and the kids." "O.K., Jim. Good luck." *Pow!* Such dialogue requires little acting ability, so money could be saved on supporting players once a "name" lead had been cast. Similarly, empty-headed dialogue, screeching prowl cars, and gunslinging demand little rehearsal—how many ways can a police car screech?—so the participants could run through their lines while the set was being prepared and then run through the scenes themselves without wasting time, which is a bookkeeper's term for rehearsal. Corners could also be cut by using the same group of secondary actors in various roles—union regulations to the contrary. The man whose face can't be seen because he's wearing a wide-brimmed hat and wiping his brow with a sheet-sized handerchief can turn up as a bartender, service station attendant, or toll collector three scenes later with few if any viewers the wiser. A piece of scenery snipped out of last week's extra footage can be spliced into this week's show; a rock is a rock is a rock.

As if all this weren't sufficient, there is an additional important reason why programs made for syndication are especially inferior. They must be sold in perpetuity, to the great station maw, and therefore they cannot contain a thought, word, or deed that would date them; what is topical today may be old hat tomorrow. They cannot be controversial; they must be salable everywhere. They cannot be realistic in gesture, dialogue, plot, or prop; the same show must be equally salable to cigarette, cigar, and pipe tobacco manufacturers, to competing lubricators, to gas-heated and oil-heated areas. The restrictions on material are so encompassing that, in the end, there is no material—just the bread-and-butter, grassroots kind of shows that will go on and on and on in Raleigh, Peoria, Omaha, and other way stations between the two great mountain chains.

Since the proprietors of the Hollywood factories don't really care about the people whose eyes and ears will be assaulted by their products, it ought to be a fair assumption that the networks, the factories' most faithful customers, are equally unconcerned about our sensibilities. The evidence, in fact, is overwhelming. Consider, for example, what networks do when witlessness leads them to invest in shows that are so much worse than the average piece of non-entertainment. When Desi Arnaz and the McCann-Erickson advertising agency came a cropper on their expensive two-part pilot for *The Silent Ones,* the Counter-Intelligence Corps show, ABC bailed out part of their loss by exhibiting the pilot, "Assassination at Teheran," as a two-part *special.* What was not even good enough to base a series on was good enough to inflict on viewers as extraordinary programming; a hoodwinking operation, pure and simple. During the 1960-61 season, NBC earned the distinction of having its Tuesday 10-to-11 P.M. time referred to as "The Garbage Hour." In that period, the network displayed "Rivak the Barbarian," "O'Conner's Ocean," and "The Renegades," which were NBC-financed pilots for series that could not be sold; these clinkers were billed as "specials," too. An additional earnest of NBC's devotion to the viewer became evident when the network opened the 1960-61 season with *Klondike,* a rousing but presumably humorous treatment of the gold-rush days in Alaska. When the show sagged, the inevitable pressure came to decrease humor and increase action. When this surgery failed to resuscitate the patient, the network and Ziv-United Artists, the producer, simply shifted the cast and story line southward and began to call the mutation *Acapulco.* The two leading actors, who had been portrayed as enemies in the frozen north, suddenly became beachcomber buddies in the sunny south. "It was as if they went on the premise that absolutely no one had been watching," comments a producer who was involved. "The whole mess was an insult to the public."

THE SEX MERCHANTS

"The writers should bear in mind that most of these girls will be beautiful bitches with only one end in mind—the seduction of Barton."—*A memo on* The Man and the Challenge.

If the Russians ever claim to have invented sex, and prove it, we are still one up. We can show that we *use* sex patriotically. We *sell* with it—over television. And as any broadcasting executive worth his rating book will assure you, selling products is what keeps America strong.

As almost everyone knows, there is nothing wrong with sex. What *is* wrong, though, is the institutionalization of leering, behind-the-barn sex, and that is what television has specialized in. To the men who live or die by ratings, sex is a device to draw viewers and thus make sponsors and networks happy. When integrated with sadism, it makes what the boys in the bookie parlor call a shoo-in. Sex in television is what appears when ratings fall and the alarm is sounded. It saves the day, the job, and the client.

Television sex, or titillation, becomes habituating. Thus, ABC calls for a "hypo" of *The Untouchables,* after, believe it or not, the presentation of an episode in which a group of Mexican prostitutes is machine-gunned. A memo from Thomas

Moore, ABC's programming vice-president, complained of "a tendency of recent episodes to become talky." He added that "as you know, there has been a softening in the ratings. . . ." Quinn Martin, who produced *The Untouchables* for the Desilu studio, had already commented, about an earlier episode: "This scene is the roughest I have ever seen. I don't know if we can get away with it, but let's leave it in. Have a feeling you may have to kill the girls off-camera." Martin's memos are a collector's item. He also wrote one in which he complained about the repetitiousness of scenes depicting murder by automobile: "I like the idea of sadism, but I hope we can come up with another approach to it." This sequence of low ratings, concern, and call-to-arms has occurred so many times it has become standard operating procedure. Witness, as an example, the chronology of events that overtook a failing CBS series.

Malibu Run, which the network co-financed with Ziv-United Artists, first appeared as *The Aquanauts*. The one-hour show's original producer, Ivan Tors, later testified before a congressional committee that CBS's vice-president for programming, Oscar Katz, had told him *The Aquanauts* would be shown at 7:30 P.M., "when children and parents see pictures together." Following plots that were par for the chase, the program's two leading characters strapped on scuba tanks each week, descended into the deep, exuding a string of air bubbles, and there grappled with the elements or with wayward humans. As series go, *The Aquanauts* was a largely harmless if heavily hoked saga of underwater life. Evidently it was too harmless; it did not deliver adequate ratings against its major competition, *Wagon Train*, in what a CBS man called "a tough competitive" time period. Consequently, sponsors grew restive over their investment. And so did CBS and the producing company, Ziv-United Artists, which had sunk some $300,000 into the failure. ". . . unless something can be done about *Aquanauts*," said *Variety*, "it won't be back." The executives rang the alarm and, immediately, a new producer—

presumably a specialist in rejuvenation injections—was dispatched to Hollywood.

An episode called "The Frankie Adventure" was one of the products of these injections. As a showcase for naked brutality, it dealt with a gang of depraved youths who were led by a sneering, bushy-haired hot-rodder, and with the brave efforts of the series' twin heroes to save the honor of Frankie, an emotionally scrambled young lady who was messing with the toughs. The show's first display of savagery occurred on a beach, where the gang used Frankie to lure a young man into flirtation. She was out of the mood at first, but when the head hoodlum ordered her to "move it," she moved it—*it* being her shapely body. She strolled before the young man (closeup on her fine legs) until he offered her a cigarette and struck up a conversation. The gang leader then appeared and accused the youth of tampering with his girl friend. This set the stage for a beating whose bestiality at least equaled anything that has appeared on television. As the scene closed, Frankie curled her lip and remarked, "I hate men who fold up!" After considerable hot-rodding on the open highways, the plot worked its way into a roadhouse, which one of the heroes was trying to induce Frankie to leave. Our strong, silent type was then restrained while the gang leader inflicted a beating even more sadistic than had taken place on the beach. In a closing scene, the gang leader smashed his car through a guard rail and plunged into the surf. He displayed groveling cowardice until he was rescued by the hero, whom he had earlier mauled, whereupon he was led away, screaming, by the police.

I tuned in "The Frankie Adventure" because the congressional committee that had discussed it had received testimony from two men who were involved in its manufacture and exhibition. One was A. Frank Reel, a vice-president of Ziv-United Artists. He said:

> I'm not an expert on juvenile delinquency. But I personally feel this episode is no worse than many others on the air. It all comes under the heading of trash.

The other witness was Oscar Katz, a CBS programming vice-president. Katz disputed contentions that "The Frankie Adventure" was all too symptomatic of what was taking place on television. He said that the show actually taught moral lessons against juvenile delinquency. Then he returned to his work, which consisted of scheduling "The Frankie Adventure" *for a re-run, again at an hour "when children and parents see pictures together."*

The Congressmen learned of even more exciting adventures of the sex merchants. Ivan Tors, the original producer of CBS's *The Aquanauts,* testified that an NBC series, *The Man and the Challenge,* was to dramatize the experiences of a doctor who, in preparation for the age of space travel, investigated problems of human endurance for survival. *Challenge* was sold to two sponsors, Winston Cigarettes and Chemstrand, but had difficulty finding a place on NBC's schedule. Eventually, Tors said, Saturday evening at 8:30 was cleared "but the price was that we could not call our doctor 'doctor,' or 'scientist,'" because such people were not glamorous, "and we had to put a great deal of sex and violence into the show." The producer testified that the advertising agency man who delivered this message told him that this price had been set by Robert Kintner, NBC's president, and David Levy, then the network's vice-president for programming. (Tors recounted that the ad man "said he was against sex and violence himself. All he would like to have from me is some women in the show because he is selling nylon and this is very important.")

The Man and the Challenge began its run on NBC as a rather interesting series with strong appeal for teen-agers, and it appeared that Tors had successfully resisted the pressure. Before long, however, he received a letter from an NBC executive in Hollywood, part of which read:

> New York has indicated to me recently their concern over the absence of sex in [six script outlines]. I have read only the last, and I think its subject matter is so provocative that

you need not concern yourself with its absence of sex. However, apparently New York prefers this to be an exception rather than the rule.

Ziv-United Artists, which was making the series for NBC, maintained that *it* was no sex peddler, but this position was contradicted by a memo from a Ziv-UA executive to the company's president. The circular proposed, as these excerpts show, a rather remarkable characterization of Barton, the lead of the *Challenge* series:

> Barton is the bright-colored fly on the hook that will attract women. And physically he comes equipped for it. We should undress Barton as much as possible in every episode. He has a fine physique, and those rippling muscles should be displayed at every opportunity.
>
> Barton has no time for women. They fight for it, some succeed in getting it, but mostly he's off again in pursuit of his next brush with death. To Barton, girls are substitutes for danger and when sufficiently enticing danger comes along, he leaves 'em. That's for women.
>
> As for men, it's the old standby—girls.
>
> I am sure that with sufficient time these scripts with the girls properly integrated organically can be extremely exciting. The writers should bear in mind that most of these girls will be beautiful bitches with only one end in mind, the seduction of Barton.

The sorry saga of *The Man and the Challenge* was closed when the congressmen read a letter, written *after* the Ziv memo, by Don Durgin, an NBC vice-president. Addressed to the Doyle Dane Bernbach ad agency, it expressed NBC's desire that *Challenge* be set back a half-hour from its 8:30 time period, in which it appeared opposite *Leave It to Beaver,* so that the number of young people in its audience could be increased.

As producer Ivan Tors concluded his testimony, he provided what may have been the most numbing note of all. "Now, I am a capitalist myself," he said, "but I feel that mental health should come first and dividends next." He may have been concerned that his opposition to the sex merchants would mark him as an agent of the Soviet Union.

It has become obvious, as a result of all these incidents, that the networks and their Hollywood associates are less interested in intelligent attitudes toward sex than in eroticism as a television commodity. That is a logical explanation for the fact that writers on one of the "doctor drama" series were given this peculiar notion of what hospital interns are like:

> They're a sexy bunch of bastards and they shag nurses, clerical workers, and almost any female they come in contact with—except patients.

Parents with children in medical schools really ought to get them out of such a profession while there is still time.

Whenever congressmen make their spirited and sporadic condemnations of the outrages of television, the suggestion arises that "the bureaucrats" are attempting to impose government censorship. The bureaucrats of television thereupon re-state their attachment to liberty and the free-speech provisions of the First Amendment. Moreover, they point out, there is no need for "outside" censorship because the problem is already being solved as an inside job. There are the networks' "editorial departments," which review scripts and films of shows intended for network exhibition, and there is the Television Code, administered by the National Association of Broadcasters, which defines standards for acceptable commercials and programming. The vigorous work of these agencies, broadcasters insist, insures that sex, violence, and poor taste are held to an admirable minimum.

Although they employ different titles, all three networks maintain "continuity acceptance," or censorship, departments in both New York and Hollywood; they are usually pointed to as effective and independent. A CBS vice-president, Joseph Ream, has declared that his department "is not a captive office boy of management." He added that "these people get in from the beginning." They got in on "The Frankie Adventure," and either it received their approval or their approval was irrelevant. An NBC vice-president, James A. Stabile, has said that his editorial group "does a good job of turning down unacceptable or tasteless material." His group either did not turn down a revenge-theme episode of the *Whispering Smith* series in which a mother was shown horsewhipping her son and shooting her daughter in the back, or it concluded that this material was tasteful. And while Oliver Treyz has described ABC's editor-censors as "absolute boss," one of them in Hollywood must be dubious. When one *Untouchables* script was submitted for approval, she wrote: "Please note I think we are killing too many people per episode." She then specified "merciless beatings and other incidents of gore" in the script. But an executive producer at Desilu circled her comments with the notation: "Don't worry about this section." Moreover, when 20th Century-Fox made a *Bus Stop* episode for ABC that starred rock-and-roll singer Fabian as an animal-like, unrepentant, teen-age killer, the script was not even submitted to the network's continuity acceptance department before shooting of the film began.

It seems, on the evidence, that there was more reality in a speech by Hendrik Booraem, Jr., an official of the Ogilvy, Benson & Mather advertising agency, in which he observed that continuity acceptance departments "are put in the position of judging material to which their own managements have given prior approval." Booraem, whose comments upset his audience of radio and television executives, also challenged the effectiveness of the National Association of Broadcasters' Television Code, a proclamation that endorses "God, His attributes and powers," and decries the favorable depiction of divorce, suicide, crime, profanity, obscenity, smut, vulgarity, illicit sex relations, narcotics, "the consumption of liquor in American life," gambling, fortune-telling, phrenology, cruelty, horror, rigged quiz shows, discourteous or distasteful commercials, and other nihilistic activities. Booraem was less than impressed by the fact that almost four hundred television stations subscribe to this Code. The National Association of Broadcasters, he said, "is dependent for its support on the very people it seeks to regulate . . . and it cannot bring to bear sufficient weight, either of economic power or of public opinion, to force the offender back into line." He revealed that although most Hollywood studios affix the Code "Seal of Good Practice" to their films, some leading executives of these companies are not even aware that they are subscribers.

An encounter with the Hollywood office of the Code leads to a suspicion that such ignorance causes little loss. The office supplements network censorship by reviewing scripts and films of programs made specially for syndication. It is directed by Frank J. Morris, a man whose capacity for viewing television films is infinite. Episodes of such programs as *King of Diamonds, Manhunt, Shotgun Slade, Miami Undercover, Lock-Up, Squad Car,* and *Tallahassee 7000* are all in a day's work for Morris. Similarly, his patience is virtually boundless when applied to the producers whose works he must audit. "The men I deal with are almost uniformly co-operative," he once said. "They want to make good, acceptable television shows. They also want to make a profit. If they can do both, they're only too happy to try."

A forceful advocate of his sentiments, the Code director revealed that he had recently prevailed in a dispute with what seemed to be nothing more than a highly personal viewpoint. The show in question dealt with German atrocities during World War II, and annoyed Morris in that numerous references were made to "Germans." "They should have been saying 'Nazis,'" he explained, "and I got them to change it. After all, it was the Nazis who committed atrocities, and not all Germans were Nazis. At the time this took place, our government was involved in delicate negotiations with Adenauer, and I didn't think we should let this kind of thing happen." Thus Morris demonstrated again the apparent impossibility of censorship ever to justify itself. The Television Code lets broadcasters place its seal on sadism and depravity, while its

Hollywood director appoints himself unofficial Secretary of State and political censor and establishes *his* view of German national responsibility—the gospel according to Morris.

Another of Morris's judgments concerned a network series over which, unfortunately, he felt, he lacked jurisdiction. The series was CBS's *The Defenders*, and the episode at issue was "The Accident," a provocative show dealing with the refusal of parents, who were members of an extremist religious sect, to allow their critically injured son to undergo surgery. Morris felt that the theme was sensationalist, but worse, that it might "drive people away from churches. Religion," he said, "should not be the subject of drama. It should be discussed in a public affairs round-table." The possibility that substantive drama *should* deal with religions that prohibit life-saving surgery was not given much weight by the Code director.

The net result of Morris's premises and activities as a Code official reinforces the inescapable point that television needs no censors, industry or governmental. It needs men of intelligence, knowledge, and courage who will program what they think is wise, informative, and truly entertaining. No "review" committee will ever improve on this approach, just as smashing fists and sexual suggestiveness will never be able to hide the need for imaginative, thoughtful writing. As has been noted by Hal Humphrey, a discerning Hollywood-based television columnist and critic: "If that much programming has to be based on crime and its byproducts, then the medium is admitting that it has given up the battle for quality. Crime shows generally are the easiest kind to dream up. To confine the necessary conflict in all drama to the non-violent type requires genuine creative talent."

Not all television executives in Hollywood endorse the cynicism and shallowness that grip their industry, of course, but almost all are victimized. This state is probably inevitable, given the film industry climate, which has nothing to do with the weather. There are degrees of depression over this condition, as well as varying expressions of guilt, emotion, and rationalization of the understandable conflict between conscience and cash. Some producers invoke the crude, ancient, but evidently still useful contention that "If I don't do it, it'll still be done, but somebody else will collect the pay." Some employ the new practicality: "What the hell—it's just the way this game is played." There are those, too, whose consciences will not permit such a confession; in these cases, the conscience remains at home while the body is at the office plying the trade: "I have to approach this like a hired plumber. They tell me what to do and I do it." And still others derive tranquility from the conviction that they are accomplishing something subtle yet magnificent: "I manage to get a lot by the agency guys. For example, did you see the show in which . . .?" In connection with this sad problem, I shared a sandwich and an eerie conversation with a passionately honest man who had produced an intelligent series. He said:

"We set out in one episode to show that narcotics addiction was not a crime but a disease, that it was much less a police problem than a medical problem. We also wanted to make the point that if addiction were handled properly, narcotics would be available to the addict while he was undergoing treatment, so he wouldn't be driven to the underworld for his supply. We had trouble with the agency and the sponsor [a soap manufacturer], of course. The sponsor's people said they wouldn't pay for the show, and if the network played it, they wouldn't pay for the time, either. But we went ahead and made it, and when they saw it we had some arguments, and we made some changes, but our major points remained intact."

Because of the position of the Federal Bureau of Narcotics, whose police tactics have obliterated the narcotics problem at least fifteen hundred times and will undoubtedly obliterate it fifteen hundred more, I was startled by the producer's refreshing approach and asked to see the shooting script of the show. As I read through it, I noticed that at three or four junctures in the story, where the producer's points would logically have been made, the color of the pages changed. On these *revised* pages appeared the more or less standard approach to addiction; there was no reference to a controlled medical supply of narcotics to keep the addict out of the hands of the underworld pushers. The producer had not made his points at all, but this eminently honest man was convinced that he had struck a blow for enlightenment and I could not muster the cruelty that would have been necessary to disabuse him. His need for a sense of accomplishment was further demonstrated when he remarked proudly that he had done a show around the theme of miscegenation; he failed to tell me that he had been forced to specify that the action involved not a Negro but a presumably less controversial Indian. This producer's strong desire to create thoughtful drama will no doubt persist. His capacity for self-delusion will also persist, but it is not to be sneered at; it is merely a fact of life—an expression of the terrible dilemma of an honest man working among rabbits.

Some Hollywood producers, however, seem thoroughly unaware that ugly problems of morality even exist. Among these is Ozzie Nelson, a grand master of the formularized "family comedy." Ozzie (he belongs to America; we may use the familiar) has surpassed the speed of sound and the climbing of Mount Everest. They said it couldn't be done, but Ozzie has done it—over a decade, he has produced the same show at least three hundred times. An anthropological study could profitably be devoted to *Ozzie and Harriet*, a neatly machined homily with all the stylization of a ballet. It portrays American middle-class life as a pleasant series of confusions involving the family car, moon-spoon adolescence, moon-June marriage, and do-it-yourself mishaps. The Nelsons are insulated from the disturbances of reality; vacuum-packed, they are affected by the jocular but not the nuclear. I have asked numerous people simply to tell me what Ozzie does for a living, and none has been able to report ever seeing the man leave for, return from, or describe his work. Ozzie is also a square; when he invites a neighbor in, he doesn't say, "Let's have a beer," or, "How about a shot of booze?" He says, according to a Hollywood writer who held his head and screamed, "Why don't we have a glass of milk and a cookie?" The Oswald George Nelsons are to the world what the ship is to the sealed bottle—it is difficult to figure out how they got there in the first place.

One day Ozzie explained himself. Appearing as a witness in a programming inquiry conducted by the Federal Communications Commission, he responded to curiosity about sponsor meddling by genially pointing out that "ours is the type of show for cowardly sponsors." The hearing examiner raised an eyebrow—the frankness was tingling—and Ozzie hastened to explain that he had said this "more or less facetiously." He finally settled on the position that "We don't walk away from subjects that might be controversial—if they're good, healthy, happy subjects." Perhaps saving his finest humor for the witness stand, he remarked, "We send our scripts to our sponsors, but I don't think they read them, because it kind of spoils the show for them."

Ozzie warmed up as he testified, and eventually he was a relaxed, philosophizing witness, relating television criticism to creeping socialism. He said:

> . . . I hope we all share the feeling that whatever ills or shortcomings television may have, that television is given a complete opportunity to work these out for itself, within the industry, because as an individual, I am extremely sorry about the socialistic tendency that our government seems to be taking in the last twenty years. I hope this [FCC hearing] is not another chopping away of free enterprise and our way of life.

When Ozzie was told that ministers, educators, philosophers, and others were constant critics of television, he demonstrated an approach to morality that is rampant in the industry. Utilizing material he has never regaled his audiences with, he said:

> Now, it could be that a lot of these people you are talking about are idealists, and have two sets of standards—one, a realistic set of standards that typifies our way of life; another, a theoretical set of standards that they wish our life repre-

> sented. We, as people who must entertain or die by the number of people who tune in, have to take a realistic viewpoint. We cannot take the philosopher's viewpoint, or possibly the educator's, or the person who might be a well-intentioned person but whose ideas are not realistic.

Realism is expensive in Hollywood and therefore lean in availability. Sometimes it has to be divined as such, when it emerges as impatience with the week-by-week nonsense that is supposed to make use of a man's talents. Occasionally it is the actors who express the frustration. Robert Stack of *The Untouchables* exhibits pique when he is asked to take all of his cops-and-robbers stage directions seriously. On the set at Desilu, as he barges into a room with gun drawn to confront a gangster adversary, the director breaks in to remind him that he was supposed to kick the door in, not merely push it open. "We kicked the last door in," Stack mutters. "Do we have to kick them all in?" The answer is silence and the shooting progresses, with machine gun and camera. Actor Will Hutchins, who played his way through the title role in *Sugarfoot* for four years, said, on hearing that his series was to be canceled, "That's O.K. with me." His work gave him "a kind of an empty feeling," he said. "Does it really mean anything? Only once in a while do you get a good feeling." He wants to do something "worth while."

The most scathing denunciation of the Hollywood junk shop has come from Darren McGavin, who helped fashion two pieces of scrap metal known as *Mike Hammer* and *Riverboat*. On his way out of the studios and the medium, McGavin talked to a magazine writer and unburdened himself. "You watch television?" he asked. "It's bang-bang, pow-pow. You chase Indians from one hill to another. And then what do you do? You move to another hill and chase Indians again. This is acting? It's like asking a cabinetmaker to build outhouses. You lose your self-respect. I hate everything about television. It makes you feel ashamed of yourself. In the end you feel humiliated."

Bang! Pow!

9 DELIVERING THE GOODS

"We sit with the writers. We have a conditioning . . ."—Nicholas E. Keesely, Lennen & Newell advertising agency.

Many of the men and women employed in television today are semiconscious during working hours. Having watched a succession of dreams being shattered by a procession of banalities, they have withdrawn their emotion. "This job used to be my whole life," ruminates a man at one network. "Now I put in my time and save my energy for other interests." This man no longer reacts sharply to programming outrages. "What's the use?" he says. "I'm numb."

There was a time, before the great anesthetic was administered, when television's inhabitants were stirred by outrage; they tried to derail nonsensical ideas and protect the medium from capture by fools. It was during those days that Goodman Ace, the dean of radio and television comedy writers, became alarmed by the size and content of his mail. He was being inundated by enthusiastic suggestions for improbable situation comedies. Since the letters came from amateurs, and since their suggestions were hopeless, Ace felt it wise to plunge a professional finger into the dike. He was writing highly readable television commentaries for the *Saturday Review* at the time, and in one, he chided his correspondents:

> There is an occupational bit of comic byplay among professional writers who, when they meet in conference to create a new idea for a television show, always start off with, "How about making it a theatrical boardinghouse, where anything can happen and usually does?" Which gives another writer an idea. "How about making it a ten-family apartment house, where anything can happen and usually does?" Which suggests to another writer: "How about a trailer going cross-country, where anything can happen and usually does?"

Having demonstrated the difficulty of taking such thin, one-joke ideas seriously, Goodman Ace relaxed, confident that the populace could sleep in safety. Which only shows that, in television, eternal vigilance is the price of sanity. For even as Ace was discouraging the amateurs, professional writers in Hollywood were developing a wardful of emaciated theatrical-boardinghouse ideas. These grotesqueries soon drove out the troublesome reality dramas, and, by now, thinness, improbability, and unreality have become basic requirements of situation comedy. Anyone who doubts this should trap an audience and recite: "How about three chimps in a family's house, where anything can happen and usually does? How about making it a talking-horse show, in which anything can happen and usually does? Or a middle-aged woman student in a college classroom? Or a maid who runs her employers? Or a French girl who marries an American and has endless difficulties in supermarkets and department stores, where anything can happen and usually does—*every week*?"

These are the formula-format series, which, between situation comedy, "family" comedy, western, action-adventure, and private-eye, occupy about 90 per cent of television's evening hours. They comprise almost all that is left for writers to work with, and they are so faithful to schematic diagram that they have caused many writers to consider an emotionally upsetting question: Is this writing? A number of these writers do their pondering during trips to the bank, of course, but they do ponder.

The question is not posed by those who recognize as "literary" only that work which is reasonably original and meaningful. It is asked by Hollywood writers who are delivering the goods for television today; they understand that various levels of performance exist, even within the mass media, because they operate on many levels themselves. But when they are confronted by a writing form that all but excludes writing, they become concerned about what might be happening to them. ("Half your pay is for what you do," states an ancient Hollywood epigram. "The other half is for what they do to you.")

The series formula locks the writer into a carefully padded cell. He cannot write his idea for a story (even within all the perimeters erected by the tradesmen) because somewhere between two-thirds and three-quarters of his role has been usurped before he reaches the typewriter. He cannot write about people he has been thinking of as characters; he must write about mommy, daddy, and their children—because they are the show. He cannot endow them with personalities he would like to explore; their personalities were molded long ago by the studio, the network, and the sponsor, and are not, of course, subject to change from week to week. And he cannot violate the laws that closely govern their existence on television; he must dramatize this week's "problem" quickly, allow for a commercial interruption, thicken the plot with familiar, acceptable misadventure, allow for a second commercial, solve the problem in a familiar, acceptable way, allow for a third commercial, and exit with a bit of familiar banter or homily. If he violates these rigid laws, he does not have a show, and if his violations are chronic, he does not have a career.

Some veteran writers have observed that ignorance of the series' basic premises, and therefore of television's current premises, leads to demands for improvement of a product that contains built-in protection *against* improvement. Edmund Hartmann, a former national chairman of the television writers' union, the Writers Guild of America, has said that comparing the medium to the Old Vic "is something like complaining that a chicken is not a peacock." When it is understood that television "is entirely devoted to a specific form of advertising, namely brainwashing," he pointed out, the success of the medium must be assayed on other than cultural grounds. Hartmann explained: "Madison Avenue and the agents thereof have become bad words in Hollywood, synonymous with stupid, routine, cliché, or debilitating. Nothing could be farther from the truth. These men are geniuses. . . . They persuade corporations to invest millions of dollars in TV programs for the purpose of brainwashing the customers. They understand they are in the chicken business. Peacocks, that's a different racket altogether."

Most of the writers who made up the "live drama" group of early television have elected to stay out of the chicken business. Playwright Paddy Chayefsky explained why when he said, "In television, the writer is treated with a peculiar mixture of mock deference and outright contempt. He is rarely consulted about casting, his scripts are frequently mangled without his knowing about it. . . ." And David Davidson, another chairman of the Writers Guild, has pointed out that, under present conditions, "the writer who cares about what he writes for television is left completely devoid of excitement." He has been told, explicitly and repeatedly, "Thinker, go home!" As an example, when Daniel Melnick, an ABC programming executive, was asked to comment on the mass exodus of writers who could not stomach series-grinding, he replied bluntly that his network's staple fare, *Surfside Six, Adventures in Paradise, Hawaiian Eye,* and *77 Sunset Strip,* required "a different kind of writer—one who doesn't have a burning desire to make an original statement."

Few writers afflicted with burning desire (and it *is* an affliction) would contradict that manifesto. But many would also point out that the "different kind" of writer fails to produce anything worth repeating in another medium, such as the Broadway theater. Before television began to abuse the language by referring to *National Velvet* and *Divorce Court* as "drama," its works bore recapture. It originated such plays as *Middle of the Night, Face of a Hero, Little Moon of Alban, The Miracle Worker,* and others. It also gave Broadway *All the Way Home,* a play that was awarded a Pulitzer Prize but encountered difficulty winning public support. In network offices, where executive guilt is not unknown, this misfortune became fortuitous. When David Levy was vice-president for programming and talent at NBC, he used it to justify the burial of meaningful drama. "The audience just isn't there," Levy said. "If these writers want to work in television they must accommodate themselves to the current tastes of the public."

The taste of the public is not even remotely involved, of course. Writers must "accommodate" the taste of the sponsor and his advertising agency. They know this because they *have* accommodated, and because their overseers have embarrassed them in public by explaining how they have been subjected to thought control. Nicholas E. Keesely, the vice-president of the Lennen & Newell advertising agency, described the process rather chillingly when he told the Federal Communications Commission:

> There is a tremendous science and skill, I think, put behind most of these shows on the part of most agencies. . . . [A] man is assigned to supervise that show . . . and sit with the producer and lay out what we think will . . . make sure that the show is along certain lines in the best public interest. We cover policy and good taste and controversy, and good writing. Before we buy a show, we try to find out who the writers are. We sit with the writers. We have a conditioning, a series of meetings. . . .

Since it is well understood that "conditioning" teaches the writer that his mission is to attract as many of the buying population as possible, thoughtful writers depart the medium rather than submit. They have departed in such numbers that the Writers Guild once had immense difficulty in gathering just thirteen high-quality scripts for a projected anthology series. Some stay, but their discomfort is extreme. Many, said a report of a committee of the Guild, "use an apologetic tone when referring to their occupation, often following up the 'admission' by quickly explaining future plans in motion pictures, novels, or the legitimate stage." Among those who leave, returning intermittently but usually briefly, some supply stirring exit lines. Robert Alan Aurthur (*A Man Is Ten Feet Tall, A Sound of Different Drummers*) commented on the networks' insistence on regarding an audience of millions as an empty theater: "How extraordinary a world is television—a place where you can flop in front of 20,000,000 people and be told that nobody was watching!" Horton Foote (*The Night of the Storm, A Trip to Bountiful*) contributed a poignant note when he said: "You can't imagine how depressing it has become. It's almost like being rejected by a lover, because at one time we *did* feel very much loved and wanted."

After driving quality writers out of television, network executives sadly explain that they can't produce quality programs because they can't get quality writers. CBS has discouraged its full share of creativity, but this accomplishment did not prevent one of its program vice-presidents, Michael Dann, from complaining that he had difficulty signing up good writers for a series that was to be free of sponsor interference. He was offering $7,500 to $10,000 a script, too, and he appeared surprised that few had remained on the scene to await his offer. This is a charitable interpretation of Dann's reaction, for he must have been aware of the impact of the much publicized saga of David Evans, a man who wrote something interesting and thereby wrote himself out of work.

When I talked with Evans in Hollywood, he was still somewhat bewildered by his plight. As an English novelist and film-writer, he had come to Hollywood to write the screenplay of one of his books, *Sand Against the Wind,* which dealt with "an atheist who gets his comeuppance at Lourdes." Evans was versatile, and television was in Hollywood, so before long he had written for *The Reader's Digest* show, *Bourbon Street Beat, The Verdict Is Yours, The Texan, Whiplash,* and *Telephone Time.* A script for the last show caused his difficulties. It was called "The Gadfly," and it was, Evans explained, "an attempt to capture the real spirit and meaning of Socrates." In addition to being entertaining, "The Gadfly" won the 1958 award of the Johann J. Smit Foundation, conferred for "the most valuable contribution to peace and human understanding."

Almost immedately, Evans's telephone stopped ringing. No producers called; no work was assigned. Eventually his embarrassed agent told him: "You're too good for television. You're too erudite. They hear you've been to Cambridge and you've had books published. And then you write about Socrates. They just worry about you."

Evans himself took some soundings on the matter of Socrates and discovered that the man was not universally known in the industry. "Some people thought he was the one who took the elephants over the Alps," he reported. "He was also identified as a Roman gladiator and a Spanish general." Evans lives in a small apartment in Beverly Hills now, wondering how he can overcome the error of having ventured into the realm of Socrates.

Evans might have avoided his blunder if he had had the benefit of a conversation in which I learned the difference between troublesome and co-operative writers. A producer was explaining his major problem as a matter of time. "It's not the scripts," he said. "They're a dime a dozen. It's the deadlines—getting the stuff shot and moving on to the next one. That's why I can't take time to work with troublesome people who feel that every line is sacred. A writer has to co-operate if we're going to get the work out."

This producer has found the ideal co-operator. "This fellow is a wild man," he said. "He writes like lightning. He comes in and says, 'What do you want?' I tell him, 'I want three scripts in ten days. Do so-and-so, and so-and-so, and do the Macomber story again.' He goes home and ten days later three scripts are sitting on my desk. The revisions are easy. I say, 'No, do this scene this way.' He says, 'Oh, yes, I should have done it that way.' He whips out the revision and we're in business. He doesn't argue. He hasn't a thought of his own. He hasn't put any part of himself into the script and so he has nothing to argue for or against. He's a valuable man. He gets the work out."

For such reasons, many Eastern writers characterize the Hollywood goods-deliverers as "hacks." This label is understandable and appealing, but it skimps on information. The "Hollywood hacks" make up a broad-spectrum group, consisting at least of writers who are: (1) doing their best and trying to do it better, (2) making the best of a bad bargain and stifling their consciences, (3) grinding out lucrative slickness and defending their sins and the industry's, and (4) producing lackluster work but producing it on time, which, as has been pointed out, is sometimes *better* than producing it well.

There is a certain fluidity in and between these groups, naturally; with money in the bank, some writers muster the courage to resist the more disagreeable assignments. Lacking money and being human, courage ebbs and the capacity for self-deception increases. There is room, too, for honest differences of opinion over the nature of some programs, but this is a minor affair, having no relation to the general truth that witlessness is heavily in demand.

Even producers display dissatisfaction with the result. Hubbell Robinson, formerly and now again a CBS vice-president, erupted in *TV Guide* with the story of a writer who had been told by a producer: "Don't write it too good. If you do, we'll never sell it." Robinson then spread the blame more or less evenly. "Unfortunately," he said, "there appears to be a large supply of scribblers quite willing to not write 'too good,' or perhaps incapable of writing any other way. Whatever the reason and despite ratings or sales, most discerning critics are agreed the bulk of television writing is shoddy, lacking in inventiveness and imagination, failing almost entirely to apply resourcefulness, perceptiveness, understanding, and interpretation to the overwhelming concerns and anxieties of our times. This is an abdication of one of the dramatist's classic roles in society."

Robinson, in the tradition of well-intentioned producers, then misplaced the blame. He accused writers of failing to emulate those who dissected their societies in the dramatic form—Aristophanes, Ibsen, Molière, Galsworthy, O'Neill, and, in more recent times, the "Chayefsky group." But writers know that David Evans dissected Socrates and was injured, that O'Neill's *The Iceman Cometh* was almost disapproved by the Television Code, and that the Chayefskys were given their walking papers long ago. Given these circumstances, it seems illusory to long for a battalion of writers to appear on white chargers and slay the corporate dragon.

The question remains: Which came first, the chicken business or the featherbrained writer? Early in 1961, some highly experienced members of the Writers Guild—the committee that noted the defensive posture of Hollywood writers—studied this question and assigned the major portion of the blame to the "crippling artistic restrictions which face the television writer in pursuing his profession." The committee's report said in part:

> . . . there are no totally independent artists. Every medium suffers multiple controls via dominant religious and political philosophies, evolved social customs and tastes, and statute. But there are certain minimum freedoms which must be guaranteed, beyond which neither art nor self-respect is possible. These minimums have been violated in television.
>
> Our medium has become dominated by a network-agency-tradesman combination tending totally toward censorship and totally against writer independence and creativity. In ten short

> years, freedom of expression in dramatic television has been reduced to an area so small that pride in accomplishment is all but impossible.
>
> Like an assembly-line painter in a giant porcelain factory, the television writer is encouraged to exercise talent and individuality in color selection and brush technique only as long as he does not stray from the catalogue of approved designs. If he does stray, the work is "corrected" after it leaves his hands. Although . . . there are some exceptions, the system can only tend toward cliché-ridden product without artistic unity or integrity.

These problems of morality and individual responsibility have gnawed at professionals in Hollywood for many years. Movie writers perennially agonized over the fullness of their swimming pools and the emptiness of their scenarios, and it was as much as twenty years ago that Theodore Dreiser contributed a trenchant appraisal of the place. When Clifford Odets, who was writing the screenplay of *Sister Carrie,* told Dreiser that the studio might junk his scenario because it wasn't "commercial," the old man replied, "But they're really cocaine sellers out here. Are you surprised?"

Not wishing to see its deliberations drowned in a sea of self-pity, the Writers Guild committee commented somewhat starkly on the defense of Adolph Eichmann: "(1) He only followed orders; (2) Someone else would have done it if he hadn't." If this seems strong tea for a writers' klatch, the committee was even more emphatic in saying: ". . . the writer cannot escape direct responsibility for what is communicated to the viewer. . . . [He] has no obligation to grapple with eternal truths every time he approaches the typewriter. But if he does write a script purporting to mirror life but instead writes to the prejudices and merchandising needs of his patron-sponsor, that writer is simply a liar. If he compounds this by rationalizing that he bears no responsibility for his act, he is also a hypocrite. If he refuses to speak out because he fears it may imperil his income, he is a coward. And if he thinks that his crime is only a misdemeanor, that the torrent of images and thoughts being televised has no effect or bearing on the shape, direction, and security of his family, his nation, and mankind, he is a fool."

It was not the function of the committee to point to specific individuals, networks, or studios, but the submission of exhibits was unnecessary. Evidence of financial enticement, dual morality, and cynicism is omnipresent. A writer who has done fine work in other fields but persists in satisfying the wants of the television junk-dealers told me: "I love the Mozart Quartets, and I get real pleasure out of being able to buy them all, for cash. So I turn this stuff out during the day and listen to Mozart in the evening." The case of Roy Huggins, who wrote and produced many episodes of *Maverick*, is illustrative, too. In 1959, *Time* quoted Huggins as saying, "Television is for younger men—about fourteen years of age—and I'm getting out." Two years later, as a vice-president of 20th Century-Fox Television, Huggins took a wider view of matters as he accused Newton Minow, the FCC chairman, of being "completely irresponsible" in his vast-wasteland indictment. "It requires so many millions of viewers to pay for a television campaign," Huggins explained to a gathering of colleagues, "and by experiment we have found out what kind of shows will produce that kind of audience." It was 20th Century-Fox that produced a sadism-and-smut episode of *Bus Stop* so bestial that Jack Gould of *The New York Times* called it "a disgraceful and contemptible flaunting of decency, an indescribably coarse glorification of vulgarity to win an easy rating."

The lure of the greenback was well demonstrated in an experience of Ernest Kinoy, one of television's pioneer dramatists. In early 1961, Kinoy was asked to see a producer about writing a pilot for a projected show, *Breakdown.* Later, he related the incident this way:

> As soon as he handed me the presentation and I saw the juicy one-word title for the series, I knew what I was in for . . . two guys, a heavy jazz beat in the background, sports

> cars—the whole thing, including the luscious girls. These two guys weren't cowboys, they weren't private eyes, they weren't lawyers, they weren't even driving a Corvette around the country. They were psychiatrists.
>
> Each week they handle a different patient—and get to the bottom of a different psychosis. . . . I kept reading and then I put it down. [The producer] asked me for my reaction, and I told him—point-blank. I argued with him for about twenty-five minutes, but I just couldn't make him see that this would destroy whatever progress had been made—small as it has been—in educating the public on the question of mental health.
>
> Anyway, I refused to write the pilot. But this didn't disturb him one bit, because somebody walked in the next day and said he'd do it. . . .

No doubt there will always be someone to "do it," but those who worry about the consequences are not deterred by such fatalism. The Writers Guild committee conceded that for the man "content to be a bench-worker, concerned mainly with a comfortable income, with little interest in his medium and its effect on his society, the current system is endurable. But for the majority of men and women who come into writing because it satisfies needs within them to create, comment, and communicate, television has become a gold-plated ghetto."

When five writers—count 'em, five—can be used on *Mister Ed,* the talking-horse show, gold-plated is understatement. The man who "adapts" can hustle from studio to studio in his choice of sports cars and get some money into the stock market without much delay. David Davidson has remarked that "it is a sad truth that never before in history have writers been paid so much for writing so badly," and the statistics bear him out. Before the invasion of big-sponsor money, many writers were paid as little as one hundred and fifty dollars for all rights to a one-hour original script. During 1960, in contrast, a large number of television writers earned between $30,000 and $70,000, and a not inconsiderable number made more than $100,000. The possibilities are enormous, as witness the pay scale of *The Untouchables.* With approximately

$120,000 spent to produce this show each week, a writer can earn $4,000—the Writers Guild contract minimum is $2,200—for supplying the words that fill the time between machine-gun bursts. For a first re-run, he receives an additional $1,400, for a second, $1,200, for a third and fourth, $1,000 each, and if it is ever played again, another $1,000. In addition, the studio deposits 5 per cent of the original payment, or $200, into a pension fund for him. Who said crime doesn't pay?

Not everyone would take such a sour view, of course. A writer for *The Untouchables* has remarked, "Frankly, I've never had it so good." He has developed a method of convincing himself that he is teaching morality to the viewer. "We start our story conferences by thinking of a character," he says, "someone with a particular trait to which the audience can relate. Greed is an example of such a trait. Once we've decided on the character trait—the flaw—we relate it to the format. In the case of greed, the character would have to own something, or try to acquire something, which would involve the Federal authorities and Eliot Ness. Something like whisky or narcotics."

Other writers find solace in equating concern with incompetence. "I look with a very jaundiced eye on writers who bleat about the lack of opportunity," says one. "This business of looking down your nose at the so-called Hollywood hack is ridiculous. The guys who don't write format can't write format." He is undoubtedly correct. Some people just can't write format.

From time to time, sounds emerge from network offices that lead the unsuspecting to believe that television really wants to break the formula-format habit. CBS's Michael Dann says that "we must intensify our efforts to create the atmosphere and form in which new writers can develop. CBS, for one, hopes that we'll do infinitely more. We're going to do everything possible to keep original drama in our schedule." Less than six months before this statement, CBS shut off its Television Workshop, which had been hidden away in the Sunday noon-time period. Similarly, NBC periodically genuflects before the need for new ideas and new talent while providing no opportunity for them to develop. When the network's executives decided once that the time had come to talk about "freshness" again, they directed a now-famous memorandum on the subject to their operatives in Hollywood. The Hollywood executives yawned as the familiar phrases rolled in on the teletype, but their boredom soon turned to amazement when the memo refused to stop. When it ended with eighteen feet of teletype paper on the floor, they could not contain themselves and suggested that its receipt be acknowledged with the reply: "Arrived garbled. Please repeat." Someone pointed out, though, that anyone who would send such a message might well take this reply seriously. So the acknowledgment was amended to: "Opening thoughts O.K., but last fourteen-fifteen feet garbled." The moral of the story is that it is difficult to make a Hollywood professional sit still for nonsense; nonsense is something he knows all about.

ABC, the "counter-programming" network, is sometimes under the impression that it, too, cultivates fresh thinking. But its owned-and-operated station in Chicago, WBKB, has indicated that new writers had better be, above all, practical. In a bulletin known as "Advice to Aspiring TV Writers," WBKB said: "A. Evolve a story-line idea for some series currently on the air. B. Watch this series and formulate in your own mind techniques employed, types of plots avoided, etc."

Goodman Ace, who has fought the losing battle for innovation and now writes material for Perry Como, has had many opportunities to observe the networks' infatuation with weary ideas. As early as 1946, he was installed on the eighteenth floor of the CBS building and commissioned to think new. He thought, and eventually suggested, among other things, that a quiz show might be developed around Groucho Marx. Impractical, he was told. One day he remarked that if an atom bomb ever fell on New York, the best refuge would be on the eighteenth floor at CBS. "There's no radioactivity up there," he said.

Not that Ace singles out CBS as a target. After NBC first staged *Peter Pan,* he wondered what would have happened if the play had been presented to an executive conference as an unknown property. Ace saw the meeting this way:

1ST PRODUCER: Well, the next thing on the agenda is this *Peter Pan* script. Has anybody read it?

1ST EXECUTIVE: I read it.

1ST PRODUCER: How'd it strike you?

1ST EXECUTIVE: It struck me as long. Get the writer to cut it to about twenty-six minutes and with a three-minute commercial we might be—

2ND PRODUCER: How about doing it as a spectacular? I haven't read all of it, but if it's long, that's what a spectacular has to be. We're halfway home to start with.

1ST EXECUTIVE: Wait a minute—that rings a bell. Peter Paul Mounds is looking for a big one-shot. And with that title—*Peter Pan,* presented by Peter Paul Mounds—or maybe we can change the title of the script to *Peter Paul!*

2ND PRODUCER: Wait a minute—hold everything. I just been reading some more of this script. Did you see this line where Peter Pan turns to the audience and asks if they believe in fairies?

1ST PRODUCER: Yes, what about it?

2ND PRODUCER: Oh, come on Harry, how are you gonna get away with that? You think NBC would let a line like that go through?

1ST EXECUTIVE: Well, that can always be changed to, Do you believe in gnomes?

Goodman Ace doesn't write that kind of comedy for television. The networks wouldn't know what to do with it, as neither CBS nor NBC knew what to do with the contracts it had with Mort Sahl. The "new comedy" sweeps America, but it is largely found in night clubs and on recordings of night-club routines. Mort Sahl explained the reason for this when he told of how the networks attempted to utilize his talents. He wanted to do a show something like *Wide Wide*

World (at which he would be positively masterful), but, he said, "In 1956, when everyone was talking about George Gobel, it was how would I like to do a comedy show like his? The next year it was emcee a quiz show, then a judge on a divorce-court show. You could tell the year from the kind of show they were pushing." Steve Allen came back to the medium, but was carefully insulated from adults by virtue of an early time period; he quit. Bob Newhart is seen, true, but his incisors reveal less of the original sharpness and his colleagues fear for his safety in the jungle.

Television is more comfortable with Joey Bishop as a press agent stumbling through a contrived plot each week, Danny Thomas working the tired and true situations each week, Donna Reed making her way determinedly through nursery-level homilies each week.

It is the *each week* aspect of his chore that makes many a writer wonder why he ever chose such a method of earning a living. Each week he must figure out new ways of doing old things; moreover, he must move his characters around in ways that the producer understands because he is accustomed to seeing them move in those ways. "The whole thing is popped out of a can," one writer observed. "Change the names and the lines can fit any show, any week. 'Drink your milk, Dennis.' 'Look out, Ozzie, that thing'll fall on you—oh, Ozzie!' 'Gee, grampa, do I *have* to?' 'Aunt Kitty's coming for a visit, Pete.' You think it's fun turning these things out? I've lost my hair and I think I'm losing my mind."

This comedy writer, who does not laugh, described a number of devices that the grind has forced onto the artisan. The most interesting is the "treacle-cutter." "You see," he said, "comedy has to say something to be funny, but in television every time you say something, somebody worries that you said too much. Therefore, you have to devise a little Sunday School lesson at the end of the show—a sermon against beating dogs or talking back to parents. But a moral of that kind has no place in comedy. It's puffed up and sticky. It's treacle.

So you have to work out a *second* ending to cut the treacle—a silly line after the commercial, or a brief sight gag. It gets the actors out of the syrup they're walking in. That's the treacle-cutter."

No picture of the television writer's life would be complete without reference to a dread institution, the political blacklist, reports of whose passing are exaggerated. Scores of writers in Hollywood are working under various forms of anonymity because their true names may not appear on studio payrolls.

The practice of subjecting actors, directors, producers, and writers to private loyalty tests originated shortly after May, 1947, when three former FBI agents began publishing a weekly newsletter known as *Facts to Combat Communism, Counterattack.* Three years later, the trio issued a thick booklet called *Red Channels, the Report of Communist Influence in Radio and Television,* which listed the names of approximately one hundred and fifty persons whose politics were suspect to the compilers. In the course of their distribution, these publications affected hundreds of people, some of whom were highly prominent and many of whom were canceled out of shows.

But *Counterattack*—to be fair to it—was more than a narrow show-business disinfectant; its range of interests was sweeping. It once referred to Trygve Lie, secretary-general of the United Nations, as "Stalin's choice," and at one time or another bared its intensely patriotic fangs at the Standard Oil Company (N.J.), the Yale Law School, the *New York Times,* the New York *Herald Tribune,* the Associated Press, and *The New Yorker, Fortune, Look,* and *Atlantic Monthly* magazines.

There were apparent oddities about *Counterattack* and *Red Channels.* The firm that published them, for example, offered to sell "derogatory information" about show-business personalities to sponsors, advertising agencies, and the television networks, and a refusal to buy was sometimes followed by an attack on a program in which the recalcitrant had an interest.

Such a sequence could have been mere coincidence, of course, but those who were its victims were difficult to convince.

In any event, *Red Channels* became what Jack Gould of the *New York Times* called "the bible of Madison Avenue." When a person was named, he was in trouble unless he demonstrated a change of heart in a way that was acceptable to the three publishers. Perhaps the most celebrated case that arose from these operations was that of Jean Muir, an actress who had contracted to appear on NBC's *The Aldrich Family* series. When Miss Muir's name appeared in *Red Channels* and telephone calls were made to the network, to General Foods (the sponsor), and to its advertising agency, Young & Rubicam, her contract was bought up; John Crosby denounced this action as "appalling moral cowardice," but Miss Muir did not appear. Nor did she appear on television again until David Susskind gave her a role ten years later.

By the end of 1950, *Red Channels* was as familiar to the industry as a rating report, and many artists were blacklisted without their knowledge inasmuch as other private lists began to circulate; suddenly, they just didn't get casting calls. Merle Miller, in his study of blacklisting in broadcasting, *The Judges and the Judged* (Doubleday, 1952), quoted a CBS official as saying, "My God, it's straight out of Kafka, isn't it? These three gents have the whole damn industry stymied—three guys, count 'em."

While executives were uniformly denying, for publication, that they used blacklists, CBS instituted a loyalty statement to be signed by each of its employees (the only man known to have successfully refused to sign was John K. M. McCaffery, who was then the moderator of a panel show). Some CBS employees were so dismayed that they regularly leaked word of blacklisting outrages to the press, but the inquisition continued and grew. Philip Loeb,* who played the role of "Jake" on CBS's *The Goldbergs,* was forced out of the show. After

* Only persons whose cases have already received extensive publicity are identified here.

Hazel Scott, the pianist and singer, was listed in *Red Channels,* the now defunct Du Mont network dropped her program; an executive explained: "It was just that we felt we could more easily sell the time if somebody else was in that spot." Later, when Miss Scott was canceled out of a program on another network, the sponsor said, "She's still listed in that book, and we don't want to get involved in any controversy." When Sidney Poitier was cast in a play on the *Philco Playhouse* series, NBC attorneys confronted him with their "derogatory information." Among other things, they asked Poitier why he had lived with the late actor Canada Lee, who was also a Negro, while they were making *Cry the Beloved Country* in South Africa.

Blacklisting abated in New York only when the bulk of television production moved to Hollywood, where writers have traditionally been more of a target than actors. The studios there denied, too, that the lists even existed.

Actually, both a black and a "gray" list are operative in Hollywood. Under this distinction, a blacklist is composed of persons who have been subpoenaed by some legislative committee checking political pedigrees and who have refused to co-operate. A gray list consists of those who, after having been named as "left-wingers" or "Communists" by a co-operator, have not made their peace with the offended group. Since a gray list is an informal document at least partly reflecting the subjective judgment of whoever composed it, all sorts of people may appear on one. Interestingly, too, they may be on Studio A's list but not on Studio B's. This quickens the pace of their lives.

Black- and gray-listed writers have used three methods of circumventing the bans. At first they employed a "front." Unemployable writers wrote the scripts but someone else signed and submitted them. This arrangement collapsed under its complexities. There were income-tax problems (who should report the earnings?) and the bothersome necessity of having to sit in on story and revision conferences (who should appear —the writer or the ghost?).

The other methods are both in effect at this moment. Under one, the listed writter simply becomes someone else; his blacklisted self dies or goes to Thule, Greenland, because of a sudden aggravation of his asthma. The new self (both for professional and social purposes) takes over his work. Anyone who wonders how a new identity could move in on an old identity's work overlooks the fact that studio executives know what is going on while they deny that anything is going on. They understand that the blacklisted writer is not really dead or in Thule, just as they may even understand their own gutlessness in fearing to tell a sponsor to keep his nose out of their end of the business.

The other popular method involves the assumption of a dual personality. At home and among his friends, the writer lives under the name he inherited from his parents; at work, he uses an alias. This method has its sticky features, however, because there are times when a professional associate must be invited to the home. The guest may follow the directions to North Hollywood without difficulty, but unless he is briefed beforehand, he may be bewildered by the name affixed to the doorbell. These briefing sessions make interesting conversation—as do those the wife of a blacklisted writer says she has when she visits the set of a show her husband is working on. "Hi," says an employee. "Are you looking for—well, whatever we're calling him this week?"

But this is not to suggest that blacklisting has become a matter of chuckles and sly grins. Essentially it remains a breeder of tragedy, as evidenced by the case of Louis Pollock, a desperate man. Pollock worked on newspapers and at publicity until he entered the film industry as a promotion man and rose to become advertising and publicity manager of United Artists. In 1941, he was elected president of the Association of Motion Picture Advertisers and became closely associated with Will Hays, first head of the Motion Picture Association of America (the "Hays office"), and with the presidents of the Paramount, Universal, United Artists, RKO, and 20th Century-Fox studios. In 1945, he quit a $25,000-a-year job with United Artists to write for motion pictures. He did this successfully and also wrote a humorous book, *Stork Bites Man* (World, 1945), which has sold almost 100,000 copies.

Pollock did radio work, too, writing dramas for *Suspense, The Prudential Hour, Philip Morris Playhouse,* and *The Skippy Theatre.* When television arrived, he sold plays to *Alfred Hitchcock Presents,* one being "Breakdown," the first television drama Hitchcock directed himself.

But in 1954, Louis Pollock suddenly stopped selling material either to motion pictures or to television. Movie scripts were invariably returned with the terse comment, "Not interested," and television story editors declined to see him. Pollock knew about blacklists, of course, but he also knew that he could not possibly be on one, since he had never belonged to any organizations but the Writers Guild of America, the Authors' Guild, and the Arlington Terrors, which he describes as "a Montreal gang of twelve-year-old stinks who used to wet-pack their snowballs." A few writers cracked jokes about the blacklist, but he only laughed with them. His sole choice, he says, was to "keep writing and to try not to believe that in some mysterious way my work had slumped." Between 1954 and the end of 1961, he wrote ten movies and thirty television plays, and still has them, unsold. True, he did sell a script in 1957 to CBS's *Lineup,* but a few weeks later the program's story editor told him that he "somehow didn't have the knack of television writing."

Since professional success is the keystone of many relationships, Pollock steadily suffered the loss of both friends and influential agents. He wrote for magazines to earn food money but finally decided he owed it to his wife and two sons to return to advertising and promotion work. Then he was rebuffed by men he had known for twenty years; one turned and walked away from him in a Hollywood restaurant.

Pollock still didn't know what had happened but, being human, he was deeply affected. His blood pressure rose, he began taking sleeping pills, and he secretly used his wife's tranquilizers. "I became panicky," he says, "and was plagued day and night by the fear of complete destitution. I was not for some months able to sit down and write another word on the typewriter."

In October, 1959, Pollock found out what was destroying him. While talking to a studio executive who was not involved with writers, he remarked that he had been blocked out of his profession, and unaccountably. An hour later, the executive telephoned him at home and asked him several odd questions. Had he had been born in Hungary? Was his wife's name Lillian? Was he fifty-seven years old? Had he ever sold newspapers in Los Angeles? Had he ever been a prizefighter? Had he ever run a clothing store in San Diego?

The answer to all these questions was no.

The wrong man had been blacklisted by the diligent protectors of American security. On April 17, 1954, a man whose name was spelled Poll*a*ck appeared before the House Committee on Un-American Activities, in San Diego, and refused to answer questions concerning his politics. Louis Pollack had no connection with Hollywood, but his name was dispatched to the studios by those to whose informational services the studios subscribed. Louis Poll*o*ck was ruined; the error took his income, his home, his savings, and—who can say it has not taken some of his life? I cannot, for I have seen him.

But at least the error had been discovered. Pollock engaged an attorney who informed the House Committee of what had transpired, and shortly afterward he had a letter explaining that the committee had nothing against him. There was a hitch, though—and it seemed to be a slight one. Since the industry officially denied that blacklists existed, and copies of such rolls were not posted on telephone poles in Hollywood, there was no direct way of informing the studios that Louis Pollock was not Louis Pollack. Pollock called a press conference at the offices of the Writers Guild and revealed his bizarre story; it made the front pages of many newspapers and, he thought, "I was now at last out from under a shadow I never knew had fallen on me."

When the William Morris agency agreed to represent him once more, it seemed as if old times had returned. But when he submitted a story to NBC's *The Deputy* series, it was turned down despite a preliminary report indicating it would be bought. He sent a story to the *Laramie* show, was told he could count on its acceptance, and was then informed that neither NBC nor the business office of the studio, Revue Productions, would approve the purchase. Somewhat dumfounded, he telephoned the assistant producer of *Laramie*.

"I asked him if he could be sure the objection was because of the subject matter of the story," Pollock says. "He expressed surprise and asked what other reason did I think could be involved. I reminded him about my blacklisting case and he immediately volunteered to check my status. Hardly ten minutes later he phoned back, sounding quite astonished, and told me he had put my name to an NBC network representative and had been informed that I was 'negative' or still on the blacklist."

Pollock discovered that he was indeed still on a blacklist; now he was considered a troublemaker because he had made a public issue of his misfortune. When I talked to him in Hollywood, he sat in the living room of his small apartment, resembling a shattered figure from—as the CBS official suggested—*The Trial.* Louis Pollock has been tried and condemned by the blacklisters, and doubly punished by the studios for having pleaded not guilty. He is bewildered; no one has told him why he must die.

10 THE PEDDLERS

"Don't let romance fade . . . fade . . . fade . . . away!"—*Colgate Dental Cream.*

At an advertising agency that spends $50,000,000 a year in television, an executive explained how commercials create strength through joy. "Consider what life would be like without them," he said. "What do you talk about at parties, after all? You talk about the new refrigerators and the new cars, don't you? The new products. Everybody does. That's what interests people. That's what makes the wheel go 'round."

A mulish optimist, I elected to view this judgment as slippage on the part of a Madison Avenue practitioner who had been working too hard. Not long afterward, though, intelligence from a social watering hole forced a reconsideration of this case for cheerfulness. At a dance in Newport, Rhode Island, an elegant couple asked conductor Lester Lanin to play "Mr. Clean." Baffled only briefly, his band was soon giving Procter & Gamble's household-scrub commercial a rousing Dixieland treatment, following which it rendered "Robert Hall," a cantata of suits and slacks, and other tone poems of the jinglesmiths. The socialites' reaction was so enthusiastic that Lanin produced a long-playing record, *The Madison Avenue Beat,* composed of fifty-eight broadcast commercials from "Double Your Pleasure" to "New-port Fil-ter Ci-ga-rettes."

This development suggests the possibility of a completely new entertainment form consisting of programs that would shun savagery and silliness and be constructed entirely of instructive and diverting sponsors' messages. "The Girl with the Fast-Acting Cold Remedy," for example, or "Nuzzle Me, My Nicotiney Baby." On Sunday afternoons, eggheads could enjoy a debate, "Do Segregated Clothes Get *Really* White?"

With such programming, we would have the ultimate in Willy Loman television—pure peddling, untouched by human creativity, or sellevision.

It would be wildly alarmist, of course, to imply that sellevision is imminent; thus far, only primitive attempts have been made to lace sponsors' products into story lines. The script of *Dennis the Menace* calls for Dennis to drink soda pop, but the sponsor, Corn Products Company, makes Bosco, so Dennis drinks Bosco and milk. Dennis is supposed to eat a meat sandwhich, but Corn Products makes Skippy Peanut Butter, so Dennis eats a peanut butter sandwich.

This blatancy is still embryonic. For the moment, at least, ABC, CBS, and NBC seem content to identify overt commercials and flank them with programming that is only indirectly an inducement to enter into the happy, happy buying spirit. Pressure for Anacin-gargling heroes and Revlon-decorated heroines may mount, however, when more package-goods advertisers conclude that they may not be getting enough return for their money. The fact is that the mass-product commercials may soon be in trouble. Although Madison Avenue continually reassures corporate advertising managers that they are getting their money's worth, and corporate advertising managers prayerfully relay this dogma to corporate directors, some corporate directors are beginning to wonder if they have been maneuvered into a lobster trap.

The strident claims and counter-claims of the peddlers neutralize each other, but no one can quit, or even let up for that matter, for fear that his competitor will continue. Thus, the only way to protect the investment is by increasing it, by buying even more commercials and giving the viewer an even worse headache. No exit.

The viewer? He feels pain; there's no doubt of that. Otherwise, 2,500,000 people would not have purchased "blab-offs," electronic marvels that end the blare by switching off the sound portion. (One manufacturer of television receivers bought a full page in a Chicago newspaper to complain that these devices were "un-American and unsportsmanlike," and to urge Congress to outlaw them.) Most viewers, however, endure the pain of super-commercialization as they do other troubles they regard as resistant to their powers of reform. They have been so cowed, the honest, gentle souls, that they can even be counted on for philosophical tolerance of their earaches.

But it does not follow in these dreary circumstances that the viewer is witless, Madison Avenue to the contrary. He knows some and suspects others of the following:

1. He is being burdened with far, FAR, FAR too many commercials.
2. Too many are either offensive or too ridiculous to be taken seriously.
3. Some commercials are a menace to our health.
4. Some are false and misleading.
5. Many are a waste of *our* money.

For imaginative ad men, the arrival of big-time commercial television was a call to the colors. They had, as a matter of routine, intruded themselves into magazines, newspapers, radio, matchbooks, commuters' timetables, buses, trains, streetcars, sports arenas, theaters, and even medical journals. They had protected us from the glare of the countryside with billboards, and they had even hired airplanes to scrawl smoky messages in the skies. But for ad men these were pedestrian efforts, the sort of day-to-day job they might be fired for *not* doing. In a narrowing land of innovation, their last really resourceful accomplishment was the erection of a huge, bright neon sign on the bank of New York's East River, across from the United Nations, so that delegates from the ignorant countries of the world could murmur, "What means Pepsi-Cola?"

As a consequence of these numerous affronts, computing men compute that the "typical American" is exposed to over 10,000 advertisements each week. Other computing men estimate that of this Gargantuan number, the "average television family" ingests about six hundred in the form of commercials during the thirty-five hours it is said to devote to its electronic bliss dispenser every week. When this figure is reduced to seventeen and a half commercials per hour of television, it seems unrealistically high, but when the number is subjected to clinical test, to borrow an elastic phrase, it is all too valid. The clinical test took place on an autumn evening between 8:29 and 9:29 P.M. The observation post was Channel 4 in New York, NBC's outlet, and the program was the first of the *Dr. Kildare* series. (*This* Dr. Kildare was seen over television in 1961, not in a motion picture theater in 1936.) Curtain:

At 8:29, NBC advertised a forthcoming program. Then came commercials for the Chemical Corn Bank and Maxwell House Coffee, followed by a public service announcement on behalf of the Federal Housing Administration. Troubled Dr. Kildare appeared, but only for three minutes; he was interrupted by the preliminary announcement that his story was being presented by Bayer Aspirin, L&M Cigarettes, and Listerine Antiseptic. Back to the story? No—a one-minute commercial for the aspirin (with references to doctors that blended with the Kildarean medical motif). At 8:48, the drama paused for a cigarette commercial, and at 9:02, for a mouthwash message. At 9:03, NBC promoted one of its own shows, then presented commercials for Yuban Instant Coffee and Ipana Toothpaste. Before returning to Dr. Kildare, whose travail was growing dimmer with each interruption, NBC revealed that *this* half of the show was being dispatched by Phillips Milk of Magnesia, Lustre-Creme Shampoo, and Chesterfield cigarettes. (A total of seven announcements unbroken by programming.) At 9:13, time out for magnesia adulation, and at 9:24, for shampoo worship. Godliness then gave way to cleanliness, in the form of a Palmolive Soap commercial. At 9:26, cigarettes, and at 9:27, Mitch Miller, behind his ecstatic grin, invited us to sing along with him later in the evening.

Grand total: twenty-one commercials—count 'em—within one hour, if it is thought appropriate to include NBC's advertisements for itself. The inclusion of these "promos" is not really inappropriate inasmuch as all the messages make up the price that must be paid for entertainment.

The American people, who rank with the most patient and generous in the world, have long been accustomed to buying broadcast service with a valuable asset—their attention. Our American corporations are indulging uncommon ineptitude and charity, for they are spending over $1,600,000,000 every year to purchase attention through television alone. George Washington Hill, model of the modern huckster, who was president of the American Tobacco Company, explained such investments during the salad days of radio when he said: "Taking 100 per cent as the total radio value, we give 90 per cent to commercials, to what's said about the product, and we give 10 per cent to the show. . . . I don't have the right to spend the stockholders' money just to entertain the public."

Merchandiser Hill was a dragoon of the hit-'em-again, they're-still-breathing army of advertising, which pioneered the tactic of driving audiences to the gates of insanity through repetition—an obvious improvement over the Chinese water-torture method. The cigarette maker is credited with the paternity of such historic declamations as "L.S./M.F.T., L.S./M.F.T. Lucky Strike means fine tobacco. Yes, Lucky Strike means fine tobacco." (It is alleged that when he died, a show-business paper reported: "George Washington Hill is dead. Yes, George Washington Hill is dead.")

Although Hill is repetitiously and thus absolutely dead, his memory lingers. But his spirit has, in many cases, been uplifted, so much so that at least three types of commercials may now be considered downright progressive:

The gusher. Ad men have concluded that whenever people see, hear, or think of water, they are impelled to buy cigarettes. Either this is incontrovertibly true or several cigarette manufacturers are sending a barrel of money up the river, and I choose, of course, to disbelieve the latter. I have seen my friends confronted with all sorts of television water—bubbling, racing, rippling, shimmering, pacific, tingling, and gushing water—and invariably they have excused themselves and gone out to buy cigarettes. If this documentation is insufficient, I can offer movies of my wife and myself emerging from numerous swimming pools, exciting droplets coursing down our cheeks, staring into each other's eyes with our original devotion, inhaling deeply of tobacco smoke, and renewing our vows. For us, love is a Turkish water pipe on a twenty-one-inch screen.

The thriller. This breed of commercial utilizes the suspense form. It begins with Mums offering Dadsy and the boys a new pancake syrup. They stare at it apprehensively, thus instilling in the viewer a sense of anticipation. Will the family go for Mums's supermarket discovery? Will they love her after breakfast, or open her arteries? Will this be a cataclysmic syrup expectoration? Dadsy and the apple-cheeked boys slice their pancakes with tentative gestures, lift a forkful to their lips, and activate their mandibles. The viewer is chilled with the dampness of excitement as Dadsy looks up. His Adam's apple ripples as the syrup slides home. Mums waits, naked fear revealed in her eyes. Dadsy smiles. So do Joey and Pete. "Gosh, Mums," they exclaim, "this pancake syrup is delectable! You certainly are an intelligent and resourceful marketer, with a keen eye for value and deep-down goodness, as well as lasting quality, Mums." Joey and Pete look as if they wish *they* had married their mother, the sponsor has won a close contest, and the viewer has had a suspenseful evening. Only an egghead or a malcontent would complain.

The johnny mop. Television commercials have exposed the stuffiness of architects, who have traditionally created a special room in the house for personal use, isolated it further with a door, and named it "bathroom." This Victorian nonsense has now been challenged in several ways. Women may be seen rubbing toilet paper across their cheeks and smiling right in the living room. People who give off odors, like lower-order animals, may learn about deodorant application without leaving the sofa, and thus stop driving friends, clients, and countrymen away. And halitosis-ridden girls may do their homework before the television and receive due warning: "Don't let romance fade . . . fade . . . fade . . . away!" These public service messages have struck valuable blows against priggishness, yet they are not universally appreciated. The enemies of frankness harass and snipe at them, and have already robbed the viewer of his right to hear about hemorrhoid suppositories, and to see brambly hair being erased from women's legs. Reaction never sleeps.

In view of a widespread tendency to make light of the tribulations of advertising men, it is not surprising that the men who make the commercials are not the most self-confident in the world. When they impetuously polled people on whether they'd like their sisters to marry ad men, only 4 per cent replied affirmatively, and that didn't help matters. Actually, they are a misunderstood breed. Many people think, for instance, that commercials are fashioned by a few people who sit around awhile and amuse one another. Not so. They are made by many people who sit around a long time and annoy each other. It is inevitable that this should happen, because there are so many conflicting views of what will sell soap, cigarettes, and flaky flaky biscuits, and where sales efforts should be concentrated. An example lies in the conviction once expressed by a thought leader of the McCann-Erickson advertising agency: "You would find the normal, hard-hitting, average man outside the metropolitan areas was a Camel smoker" (He was referring only to commercials; another ad man with a tobacco client discussed *programming* by explaining: "No one has ever convinced me that it takes any intelligence to buy this brand [his client's] rather than any other, so why should we sponsor intelligent programs?")

When life was simpler, an ad man could produce an interesting idea and watch it progress through mechanical stages into final form. Today he is second-guessed by *wunderkind* psychologists who are helping humanity by placing their alleged insights at the service of merchandisers, *e.g.*, the motivation researchers. Thus, the ad man is told by the high priest of motivational incantation, Ernest Dichter, that a viewer will welcome a commercial that offers him "an opportunity to identify with it and which appears to represent some understanding of him, and of his needs and tastes in keeping with his socio-economic grouping." Attempts to apply such advanced thinking to corn-remover problems may account for many hypertension cases along Madison Avenue. At the very least, it causes confusion and a considerable waste of (our) money. (One commercial was subjected to psychological scrutiny *after* it had achieved remarkable sales results in a test area; the verdict: "Don't use it—it won't work.")

Examples of awesome indecisiveness are numerous, but one is particularly worthy of an award. It happened when an agency hired a film studio to shoot a commercial for a beer whose label depicted an Indian girl. After months of preparation, a script was written that called for a comedian to present an old-fashioned spiel, and for a hand to reach into the picture at the end and pour the parched barker a glass of beer. It was the hand that caused the difficulty.

"Let it turn out to be the hand of a pretty Indian girl, like on the label," said a straight-thinking conferee. The idea was accepted and the film producer was instructed to locate an Indian girl. He found one and was ready to shoot, when his director received a memo, from the ad agency, that belongs in some hall of fame. "Please find out about a lion immediately now!" it said. "Do it—just do it! NO QUESTIONS! NOW! NOW! NOW!" It developed that the client had crudely suggested that he was trying to sell beer, not pretty Indian girls. So the director found an aged, toothless lion and the producer was prepared to roll his cameras, when he received a telephone call from the agency. "A live lion is too dangerous. Use a stuffed lion." The director found a stuffed lion, whereupon the agency said, "Not lifelike enough. We'll use a pretty Indian girl." And so the commercial was made.

I found it difficult to believe that the production of some of these relatively brief epics could cost as much as $25,000 (a quarter of a billion dollars a year goes into their manufacture), but that was before I watched a rather modest sample facing the cameras. It involved the efforts of troupers Enid Markey and Tom Pedi to convince the American woman, on behalf of Procter & Gamble, that washday is funday when Dash is the detergent of choice. The seasoned actors were surrounded by a director, two cameramen, a prop man, a sound man, two lighting men, a script girl, and miscellaneous others on the payroll. A make-up man patted Miss Markey's face, an electrician slapped a balky lighting fixture, a bell rang, and silence fell on the studio. The camera whirred.

"Madam," said appliance serviceman Pedi, "when I say carefree washdays, I mean you can place your *confidence* in this package."

"But I want clean clothes," replied housewife Markey—in what struck me as a non sequitur.

"Cut!" yelled the director. "Darling," he said, "*clean* clothes. *Clean!*"

"*Clean!*" said Miss Markey. She and Pedi composed themselves, the director smiled, all hands resumed battle stations, and the cameras rolled.

"But I want *clean* clothes," said Miss Markey. "I want them *clean!*"

"Wonderful, darling," said the director. "You're doing it fine, Enid darling. Perfect." He paused. "We'll try it just once more, honey."

They tried it seven times more.

If this amounts to a Cecil De Mille production for a shoelace, it is not resented by people who must eat—actors, for instance. "My timing is superb," reflected an excellent character player. "I came to New York just as they were burying live drama. I had one beautiful part on a *Robert Montgomery Presents* and one nice role on a *Studio One.* Then I considered the possibility of playing a clown at supermarkets on Saturdays, or of starting a newspaper route in the suburbs. But my agent called with a terrific role. I was to play an attendant in a car-wash parlor who discovers that you can plug a shaver into a car's cigarette lighter. I did it. Like Marlon Brando and Errol Flynn I did it. And every time that commercial was run, I got a residual check in the mail. Grocery money. God bless something."

The saga of Julia Meade is similar, if headier. Julia studied at the Yale School of Drama, played stock theater, and finally entered television as one of the pretty girls who relax audiences and dispense prizes on game shows. She entered the world of commercials in the late 1940's through the *Ed Sullivan Show,* and as a champion pitch girl, has earned over $100,000 a year many times since. Miss Meade may never achieve the riches earned by Betty Furness, the skilled refrigerator-door opener, but she is content; art is long and life fleeting.

The television commercial was born and broadcast before most of America knew that television itself existed. The date was July 1, 1941, five months before another date that shall live in infamy. At ten seconds before 2:30 P.M., NBC's New York channel, then WNBT, switched off its test pattern, displayed the time on a Bulova clock, then telecast a baseball game from Ebbets Field. At 6:45, Sunoco gasoline sponsored Lowell Thomas with his version of the news, and later that evening, Lever presented *Uncle Jim's Question Bee,* with a commercial for Spry. Procter & Gamble retaliated with Ralph Edwards' *Truth or Consequences,* and before the station signed off with "The Star-Spangled Banner" at 10:57:19, viewers—an estimated 4,500 of them—received the correct time from Bulova again. WNBT collected three hundred and twenty-two dollars in commercial fees, a heavy loss for the day but no cause for concern; the pot of gold was clearly visible on the horizon.

The eruption of World War II upset the timetable; but the war did end, and so did delays in the production of television receivers and transmitting equipment. The years that followed saw more and more national advertisers recognizing the sales power of the new medium. At first they scrambled for position by sponsoring entire shows; a half-hour program could be had for the truly economical price of $1,000,000 or less a year, including network time and talent costs. But as prices rose, fewer corporations could afford steady network television, so costs were split under alternate sponsorship arrangements. Eventually, many programs found themselves with three sponsors, and finally, when the cost of a half-hour program got beyond $5,000,000 a year, only a handful of firms could afford "their own" program. The networks solved this crisis by selling "minutes"; they would produce a show themselves and simply drop in various commercials.

And all the while the commercial clamor was increasing, for in addition to commercials on network shows themselves, there was the gigantic institution of "spot" advertising. A "spot" is a commercial dropped into the interval between programs, the "station break" (whose original purpose was to permit stations to comply with Federal law by stating their call letters). The term "spot" once referred to spots on the map; a brewer whose market was restricted to the Northeast would buy spot time on stations in the Northeast. In present usage, the term applies to any commercial inserted between programs, or sometimes to rather unnatural breaks built into programs. Spot is big business, accounting for almost 40 per cent of all television advertising.

Understandably, then, the broadcasters' problem soon changed from one of finding enough advertisers to one of finding enough places to put advertisers; the problem was solved by putting them everywhere, at every conceivable opportunity. The high, or low, point in this process was probably reached when the events surrounding the inauguration of President Kennedy, in January, 1961, were brought to us by Purex and the Savings and Loan Foundation, Inc. The swearing-in ceremony was free of sponsorship, but the mark of the household bleach was inevitably on the entire affair and would not rinse. Worse, if possible, the inaugural ball was sponsored by a hosiery mill, and we have been shown the Kennedys' life in the White House by grace of Procter & Gamble's Crest Tooth Paste.

The rewards of over-commercialization are stupendous and therefore irresistible. In broadcasting, every motion of the second hand is worth many dollars, and increasingly, every motion has been made to count on the cash register. The way in which this has been accomplished is illustrated by the fate of the station break. In 1948, it was fifteen seconds, during which stations presented a spot commercial. Three years later, the interval was increased to twenty seconds, which lengthened the commercial; and in 1956, to thirty seconds, which allowed two spots, and in many cases, three. Each time the break grew, a commensurate amount of time was snipped, ethically or otherwise, from the programs that surrounded it; not even television can get more than sixty seconds out of a minute.

The climax occurred in early 1961, when ABC announced it was increasing its break to forty seconds. Madison Avenue emitted fierce growls, with the president of Young & Rubicam suggesting "a direct infringement upon responsible use of free air waves granted to networks and stations by all the people." He called the plan "another step toward a chaos of commercialism extending from coast to coast." The ad man felt, in other words, that for advertisers the law of diminishing returns was becoming operative. After these brave words, Y&R and other agencies swung gracefully into line; and CBS and NBC lengthened their intervals, too.

Ten seconds do not an eternity make, but their addition to spot commercial time has garnished television's already tasty profits: It has been estimated authoritatively that the three networks, through their fifteen owned and operated stations, are increasing their revenues by about $7,500,000 annually; the five hundred and fifty other stations are conglomerately benefiting by approximately a quarter of a billion dollars a year. The viewer benefits by having more products to talk about at parties. If he becomes annoyed despite this gift, he can comfort himself with the knowledge that not everyone is unhappy. There is, for example, the ad agency man who told me why his aspirin commercial was repeated endlessly without alteration. "It's the most obnoxious commercial on the air," he said, "but that company is selling an awful lot of aspirin. Do you think it will be taken off?"

"No," I replied.

11 THE HEALERS

"If your child is having trouble with his lessons, it may not be his fault—he may need a laxative."—Phillips Milk of Magnesia.

"Were a healthy Eskimo or a native of remote Tibet to take up residence in our midst, and, with the aid of an interpreter, learn about American life only, or mostly, from the television screen," mused an editorial writer in a Connecticut newspaper, "he would have to conclude that ninety-nine out of one hundred are hypochondriacs or sick."

This alarming possibility has also concerned Brooks Atkinson, of the *New York Times*, who feels that television's medicine men may be engaged in "a crusade to stamp out mental health." Atkinson wonders whether we have been so weakened by acidity, irritated stomach walls, heartburn, tension, headaches, and constipation that little more will be required to exhaust the febrile, pain-lashed American body and hasten its delivery to the friendly undertaker.

Our leaders in television tend to dismiss such comments as competitive bitterweed, but this does not seem an adequate substitute for an examination of the facts. The problem is too serious for handling by the bookkeeper; it involves advertising that is at least obnoxious, and at most may be a threat to the health of many people. Most of the offenses emanate from the drug and "remedy" industry, which spends about $150,000,000 a year in television. (This figure excludes television advertising of toiletries such as tooth pastes and deodorants.) Much of this gigantic expenditure goes into the production of commercials whose claims: (1) skate skillfully near the line of illegality and (2) are so blatantly deceitful that they are eventually halted by government action. Getting away with the first type brings a raise to advertising men; getting caught with the second brings a slap on the wrist from the Federal Trade Commission.

I once had occasion to discuss the medical-advertising problem with an attorney then with the FTC whose desk was piled high with scripts of commercials he felt were dangerous. Most contained such phrases as "doctors," "special ingredients," "relief," "fast action," and "prescription." These are the semantic wands that snake-oil salesmen waved over gullible crowds in Gulchville until television provided an entire nation for an audience. The attorney wagged his head dolefully and said, "We can't do much about most of these birds. We don't think we could win the cases in court. Besides, all these people need is a little time. Before we could catch up with them, they'd have discarded the campaign and started a new one."

Later in the day, the attorney became uncomfortably candid. "The pressures are enormous around here," he said, "and men have to think of their futures, too." He ran a hand through his thinning hair and murmured, "You don't go out of government service with much in the bank, and there are consulting jobs in industry to be considered. It gives you something to think about when you feel like getting hard-nosed about some of this slipperiness."

The man was embarrassed; he regained his composure, and his earlier irritation, when I asked if it was not true that only thoughtless people were likely to be misled by wily claims in drug advertising.

"That's nonsense and I'm tired of hearing it," he snapped. "Thoughtful people are rarely misled by anything. Thoughtless people are misled by everything. It's the thoughtless people who need protection."

And there, of course, my man in purgatory had focused on the truth of the matter. Impressionable parents may well stuff their perfectly healthy but academically slow children with milk of magnesia when they hear the televised voice of authority deliver his dagnosis: "If your child is having trouble with his lessons, it may not be his fault—he may need a laxative." They may well rub themselves slick with liniments when their arthritis should be receiving competent, not patent, medical care. And what is their defense against the medical mystique conveyed by announcements that "men who know medicine know Bayer brings the fastest . . . relief," and that "three out of four doctors recommend the ingredients in Anacin"? They may well cram their bodies beyond tolerance with compounds that promise "fast, fast, *incredibly* fast relief" to people in pain.

Which is the more important in such cases—the right of the syrup, salve, and pill makers to operate freely in the market place of health, or the right of the public to reasonable protection by their government? As matters stand, ad agencies play cat and mouse with the law in a manner that would dazzle a student of brinkmanship. The object on Madison Avenue is to discover suggestive semantic devices that imply what the law prohibits saying, and to press the theme home until halted by government action. But government action is so tardy that by the time a halt is ordered, in the words of Paul Rand Dixon, the chairman of the FTC, a fraudulent campaign "runs its merry course until it dies of exhaustion and is buried by its sponsors."

The case of arthritis—a word heard frequently enough on television—illustrates the problem. For years medical authorities have conceded that they do not understand the basic nature of this disease and can therefore offer no cures. Nevertheless, the Arthritis and Rheumatism Foundation estimates, arthritis sufferers waste over a quarter of a billion dollars each year in a vain, tragic search for a potion that will give them peace. "The most that can be expected from any proprietary drug, remedy, device, or other treatment for arthritis on the market today," the Foundation has said, "is *temporary* relief from the *minor* symptoms of the disease. And for the most part, this can be purchased for the price of a five-grain aspirin tablet, the homely hot-water bottle, or a good long soak in a warm bath."

Despite such pronouncements, the television networks steadily lowered barriers against commercials for arthritis balms while understanding that the Federal Trade Commission must fight its way through a legal mare's nest before it can halt deceptive and misleading claims. Considering the impact of a television campaign, by which most of the nation may be saturated almost overnight, how quickly should the FTC be able to take effective action against fraud? One month? To insure that due process of law is observed, would three months, or perhaps even six months, provide a reasonable period of time?

In this spirit of flexibility, consider the FTC's experience with three liniments—Mentholatum Rub, Heet, and Infra-Rub—products whose television commercials made use of shooting flames and piercing arrows to represent the pain of arthritis and the penetrating quality of their balms. The FTC found their claims "unfair and deceptive," but needed thirteen months to prohibit the manufacturers from broadcasting their messages. Any company that cannot make the most of a year's television advertising would be well advised not to use television at all.

Yet the meticulously fair among us may feel that a considerable business investment should be guarded against capricious interference, and that under such circumstances a year's delay is not unconscionable. Their charity may be affected by a glance at the Dolcin case. Dolcin is a tablet described by its makers as "the best friend of arthritics and rheumatics"; it has sold at the rate of $1,000,000 worth a year. The pill came to the FTC's attention during a radio advertising campaign in 1949, when its manufacturers claimed, among other things, that it was "not just a palliative masking pain and discomfort for a few hours," but was "designed to relieve pain promptly" and give "prolonged relief." Dolcin was recommended for "children's so-called 'growing pains'" and was said to be suitable for persons who reacted adversely to aspirin. Moreover, users were urged to continue taking the pills for weeks and months.

The Trade Commission issued a complaint against Dolcin in August, 1949. The company challenged the action and received, as the law required, a full hearing before an FTC examiner. Two years and five months later, in January, 1952, the examiner ruled that Dolcin's advertising was indeed unfair and deceptive. Dolcin appealed the finding and obtained a hearing before the full commission, which rejected the appeal in December, 1952. Having exhausted its opportunities before the agency, the firm appealed to the courts. In July, 1954, four years and ten months after the complaint was issued, a United States Court of Appeals rejected the appeal after slightly modifying the FTC's order. Dolcin was told to comply with the order forthwith; instead, it continued to make its claims and asked the court to reconsider. That action delayed the resolution of the case another seven months. When the court turned down the company's request, it went back to the FTC to present "new evidence." Finally, in October, 1956, seven years and two months after the complaint was issued, Dolcin was ordered to stop. (Before the case left the courts in December, 1957, the firm's officers were found guilty of criminal contempt for persisting in their deception after the first court decision in 1954.)

My own estimate is that over 300,000,000 Dolcin tablets were sold while the due process of law was being observed in its finest detail.

Lest anyone feel, however, that Dolcin represents a singular case, there is the remarkable saga of Carter's Little Liver Pills. This laxative was advertised back in 1883 as a most potent medicinal: "Sick headache positively cured by Carter's Little Liver Pills. We mean cured, not merely relieved, and can prove what we claim. There are no failures and no disappointments. . . . Carter's Little Liver Pills also cure all forms of biliousness, prevent constipation and dyspepsia, promote digestion, relieve distress from too hearty eating, correct disorders of the stomach, stimulate the liver, and regulate the bowels. . . ."

When Fletcher G. Cohn, who is now general counsel of the FTC, was thirty-eight years old, the Commission became interested in the marvelous little pills. That was in 1943. Cohn was fifty-four years old when Carter finally lost its case, after a trip to the U.S. Supreme Court, in 1959. He accumulated 10,000 papers and an ulcer in the course of the litigation; one proceeding was conducted in his hotel room in San Francisco, minutes after he had received a blood transfusion. Altogether, the Little Liver Pill case represents tenacity on the part of everyone concerned, including television executives. Carter made so many claims for its product that the case could be the subject of a book in itself; more important, its television commercials (sample: "Five New York doctors have found a way to break the laxative habit . . .") were accepted by television broadcasters after the case had been in litigation for a number of years, and after the FTC's initial decision had found the claims to be deceptive.

Although the firm promised relief, at various times, for persons who felt "down and out, blue, worn out, logy, depressed, sluggish, all in, listless, mean, stuffy, sour, dull, bogged down, gloomy," and more, Carter became famous in television for the claim that its pill would "promote the flow of liver bile" and thus relieve constipation "nature's way."

Today, after its defeat, Carter's drug appears on our television screens as "Carter's Little Pills." And if a viewer unconsciously inserts the censored word "liver" himself, he is neither unusual nor clairvoyant; he is simply unable to overcome the effect of long conditioning. Carter received sixteen years of due process; the public, winning a resounding Pyrrhic victory, received sixteen years of false and deceptive advertising.

With the dismissal of any lingering objections that everything is all right, or will be if we are patient enough, the conclusion is unavoidable that something has gone awry with the government's stated obligation to shield its citizens from dishonesty in commerce. The impulse is to blame the Federal Trade Commission, but it should be recognized that Congress, in creating the agency in 1914, empowered it to guard only property rights; mere injury to people was not an offense. If a businessman's illegal tactic injured another, let the offender beware; if it injured the public, *caveat emptor.* Congress did not allow the FTC to concern itself with human rights until 1938, and it has not extended itself conspicuously since then to show that brisk enforcement of the deceptive-advertising law is one of its passionate desires.

Some commissioners, moreover, have demonstrated exceeding concern for the problems of the entrepreneurs they are supposed to police. Lowell B. Mason, for example, left the FTC in 1956 and wrote a book in which he expressed grave fear that the agency was tampering with the legitimate rights of businessmen in a free enterprise economy. I was introduced to this book, *The Language of Dissent,* by Rosser Reeves of the Ted Bates advertising agency; Mason supports his contention that the "bureaucrats in Washington" are seeking too much power. (In 1960 and 1961, Bates agreed in three FTC cases to halt deceptive practices. The consent orders that Bates signed are triumphs of solicitous double talk; offenders do not confess that they have done anything wrong, but they agree to stop doing it.)

A modest hope for vigorous action against fraudulent commercials is based on the FTC's request to Congress for legal power that would enable it to move "with a squad car instead of a hearse," as Chairman Dixon puts it. To prevent future Dolcin or Carter cases, the agency wants the right to issue immediate restraining orders against objectionable practices; its adversaries could then appeal to the courts. But in discussing this issue with a number of advertising men, I found unanimous objection, usually based on the argument that "it would be dangerous to concentrate so much power in Washington." (This remark came up so frequently that I began keeping a tally of how much time passed before each man offered it; a Kenyon & Eckhardt executive won with four minutes and fifteen seconds.) The tenor of these discussions suggested that the ad men regarded Washington as the seat of Soviet, not American, government. On the other hand, the Advertising Federation of America has invested funds in cocktails for congressmen, and it is doubtful that ad men would want to lift the spirits of Russian congressmen. The situation is baffling.

Some of the mist might be dispelled if the FTC were to use the power it has, while it waits for more. Section 12 of the Federal Trade Commission Act makes it unlawful to disseminate, *"or cause to be disseminated,"* false advertisements for foods, drugs, devices, or cosmetics. No television station has ever been cited by the FTC for its role in circulating deceptive commercials, yet they have abounded. And by the time a fraudulent commercial is removed from circulation, it has usually been shown hundreds of times.

A hard-sell obesity drug named Regimen is a case in point. Commercials for this weight remover cost $1,500,000 in 1958 alone; they promised: "Lose six pounds in three days—ten pounds in a week—or your money back!" The FTC soon prohibited the claim that the drug could cause the loss of a predetermined number of pounds. Despite this, and despite the odorous reputation of weight drugs to begin with, the CBS Television Network carried Regimen spots for thirteen more weeks, NBC for seventeen more months. NBC gave up its revenue after the Manhattan district attorney seized a batch of commercials to determine whether they were false and misleading.

Yet most practitioners of the advertising trade become huffy when the subject of quick restraining orders is raised; they insist that objectionable ads emerge from a tiny minority of their fraternity. But the FTC's Dixon has noted that the blame attaches to more than "an irresponsible few," that violations have been committed by many large, well-known television advertisers. The broadcasting-advertising industry, when pressed by the threat of sanctions, suggests that self-regulation is preferable to legal restraint, but the case for voluntary decency is not impressive. Advertising groups establish "ethics" committees to discourage shabby conduct, the networks maintain "commercial copy acceptance" staffs, the National Association of Broadcasters has a Television Code Authority, and transgressions persist. The record is lengthy and reads like a Who's Who of Business.

An order against misrepresentation was issued against Procter & Gamble, for example, as long ago as 1924; during the next thirty years this company agreed seven times to halt or modify claims for products that included Drene, Camay, Chipso, Ivory, Tide, and Cheer. In recent days of television, the FTC has successfully challenged commercials for Procter & Gamble's Crest Tooth Paste, Colgate-Palmolive's Colgate Dental Cream and Palmolive Rapid Shave Lather, Vicks Cold Tablets, Aluminum Company of America's Alcoa Wrap, Standard Brands' Blue Bonnet Margarine, Mennen's Sof' Stroke Shaving Cream, American Chicle's Rolaids, Eversharp for its Schick safety razors and blades, Brown & Williamson's Life Cigarettes, and other products. The Warner-Lambert Pharmaceutical Company agreed to halt claims that its Listerine Antiseptic would protect against Asian Flu; Lanolin Plus agreed to stop implying that competitors' shampoos would burn the hair of users; auto companies agreed to modify claims for low gasoline consumption; cigarette companies escaped wholesale complaints only by agreeing to jettison loud and ludicrous claims based on miniscule differences between the tar and nicotine content of their brands.

It seems, then, in light of the speed and saturation power of television, to be far too late for self-serving "truth in advertising" campaigns. It is preposterous to believe that manufacturers, advertising men, and television executives are naïve urchins who need to be indoctrinated in the differences between truth and falsehood; they need only to be convinced that falsehood will be promptly and expensively punished.

Even some ad men agree. Max Geller, president of the Weiss & Geller agency, notes that his colleagues "need the moral crutch of Uncle Sam's regulations to resist the pressure of clients in this Darwinian jungle." And Fairfax Cone, chairman of Foote, Cone & Belding, says flatly that "the industry cannot police itself, it never could." Cone feels that the FTC, in seeking quick injunctive power, is simply "reaching for more authority to do what it is supposed to do."

But in the eleventh-hour clamor for voluntary reform, it is worth considering some deterrent measures that broadcasters might take. Two such possibilities come to mind immediately: first, television networks or stations could announce, with the final showing of a challenged or outlawed commercial, that the FTC had alleged or found it to be false and deceptive. I realize this proposition smacks of insanity (to broadcasters), but it is entirely rational; under present practice, the viewer is not told that he has been misled. Second, federal action against a commercial should be reported over the regular newscasts of any network or station that carried the advertisement. Refusal to take such action would amount to a confession that a broadcaster is withholding vital news from the audiences that bring him his considerable income.

Would television thus be undermining advertising? Hardly; it would simply be undermining *dishonest* advertising. Surely no one could object to that.

THE PRIVATE ARMIES

> *Repairman: Use Dash—*
> *Ellen: Use Tide—*
> *Wife: I don't understand—aren't they both made by Procter & Gamble?*
> *Repairman: Yeah.*
>
> —Television Age, *July 10, 1961.*

David Ogilvy is the man who tickled America and sold a great many Hathaway shirts by adorning his Hathaway man with an eye-patch. Ogilvy is president of the Ogilvy, Benson & Mather advertising agency, which channels over $20,000,000 a year into television. He is therefore not a man who was born yesterday.

In addition, Ogilvy gets to the point. There was an occasion, for example, when he explained the paramount dilemma of advertising to a group of his colleagues in Washington. He said: "There really isn't any significant difference between the various brands of whiskey, or the various cigarettes, or the various brands of beer. They are about the same. And so are the cake mixes and the detergents, and the automobiles."

Well, how do you solve such a dilemma if you are an advertising man and do not have David Ogilvy's imagination but do have clients who spend enormous sums of money on television commercials? You make commercials that show why brand A will promise more romance, guarantee more success, and promote more hair on bald men's heads than will brands B, C, or X. And you promise, guarantee, and promote over and over and over because that is all you can do for a client whose product is essentially the same as his competitor's.

Most advertising men, as well as most prominent advertisers, are unable to make a valuable contribution to this discussion because they are living in a cataleptic condition that precludes searching thought. These distraught men are vituperatively opposed to kidnaping, communism, and criticism of advertising, and do not appear to detest one more than another. They are not exclusively *against*, though; they are in favor of fun, consumer spending, and Americanism, and do not appear to relish one of *these* more than another. In fact, they consider the three to be synonymous.

The television industry agrees. It has so confused its functions with those of Madison Avenue that it arms its representatives with cuff-notes for speeches that extol bigger and better spending. The National Association of Broadcasters is the source of a number of convenient homilies for public speakers, of which this is a sample: "Higher consumption . . . raises living standards and results in a better life. Television advertising, or electronic salesmanship, helps sell everything from candy to cultivators. On both a national and a local basis, those who have goods and services for sale familiarize consumers with their wares, remind them of their needs for them, and overcome inertia against buying."

Occasionally, to suit a purpose, broadcasters reverse their field, and portray advertising as anything but powerful. This is the bashful-modesty approach that has been used by NBC's Robert Sarnoff, who says that advertising "can only propose; the public disposes, and rightly so." The purpose of this gambit is to counter criticism that much of television's package-goods advertising peddles only variations on the same theme and thus does not contribute anything of permanent value to the economy (let alone the culture).

Sarnoff pleases major advertisers with such speeches, but the most artful defense of massive consumer-goods advertising comes from his best client, Procter & Gamble, which is the league leader at the game of endowing commercials with saintliness. This skill is essential, of course, for a corporation whose chairman, Neil McElroy, once said: "We are as much in the advertising business as in the manufacturing business." Howard J. Morgens, who as P&G's president supervises its $100,000,000 annual investment in television, boosts advertising by knocking the Russians. This technique, like Ivory Soap, is a guaranteed crowd pleaser, whatever its deficiencies of logic. Morgens rebuts arguments that a lot of advertising is sheer waste with the baby-kissing idea that "the people" should decide how their nation's resources are to be allocated. He usually speaks to friendly audiences who have learned to disbelieve that in a democracy the people decide on a *government*, which then decides policy. *Government* is so dirty a word that sponsors may soon forbid its use in television scripts.

The men in the advertising agencies, on the other hand, are disappointingly unsophisticated in their defense of wasteful, clamorous commercials. Most of them rely on the weary but stubbornly serviceable premise that critics of advertising eat children and hate America. A letter to *Advertising Age* speaks with the eloquence of George F. Babbitt: "An attack on advertising is an attack on the American way of life, of which advertising is an essential part." Similarly, Arthur C. Fatt, president of the Grey advertising agency, contends that the advertising critic, or Antichrist, is simply ignorant but nonetheless a threat. "This lack of a fundamental understanding of advertising and selling on the part of some clergy, some educators, some government officials, and even some economists," Fatt says, "can be downright dangerous, even catastrophic, not only to advertising, but to the system which has brought us a standard of living envied by the rest of the world. . . . Any action which dilutes believability in advertising, which undermines confidence in selling, also tends to destroy faith in our system of individual initiative and competitive enterprise." Fatt's call to the firing squad is echoed by Harry Harding, executive vice-president of Young & Rubicam and a former chairman of the American Association of Advertising Agencies, who tells his audiences of "the genuine enemies of our free economic system who know full well that an attack on advertising is a telling blow at our mass distribution system. . . ." There are occasions, too, when the ad men broaden their target and suggest that attacks on rotten television entertainment may cause our next depression. "Tampering with television programming can derail the economy," says John P. Warwick, vice-president of Warwick & Legler. He added: "The public likes it the way it is, and it's good for business, which means it's good for everyone."

While the ad man's capacity for delivering and listening to these sloganized outbursts is awesome, there is a good reason for both their existence and their rash premises. The reason is television, which has been the major cause of increased advertising expenditures over the recent past. Since 1952, when the big money began moving over to the electronic salesman, the proportion of advertising outlays to gross national product has steadily risen. This is embarrassing because so much of the resultant ballyhoo consists not of helpful information but of nonsensical trade-mark claims. We are witnessing, and paying for, an expensive private war carried on by private armies.

It should not be surprising, therefore, that more than one thoughtful economist feels this decade will "unavoidably become a battleground between the forces tending to produce a gadget society and those pointing the way to a truly civilized community." When Alvin H. Hansen, professor emeritus of political economy at Harvard University, made that observation, *Advertising Age* said, "It is scarcely news any more when a Harvard professor takes pen in hand to beat advertising's brains out." Hansen was excommunicated along with Harvard's John K. Galbraith, another dissenter, and Arthur Schlesinger, Jr., who criticized advertising excesses before he entered government service and took the vow of silence.

The gadget promoters have turned heartily to the task of creating *their* kind of community. One of their ideological leaders, Marion Harper of McCann Erickson, has already suggested that what this country needs is a good 10 per cent tax cut. The proceeds of this windfall, he explains, would be directed to the accretion of more and more goods. (This might in turn stimulate the building industry; we would surely need more room to house the stuff.) Harper realizes, of course, that the peddlers may face a surfeited public at some point, but he is prepared for that horrifying eventuality. "Energy can be devoted," he notes, "to developing consumer values that meet minimum buying resistance. . . ."

Although it is difficult to maintain Harper's pace, it may be anticipated that he already has a budget for brainwashing commercials. Perhaps they will be of the soft-sell genre, merely suggesting that buying is better for your health. But inevitably the "irresponsible few" will present more compelling messages—perhaps a scene of a man being hung for refusing to buy solid gold golf clubs for each of his children, or of a woman being horsewhipped for donating twenty dollars to the Cancer Society instead of buying a fifth toaster.

Farfetched? Of course. But some people in advertising have an uncanny ability to make a commonplace of the extraordinary. Such a man is Rosser Reeves, creator and chief admirer of the Anacin commercials. (Reeves refers to this cretin as "the great Anacin drug commercial, with its three streams of bubbles flowing up to three boxes in the head.") He is the universal man—this yacht-racing, chess-playing, plane-flying, art-collecting partner in the Ted Bates agency (specialists in products "eaten or rubbed on or smoked"). Reeves works in a large, tasteful office, where he plans large, tasteless commercial campaigns. Just plain folks who take their families into the bathroom at bedtime and shout, "Stops halitosis!" or, "Pink toothbrush!" (as we all probably do on occasion) are talking Rosser Reeves's language. He is, in addition, the man who wrote the questions and answers for the unforgettable "Eisenhower Answers America" television bombardment of the 1952 presidential election campaign. Since these commercials were composites—the questioners were filmed later and never saw the candidate—they might be called "rigged" in today's lexicon. But Reeves would consider such an epithet tangential; he is more fascinated by his concept of the "buyer in the voting booth." He has been quoted, and doubtless with accuracy, as saying: "I think of a man in a voting booth who hesitates between two levers as if he were pausing between competing tubes of tooth paste in a drug store. The brand that has made the highest penetration on his brain will win his choice."

It would be erroneous to say that Rosser Reeves is what is wrong with television, but he makes the error attractive. As the number-one package-goods peddler of the profession, he comes closest to modeling economist Galbraith's man "who devises a nostrum for a nonexistent need and then successfully promotes both." Since Reeves does not approve of David Ogilvy's brand of imagination, he has relied on repetition. ("It is almost as if the Bates copywriters . . . said, 'Now we gotta slug the S.O.B.'s,'" commented a veteran ad man in *Sponsor* Magazine.)

It is not difficult to find a good word for Reeves along Madison Avenue, where the phrase "If *you're* so smart, why ain't *you* rich?" was probably born. He is credited with an "icy intellect" and doubters are regularly warned not "to sell Rosser Reeves short." But a challenging voice has been heard from the creative wilderness, too. It belongs to Stan Freberg, who is responsible for the rollicking (and highly successful) Chun King commercials and other refreshing ideas.

Freberg began by calling Reeves "Hercules Unchained" and went on to dub him "the dean of the gastro-intestinal school of advertising," a man who commits "pre-medicated assault on the American home." But Freberg is more than a quipster. As a stunningly successful advertising man, he doubts that people "are sitting glued to their television, just *waiting* for that movie to be interrupted by the man talking about bad breath, or the drainage of sinuses, or a frank discussion of 'regularity.'" (The Bates agency produced the outlawed Carter's [laxative] Pills commercials.) Believing that ads must be attractive and intelligent, Freberg finds Rosser Reeves "the most dangerous words in advertising."

Since Reeves is responsible for a number of television's most insistent commercials, it is worth knowing that the man from Bates has written a book, *Reality in Advertising,* in which he has confessed his addiction to a theory known as U.S.P., which means "universal selling proposition." This is Reeves's shorthand for saying that *something* must be ferreted out and harped on to make a tweedledee product seem to differ from a tweedledum twin. The fact that competitive products may possess the same attribute does not inhibit Reeves. If the ingredients of mass-produced breads are fairly similar, reach for a U.S.P.: "Builds strong bodies twelve ways . . ." If today's tooth pastes are similar in effectiveness, catch a man with our client's brand: "Don't let romance fade . . . fade . . . fade . . . away!" But most important, transmit this intelligence thousands of times over scores of television stations until it has jammed itself into the viewer's unconscious.

When semanticist S. I. Hayakawa, of San Francisco State College, analyzed the ethical quality of Reeves's book, he concluded that "moral anesthesia eventually overtakes many people in the huckstering game, but I have rarely seen it documented so conclusively . . ." A line from Reeves's rejoinder was pure, illuminated Reeves: "I have a faint feeling of embarrassment, akin to a man (unobserved) who is watching another across an airshaft, deep in some personal function."

It is a mystery along Madison Avenue why Rosser Reeves and Procter & Gamble have not embraced. Reeves is a semantic acrobat and Procter & Gamble has been an advertising juggler for many years. Many guileless observers marvel at P&G's nimbleness, a talent that stems from the firm's insistence that each of its numerous detergents is better than any of the others. It was this wheel spinning against itself that caused *Television Age,* ordinarily a non-troublesome trade magazine, to ponder the problems presented by commercials for P&G's Dash and P&G's Tide. The magazine confessed to having "this horrible nightmare in which the family washing machine breaks down. The wife puts in a service call. In a few minutes the front door opens and in rush—simultaneously—that little fat repair man in the Dash commercials and that cute thing who calls herself 'Ellen Harty, home economist,' in the films for Tide." *Television Age* envisioned the conversation that ensued:

REPAIRMAN: I see your trouble, lady. You've been using one of those icky detergents that clog up the machine works with too much suds! You should switch to Dash.

WIFE: But Ellen Harty, home economist, tells me to use Tide because its rich suds get my clothes cleaner!

ELLEN: That's right, fat boy.

WIFE: Will somebody please tell me what to do about the machine?

REPAIRMAN: Use Dash—

ELLEN: Use Tide—

WIFE: I don't understand—aren't they both made by Procter & Gamble?

REPAIRMAN: Yeah. . . .

Despite the fact that *Television Age* may yet rue its venture into satire, the magazine illuminated the problem of wasteful advertising. The specifics of this waste can be understood when one of P&G's actual commercials for Dash is studied (briefly, be assured):

CHARLIE: In response to your urgent summons, I've come to repair your automatic washin' machine.

HUSBAND: Aw look, fella, my wife's away and I'm doing the wash. There's suds all over the place. First the clothes didn't come out clean, so I put in more detergent. Now, the machine's conked out.

CHARLIE: In these automatics you gotta use the only product that has the cleaning power you *need* . . . without causin' that oversudsin' problem which can stop the machine.

HUSBAND: What's that?

CHARLIE: Procter & Gamble's unique product—DASH. For truly carefree washdays, use only DASH. . . .

(A few seconds later, after Charlie has unclogged the apparatus, he offers another truism from P&G.)

CHARLIE: DASH cleans better than any other detergent in these automatics . . . without making too many frothy suds.

It is clear from this exchange that Dash is "the only product" with the requisite cleansing properties and without undesirable side effects, that it is "unique," that "only Dash" should be used, and that Dash cleans "better than any other detergent" in automatic washers. This all seems fair enough; goodness knows, there is no argument with Procter & Gamble's technical proficiency. P&G causes the confusion when it also urges the purchase of Tide and other detergents such as Oxydol, Dreft, and Cheer. These are all P&G products, and they might well be thought of as inferior because of P&G's description of Dash as "unique" and best. (I noted that my box of Cheer said it had been "recommended by manufacturers of automatic washers," but I think too much of my washing machine to take *their* words over P&G's. I returned it to the store.)

From this confusion, only one winner and one loser can emerge. Whichever detergent is sold, P&G wins; and the television viewer pays the bill—a stupendous bill. In 1959 alone, P&G spent, to advertise Dash on television, almost $4,500,000; for Tide, almost $8,500,000; for Cheer, over $6,000,000; for Oxydol, almost $3,000,000; and for Dreft, almost $2,000,000. Total for five brands—all made by the same firm and all suggesting that washday can be almost as much fun as sex—$23,907,665. Television did not receive this entire amount, of course; about $3,500,000 of it went to the ad agencies that prepared the commercials. This may answer the immemorial question of what causes love, at least between television, advertising agencies, and advertisers.

If this war within a war were the only instance of using the consumer's money to sell him something, complaints would probably be minimal. But the private armies are staked out on many fronts. Consider that Lever Brothers, which is surely as dedicated to ecstatic washdays as is P&G, also spends millions for television advertising to beatify *its* detergents—Rinso Blue and All. And there are just as earnest commercials for Colgate-Palmolive's Fab, Ad, and Vel, not to mention Purex's Trend.

Will Lestoil clean a wall more effectively than Mr. Clean, or vice versa? Is it worth $25,000,000 in television advertising for the consumer to find out? Whose money is being spent when Anacin, Bufferin, Bayer, and St. Joseph pour $35,000,000 into aspirin commercials during a single year? And when Crest, Colgate, Gleem, Stripe, Pepsodent, Cue, and Ipana devote even more to their private but televised conflict?

Questions: Is Gardol better than Irium? Is Irium better than Gl-70? Is Gl-70 better than fluoride? Is fluoride better than Fluoristan? Is Fluoristan better than stannous fluoride? Is stannous fluoride better than Hexa-Fluoride? Is Hexa-Fluoride better than hexachlorophene? Is hexachlorophene better than tyrothricin? Or is it time for a return to the blarney days of chlorophyll?

Answer: What an incredible insult to a nation's intelligence!

No tribute to the art of insult should omit the cigarette industry, which invests $100,000,000 a year in television and which is invariably represented early enough in the evening to attract the attention of teen-agers who are watching the westerns and action-adventure shows. (A stock remark in advertising: "There are no little children any more—they're little adults. We sell to them on the premise that soon they'll be big adults and product-buyers.") Anyone who doubts that television is being used to prepare youth for smoking will take no comfort from noting that each of the following programs has been sponsored by or carried a participating commercial for a cigarette company: *Lawman, Cheyenne, Wagon Train, Wells Fargo, Tall Man, Checkmate, Follow the Sun,* and *Route 66.* But this will not surprise anyone who is aware of the tobacco firms' past performance. For years, BBD&O has been conducting college campus campaigns for Lucky Strike, and few will soon forget American Tobacco's direct appeals to youth on behalf of its now defunct *Hit Parade.*

To carry on *these* private wars over the public's television, R. J. Reynolds and American Tobacco put up $36,000,000 a year, Brown & Williamson and P. Lorillard strike back with an equal amount, and Philip Morris and Liggett & Myers stride into the arena with $27,000,000 more.

If this is what makes the wheel go 'round, we can object, but without much gusto. However, if the soap, tooth paste, aspirin, cigarette, gasoline, drug, breakfast food, and other wars are being conducted at our expense, and with a destructive effect on individual pocketbooks and national culture, then television has added more reason to its several causes for shame.

13 THE RATING GAME

> *"They hollered against doctors 500 years ago the way some people holler against ratings today."—Sydney Roslow, director, The Pulse, Inc.*

The average person is not equipped to be a magician because he lacks the ability to produce something from nothing, or from what seems to be nothing. That's why television ratings are so fascinating; rarely has so much been produced from what seems to be so little.

Most people could not even define a television rating precisely. For their benefit, a rating of 25 means that 25 per cent of everyone who could have seen a program actually did see it. Or, more precisely, the raters claim that that many people saw it.

Most of us would be too inhibited to make such a statement. If we were to look in on 1,000 operating television sets, and discover that 20 per cent were tuned to program A, 30 per cent to program B, and 50 per cent to program C, we would conclude that two hundred homes saw program A, three hundred saw B, and five hundred saw C.

A. C. Nielsen, Sr., founder and chairman of the A. C. Nielsen Company—"world's largest marketing research organization" and the dominant television rating service—is not inhibited. If he monitored those same 1,000 television sets, he would conclude, if the assumption were that all television sets in the United States were turned on, that 9,400,000 of them were tuned to program A, 14,100,000 to B, and 23,500,000 to C. As a matter of fact, or of wizardry, Nielsen's organization arrives at conclusions of this kind, without apparent difficulty, seven days a week, fifty-two weeks a year, and shows no signs of quitting.

Since many people cannot figure out how he does what he does, Nielsen is sometimes considered to be the most successful journeyman sorcerer since Merlin. But the amazing extrapolator would deny possession of any power stronger than mortal intelligence well applied. Specifically, he applies statistical sampling techniques to the human problem of who watches what on television. "It's like withdrawing one pint from a tank car full of milk," he explains. "Analyze the pint and you know the content of the whole car." Nielsen, like nuclear physicists and other complex thinkers, has had to develop many such analogies in order to communicate his science to the uninitiated.

The strains on Nielsen's patience have been extensive over the past few years, and he is exhibiting certain symptoms of testiness in his middle sixties, especially toward dullards who cannot, or intransigents who will not, comprehend what he regards as the obvious in logic. For this reason, he is rarely as annoyed with television and advertising executives who subscribe to his homogenized-pint-of-milk theory as he is with television critics who don't. The executives support the rating services; they pay millions of dollars every year for number potions which will either soothe or irritate the stomach lining. The critics, on the other hand, have almost no stomach for rating services; John Crosby, for instance, has called the Nielsen company "the closest thing we have in modern times to a witch doctor."

The raters are skilled in the art of self-defense, but for remarks such as Crosby's they have only a curled lip. And when George Jessel offers cigars or candy to anyone who has ever been contacted by a rating service, and he receives no takers, they collapse into silent stupefaction. This is understandable, inasmuch as scores of thousands of people *have* been telephoned, written to, or visited by raters (even if I never have).

The problem, as often happens, is that many people have been talking *around* the point because it takes a painful amount of study before it is possible to talk *to* the point, which is: What do rating services actually reflect, how accurately do they reflect that, and what effect should ratings—accurate, reasonably accurate, or inaccurate—have on the most powerful communications device man has yet invented?

In order to resolve those questions, the raters' work must be understood, and that is where the hard labor begins.

Arthur Charles Nielsen, Sr., before whose numbers strong men ulcerate and weaker men contemplate unemployment insurance, was attracted as early as 1923 to the notion of measuring human conduct by mechanical methods. It was then, after a brilliant scholastic, tennis, and R.O.T.C. record at the University of Wisconsin, and service in the Navy, that he organized the A. C. Nielsen Company. His desire was to help business apply to its merchandising problems "the precise and reliable procedures and measurements with which I had become familiar in the course of my studies and practical experience in electrical engineering." For a discouraging decade, business was slow to appreciate Nielsen's genius, but he broke through when he devised the first of numerous Nielsen Indexes, which continuously measure the retail sales flow of foods, drugs, and other commodities. Today these numbers are used—that is, they are bought from Nielsen—by industries that do almost two-thirds of all American advertising. These are familiar giants of the consumer-goods field, ranging from Alka Seltzer and Coca-Cola through Ivory and Kleenex to Scotch Tape and Shredded Wheat. They have made it possible for Nielsen to draw a handsome salary from his company—of which his son, A. C. Nielsen, Jr., is president—to reside in a twenty-room Tudor house in suburban Chicago, and to pay the wages of over 4,000 employees in thirteen countries, which he tirelessly visits.

The mass-goods producers have also made it possible for Nielsen to develop, or as he would probably put it, perfect, his rating services. The idea that the habits of unseen audiences could be "measured" electronically came to him in 1936, when he learned of a recording machine invented at the Massachusetts Institute of Technology. (At that time, raters relied on telephone and diary methods to extract information from listeners.) Fortunately or otherwise, Nielsen was able to buy the rights to the electronic gadget, modify it, and patent the Audimeter, which began delivering Nielsen Radio Index ratings in 1942. When television's golden goose appeared, the resourceful engineer was eager to help once more, so he adapated the Audimeter to the new salesman of the broadcasting industry, and, in 1950, inaugurated the Nielsen Television Index, a statistical report which has supplanted thinking along Madison Avenue and its subsidiary roadways.

Like Mighty Mouse, the Audimeter is small but awesome. When wired to a television set, it continuously records the channels that are tuned. It tells what time a station was brought in, how long it remained in view, and when and for how long each change was made. Since this is only a history of tuning, the Audimeter does not record who, how many (or if anyone, for that matter), was watching. And so, of course, it does not reveal viewers' opinions of what they (or non-they) have seen. The Audimeter is not a critic; it is simply an electric timekeeper.

Nielsen Audimeters are attached to 1,100 television sets in various parts of the United States; thus, television has created still another subspecies of viewer, the *Nielsen* family. Every two weeks, Nielsen families fulfill their obligation to merchandising by divesting their equipment of a small cartridge of microfilm on which their viewing behavior has been inscribed. When they feed the apparatus a fresh cartridge, they are rewarded with two pieces of silver totaling fifty cents. The information-laden spy is then mailed to Nielsen headquarters in Chicago, where it is subjected to development and decoding by a corps of intelligence machines. The elicited information is simultaneously punched onto IBM tabulating cards and fed to an impressive bank of computers. It is this mechanized trip through computer-land that once provoked Nielsen to remark: "How can anyone pit himself against a giant electronic research system?"

The ultimate destination of the giant's efforts is the desk of the television and advertising executive, who receives printed reports in living color. When he opens his brochure, he is reading the New Testament of television.

Many of television's difficulties stem from the tendency of these executives to give their Nielsen bibles a fundamentalist interpretation. What is written is the word; the whale did verily swallow Jonah, the fall of a rating point is a fall from grace, and eye-for-eye retribution must be exacted if we are to be washed of sin.

Under this dogma, the office of a network's programming vice-president becomes a pagan sacrificial chamber on Nielsen morning. If the rating of *Daddy Is a Dope* has fallen five points, the executive proceeds to the altar, or telephone, establishes emergency communication with the producer (who has guiltily been awaiting the bolt from on high), and delivers the prescribed punishment.

"Jack, boy," he says, "you have slipped badly."

"Strictly temporary, Joe," the producer ploys bravely.

"Jack, boy," the executioner retorts, "we are all strictly temporary. You have gone off five fat, screaming Nielsen points."

The producer, who has a nice family at home and would be a decent man if they'd let him be one, makes his standard bid for self-respect. "Joe," he says, "the show we slipped on was the best we've done. Not much smash-'em-up, true, but an awful lot of meat. We gave 'em something to think about."

"I didn't see the show," comes the reply, "but I read the Nielsens. You are a fine man, Jack, but your show did not get a fine Nielsen and I implore you to understand that without fine Nielsens, you cripple the show ahead of you and you murder the show behind you. Perhaps you have plans to prevent the recurrence of this disastrous event?"

The producer divines that the atom bomb is being held in abeyance; he is being offered an opportunity to redeem himself, to continue payments on the house, the freezer, the cars, the thirty-three footer, the college loan, and the addition to the house that his wife is discussing with the nice architect. "Joe," he says, "I will be frank to say I made a mistake. We've got to give 'em what *they* want, not what *we* want. You tune me in next time around and you'll see the works—I've got a massacre on the griddle that'll—"

"I don't watch, myself, Jack, but I'll tune you in when the next Nielsens arrive. Good-by, now."

The programming vice-president, who, the odds have it, would also be a nice man if he could be, then receives a call from a newspaper or magazine writer who asks him why the networks place such reliance on ratings. He clears his throat, stares out the window into the jungle, and replies: "I don't understand why you people always feel we live and die by ratings. Ratings are only one factor in our decision-making process. You see . . ."

In the executive's copy of "National Nielsen TV Ratings," as the bible has been retitled, reposes a lode of information, some of it peculiarly arrived at. The two most important pieces of data are the *total audience rating* and the *average audience rating*, which as might be expected are not the same. The total audience rating is determined by an Audimeter-film reading of the number of persons whose television sets were tuned to a given program for at least six minutes.

(Some services use a five-minute minimum.) "Thus," the Nielsen company explains, "a total audience rating of 33.2 for *Maverick* indicates that 33.2 per cent of the TV homes in the rated area were tuned to at least [six] minutes of this program."

One of the Nielsen assumptions that must remain moot for the moment is whether 33.2 per cent of "the TV homes in the rated area" (in this case, all "on" sets in the U.S.) were tuned in, or whether all that can really be said is that 33.2 per cent (or 365) of Nielsen's 1,100 Audimeter homes were tuned in. (Actually, a maximum of about 75 per cent of all television sets are tuned in at peak viewing hours; this percentage yields a "share-of-audience" figure that always differs from the rating.)

But if Nielsen's *projection* is left undisturbed for the moment, it is only to get at an even more intriguing point—the curious standard of measurement whereby persons who have tuned in only six minutes of a program are counted into its Nielsen total audience figure. Since from an artistic standpoint such fragmentary viewing does not make sense, there must be another reason for this calculation. The reason is that the total audience rating has positively nothing to do with art or entertainment. When Nielsen delivers a total audience rating to his supplicants, he is merely saying that X number of television sets were tuned in *long enough to receive at least one of the sponsor's commercials.*

An understanding of this point illuminates so much about the attitude of the television networks toward their viewers, but it also reveals the possibility of Nielsen delivering a total audience rating of, say 25,000,000 sets for a program, wherein half those sets belonged to people who watched six minutes, became disgusted, and tuned out. They will not have tuned themselves out of the ratings; they will be delivered to networks, advertising agencies, and sponsors as another validation of the premise that the people are getting what they want.

The second important Nielsen product, the *average* audience rating, is similarly endowed with awesome statistical properties. In another of the firm's baby-talk analogies for laymen, the average audience is explained in this way: "Consider a revolving door, through which a number of persons pass. A count of the number of *different* persons passing through this revolving door might be considered analogous to the *total audience* rating. . . . In contrast, a count of the number of persons in the revolving door at any given time might be considered analogous to the *average audience* rating of a program."

Nielsen is able to produce such a rating because the microfilm in his Audimeters is calibrated minute by minute. In the case of a half-hour show, the number of Audimetered sets tuned to it is recorded for each minute, the numbers are totaled, and the total is then divided by thirty minutes to yield the average audience rating. It can be seen from this that a program could easily have an average audience rating of 40 and a total audience rating of 60. The higher the disgust, or six-minute tune-out index, the higher the total audience rating. Moreover, the total audience figure tends to become higher and higher as the duration of the program increases. More people have a chance to tune in for six minutes of accumulating dismay if a program is an hour long than if it runs for only a half hour. The Nielsen company has determined that with a ninety-minute show the usual difference of total over average audience is 55 per cent.

Because of this disparity, some critics of the rating services are maliciously awaiting the day when a half-hour program will be so unbearable that 7,800,000 sets will be tuned in for only five minutes (Nielsen requires a minimum of six), another 7,800,000 for the next five minutes, and so on. On that basis, an average audience figure of 7,800,000 for the show would of course result. And since that is 14.7 per cent of all U.S. television sets (about 53,000,000), Nielsen would have to produce an average audience rating of 14.7. But since no sets had been tuned to the program for more than five minutes, he would also have to deliver a *total* audience rating of 0. On balance, therefore, malice does not seem to be entirely without virtue.

But this is not to say that churlishness is essential to a discussion of television ratings. In the case of Nielsen's average audience, the facts need no embellishment. Consider, for example, the way in which Nielsen's "minute-by-minute audience profile," which is derived from the individual minute readings of a program's audience, invites the sponsor and his advertising agency to meddle in a show's content. When the individual minutes' audiences are transferred to chart form, the sponsor has before him a record of viewer increases and decreases during his program, which is rather loosely called a drama.

If in scanning the show's "profits," he sees that he is not getting his peak audience during the first two or three minutes, he does not place his commercial at the beginning. Start your story, he tells the producer, and we'll drop the first commercial in at the fifth minute.

"We're going to interrupt for the first commercial at the fifth minute," the producer tells the writer.

"You can't do that in this story," the writer says. "It has to flow uninterruptedly for at least ten minutes in order to make sense."

The producer yawns.

The scene is repeated when the sponsor discovers that he's getting a large tune-out at the twenty-sixth minute. This time the writer protests that he's being asked to chop his climactic scene into bits, and he fares as well as he did earlier. The commercial cuts in when the sponsor dictates. (There were so many commercials on the *Playhouse 90* series that writers had to write five and six synthetic climaxes in order to retain their audiences.)

The minute-by-minute profile is also useful in destroying attempts to sandwich a bit of culture between the dog acts of a variety show. When the sponsor sees that he loses audiences from the moment an operatic or Shakespearean segment begins, he becomes upset. And if there is more than one sponsor sanctifying the dog acts, none wants his commercial placed around the repelling cultural segment. The producer is able to draw his own conclusions, as Steve Allen once did. During his rating contest with Ed Sullivan, Allen presented Elvis Presley and beat Sullivan 20.2 to 14.8. "It's a comparatively easy thing to get a big rating by booking a 'hot' attraction," Allen explained. "Presley, for example. But the show on which we presented Elvis happened to be one of our worst."

If the sponsor is so witless that he fails to grasp the profile's lesson, Nielsen has spelled it out for him in a pamphlet entitled, "Measuring Television's Audience." The author, Bernard H. Ober, an advertising man, presents a chart showing the loss of audience accompanying cultural segments on two opposing variety shows (which were probably Allen and Sullivan). He then says: "Note the effect of switching caused by a 'long-hair' presentation: the audience that had switched to the competitive variety program remained tuned to this program until a long-hair presentation also appeared on it. . . ."

Although Nielsen is primarily known for its national television ratings, the company also provides magic numbers for various local areas by regularly mailing diaries—Nielsen calls them Audilogs—to 1,200 homes. Co-operating families keep the dollar bill that accompanies the diary, write down the secrets of their television lives, and consign the results to the mails. Thus, the sponsor knows, or thinks he knows, whether they got his message in Keokuk.

To help determine whether dear diary has been told the substantial truth, Nielsen also adorns co-operating homes in fifty areas with a device known as the Recordimeter, which is connected to the television set and records the times at which it is turned on and off. If the amount of viewing noted in the diary does not generally correspond to that revealed by the Recordimeter, something is presumed to be fishy in Keokuk and the diverging diary is banished.

The Recordimeter is a versatile instrument, since it also serves to promote alertness by intermittently flashing a light and buzzing, somewhat in the manner of a tilted pinball machine. In this way, if a program puts a viewer into too deep a slumber, the Recordimeter helps revive him so he can tell his diary that he saw the program that put him to sleep. Back in the 1930's, the C. E. Hooper firm (remember the Hooper ratings of radio days?) used a pencil, strung from a control knob, as a similar stimulant; blinks and buzzes are proof, therefore, that Nielsen is young and modern in heart.

Although the Nielsen organization does not, in its view, have peers, it does have competitors in the profitable rating game; chief among these is the American Research Bureau, with headquarters in Beltsville, Maryland. ARB was formed in 1949, when television was stirring, by James W. Seiler, who is twenty years younger than A. C. Nielsen, Sr., and who, with a background of research work at NBC, can be regarded for what it is worth as more of a product of the broadcasting industry.

Seiler's strength lies in local rather than national ratings, and his weapon is the viewer diary, which goes into approximately 2,200 homes. Whether he uses diaries because he feels they are most effective, or whether he is bound to feel they are most effective because he uses them, is an interesting riddle. In describing the diary technique, Seiler has said, "We are very proud of it . . . and make no apologies for it," but some observers feel that apologies would not be inappropriate. Among such dissidents are, of course, those who do *not* use diaries, and in the spirited rating game few holds are barred when one player compares the championship of his performance to the amateurism of a competitor's. Nielsen and ARB, in particular, are inclined to publish brochures, and write letters to editors of trade journals, in which the opposition receives kidney punches.

Less partisan critics usually dwell on ARB's basic methodology—the fact that it selects its diary-keepers from telephone directories. The major contention is that random sampling is supposed to give everyone an equal chance to be selected, while not everyone has a telephone. Actually, telephone ownership does vary rather startlingly for what is widely billed as the electronic age. According to studies published by the U.S. Census Bureau in 1958 and 1959, the number of households with telephones varied from 80 per cent in the Northeast to 58.3 per cent in the South (38.5 in the rural South). In addition, there are limiting factors caused by the economically useful practice of not calling toll areas, and of being unable to contact owners of unlisted telephones. The net effect of these omissions, the critics maintain, may cause a serious distortion of rating numbers. How does anyone know, the question is, whether people who cannot be (or simply are not) reached by telephone will like *Gunsmoke* as well as those who are available?

It would be thoughtless to assume that rating services do not have a rebuttal to such reflections on the quality of their merchandise. ARB, for example, validated its diary method by establishing other random groups and then checking their viewing through personal interviews and by telephone. The agreement, Seiler explains, was "almost fantastic." Moreover, he points out, his operatives, of whom about 4,000 are on call around the country, supervise the diary-keeping through personal visits. And further yet, he adds triumphantly, his confessors do not receive any stipend of $1, as do Nielsen's. Their co-operation is presumably inspired by a letter which accompanies their diary and which notifies them that the success of ARB's survey "depends upon the co-operation of the people whose names are drawn." Seiler draws their interest (and does he influence their diary notations?) by remarking, "Television stations and sponsors use our surveys to help them produce the kind of programs that people want to see." And he thanks them for their assistance, not only on his own behalf but for the television industry as well.

I have speculated on the possible inferences that a conscientious, guileless family could draw from Seiler's suggestion that his surveys help in the production of "the kind of programs that people want to see." I would not want to manufacture any new problems for the raters, but it does seem entirely possible that the above-mentioned family would react at diary-entry time in the following way:

HUSBAND: While you're putting out the lights, dear, I'll fill out the diary for this evening—oh-oh, for the last two evenings. We didn't fill it out last night. Let's see, we watched *The Play of the Week* and *CBS Reports*, right?

WIFE: Yes, but the children saw the cartoon show. You'd better put that down. You don't want it all *that* kind of thing.

HUSBAND: You're right. Mr. Seiler did say his ratings help them figure out what people want to see, and we shouldn't weight it with our high-brow stuff, should we?

WIFE: No, it wouldn't be fair. A lot of people get a kick out of the wrestling, you know.

HUSBAND: Well, what did we see tonight? There was *Eyewitness*, and that concert show they got from the educational station. That's all—well, now wait. I'm not going to impose my Beethoven on everybody. I *considered* watching *Rawhide* for once, so I think I'll just. . . .

Are the reactions of co-operators affected? Certainly Seiler's letter implies that a diary-keeper has achieved a special status; he is no longer "average." Do his viewing habits then change? Perhaps not, but ARB's diaries provide a space for comment, and one woman respondent indicated she wanted to be sympathetic to television's problems. "We aren't too critical," she wrote, "as we know the time is very expensive. . . ."

In addition to the diary technique, which is also used to produce a national report, ARB employs an electronic measurement system which is similar to Nielsen's but has a slightly terrifying feature. This is Arbitron, described as a "revolutionary new research tool" and said to answer "the demand of the television industry for instantaneous audience measurement on an around-the-clock basis." To those blessed with the ability of extracting brightness from gloom, Arbitron could have humorous aspects. First of all, it is too modestly named. Any machine possessing its power and omniscience should have been called Our Ford. On the electronic *qui vive* for vagaries of human behavior and ever ready to report them to the merchandiser-entertainers, it shows signs of birth in the pages of *Brave New World,* but less romantic records indicate it is the creation of James W. Seiler.

Our Ford's electrode on the human mind is the transponder, a *thing* attached to approximately four hundred and fifty television sets in New York, Washington, Baltimore, Philadelphia, Cleveland, Detroit, and Chicago, cities where several channels coexist and where many detergent, drug, and Cracklespop buyers live. The transponder's sensitivity to channel switching enables it, in New York, to relay information to a central board roughly resembling a race track's Totalizator board. As the tote board periodically exposes the betting pools on each horse, the Arbitron exposes, every ninety seconds, the contending programs on which people are betting their souls at those very moments. This disparate wagering appears, after a quick trip through computer circuitry, in the form of ratings which a sponsor, an advertising agency executive, or a station manager may have on his desk the following morning. Businessmen who consider New York sinful and maintain their offices elsewhere may have their ratings telegraphed.

When Our Ford was introduced, Seiler revealed how much it could assist advertising in fashioning television after Willy Loman. "For the first time in television research history," he said, "this makes it possible to evaluate weaknesses and strengths on the basis of practically instantaneous audience reaction. . . . With television costs going higher, advertisers and stations alike have been demanding some form of research for major markets that would give them a quicker reflection of viewer reaction to their programs. Arbitron is the answer—the ultimate in fast and accurate research reporting."

Once Ford is seen in action, it takes little imagination to

envision a sponsor, his advertising agent, and their program's producer seated in the neatly appointed room in which the creature lives. Alongside an identification marker for the channels there are rows of lights, each representing an increment of viewers (x number of sets are tuned to Channel 2, a light lights). Also available are television receivers, which make it unnecessary for men with reading problems to read scripts. The sponsor's show is an action-adventure epic, and he stares at Our Ford with satisfaction.

"Look there," the ad man points out. "They're flocking to us, and *The Iceman Cometh* is drawing beans. Holy smoke, did you hear what the bartender called those prostitutes? He called them *whores!*"

"They tried to rope me in on that one," the sponsor says, "but I told 'em, I said, 'I'vegotaresponsibilitytotheAmerican peoplewholetmecomeintotheirlivingroomsasa*guest*andI'mnot goingtogivethem*smut!*' Who's going to think about whores and the seamy side and then sit down and figure out how to add a little playroom to the house? Nobody, that's who. How we doin'?"

He's doing socko. His blond lovely-boy, the star, has just pulverized a swarthy, scowling villain with a tire iron, and Our Ford is lighting up like Rockefeller Center at Christmas.

But two minutes later, Mr. Cracklespop is depressed. Through a lapse on the part of the producer, the show has gone talky and a distressing number of viewers have become restless, perhaps because the talk isn't worth the listening; the lights reveal that they're sampling other channels.

"Now look there, we get the drop-off just before the commercial! What am I, a public charity? I give 'em entertainment and when the commercial comes on they've flown the coop. Some of 'em are even sneaking over to hear dirty words on that laundryman show!" He glares at the producer. "Who're you working for, friend, Mrs. O'Neill?"

Not long afterward, the observers have departed and the room is dark and silent except for a strangulated moan from

Our Ford. Either someone left the switch on or His conscience is troubling Him.

As if Nielsen and ARB were not enough for one country's television, there are also Trendex, Pulse, and other rating services, but many of their procedures are similar. Among some interesting differences are those of Trendex, which is directed by Edward G. Hynes, Jr., a man who doesn't think raters should be criticized because low-rated shows do not survive. "When you're a nose-counter," he says, "you simply record the way the audience stacks up. It's a little appalling to be whacked over the head and told you're responsible because a program is canceled."

Hynes founded Trendex on the premise that "basically and primarily the American people do not mind answering the phone." His firm telephones American people—thousands of them, he says—in twenty major cities ranging from New York and Boston, in the Northeast, to Denver in the West, and Atlanta and Houston in the South. Unlike ARB, though, Trendex does not telephone merely to arrange for the placement of diaries; the viewing information is secured during conversations with everyone who answers and does not hang up when he learns he is talking to a rating service.

All three television networks have outlets in Trendex cities, and the service therefore provides ratings that essentially measure network competition. Nielsen provides a similar service, but a program's Trendex may vary considerably from its *national Nielsen;* Hynes is a big-city counter, while Nielsen goes down on the farm, too. Moreover, a Trendex will usually be lower than a national Nielsen or ARB report; three-network cities mean more competition and greater fragmentation of audiences. More puzzling to some people, a program will sometimes appear in Nielsen's "top ten" list and not be found in the Trendex top group at all. Solution: Trendex measures only the first week of the month. "If a show isn't on the air,"

Hynes has explained with irrefutable logic, "it can't be in the top ten."

Sydney Roslow, director of The Pulse, Inc., seems less logical, at least in his public statements. He is the man credited with the observation that some people scoffed at doctors five hundred years ago the way they scoff at ratings today. But Roslow, a pleasant man to chat with, suffers less from illogic, actually, than from an occupational trait peculiar to raters. He finds it difficult to understand why everybody doesn't understand the palpable verity of rating figures. He understands because he holds a doctorate in psychology and has been ringing doorbells and interviewing people since 1927, when he was working his way through college. After many years of sampling and polling, for the U.S. Department of Agriculture and a psychological testing firm among others, he established The Pulse, Inc., in 1941. He considers the firm's work a clear asset to television, which, he says, "is a commercial system, and I don't think we should lose sight of that."

Roslow is unpretentiously commercial himself. When he was told that a congressman had accused raters of a "soulless evaluation of the artistry of a human performance," he exclaimed, "I'm evaluating the artistry of a human performance? All I'm doing is adding up a column of figures and selling the answer." It cannot be said, though, that Roslow ignores artistry altogether; he has estimated that he watches television about sixteen hours a week and that his favorite program at one time was *Have Gun, Will Travel.*

Pulse publishes ratings based on personal interviews, but it also produces a type of "people research" that should fascinate anthropologists of the twenty-first century. After its interviewers find out which programs a respondent has been watching, they ascertain his potential as a customer for various products. Pulse is thus able to tell Mr. Cracklespop how much money viewers of his program spend on groceries each week, how many children they have, if any, and so on. Pulse has already informed R. J. Reynolds that *Maverick* delivered a larger concentration of men who smoke cigarettes than any other evening program sponsored by a tobacco manufacturer; Liggett & Myers was told that two of its shows, *The Untouchables* and *The Twilight Zone,* led among women smokers. CBS, Pulse has divined, attracts many lipstick users; NBC is popular among the hair-spray crowd; and many (but not most) women watch ABC while applying nail polish.

When distinguished radio programs were being canceled because their Hooper ratings were low, Fred Allen and other thoughtful performers denounced the numbers operation with bitterness. Today, when ratings are being used by the television networks to grind programming into a one-taste hamburger, thoughtful people—Steve Allen, Robert Saudek, Jack Gould, and others—are again disdainful. Newton Minow and LeRoy Collins are suspicious. David Susskind, George Jessel, John Crosby, and several congressmen are contemptuous. Dr. Frank Baxter, who achieved eminence as a television lecturer on Shakespeare, speaks of "the idiots who run TV and look at the ratings." Altogether, ratings have come to resemble Mark Twain's weather; no one does anything about them.

This conspicuous absence of action is due, in large part, to the marketing men's desire that the rating system be preserved. But it is also due to the bramble of complexity that has unnecessarily been planted around the methodology of the rating services; as a man from the Nielsen company put it—hopefully, I imagine—"Let's not get into the methodology of it. You can have a car and never understand what goes on under the hood as long as it drives well. As a matter of fact, it might be *better* not to know about it." This strength-through-stupidity credo has undeniable utility, but not for viewers.

Which is not to imply that statistics and Scrabble are of equal complexity. The subject does present difficulties, enough of them so that in 1960 a House subcommittee, led by Representative Oren Harris, asked experts to assess the rating services' methodology. The American Statistical Association, on request, appointed a Technical Committee on Broadcast Ratings, with Dr. William G. Madow, of the Stanford Research Institute, as chairman.

The television industry reacted with characteristic but, as usual, needless nervousness. "Suspense on Capitol Hill," said *Broadcasting,* while the Madow Report was awaited. Two weeks later, when it was delivered, suspense gave way to relaxation. Newspaper stories indicated that the committee had vindicated the raters, and Congressman Harris said that while it had revealed "important sources of error" in methodology, it had also found that "the services seem to be estimating the ratings fairly well on the average."

This unnecessarily kind interpretation of the Madow Report gave the broadcasting-advertising industry a chance to use it as a whitewash. *Advertising Age* went so far as to claim that the investigation "has indicated that radio-tv ratings . . . are technically sound." In fact, LeRoy Collins, president of the National Association of Broadcasters, was the only person of prominence to speak out against this hoax. He said: "There has been considerable apparent acceptance of the report as giving broadcast ratings a vote of confidence. Careful reading of the report simply does not support such a conclusion, in my opinion."

The Madow Report did say, "Our over-all evaluation of the rating services is that they are, on the whole, doing a reasonably good technical piece of work for the purposes to be served. . . ." The committee then proceeded to a startling contradiction which neither Congressman Harris nor newspapers saw fit to discuss; it presented findings that were devastating enough to challenge the very existence of the rating services. They showed that the basic technique used by raters *is so seriously and consistently violated as to call into question the truth of any rating delivered today.*

The matter is not nearly so difficult for a non-statistician to grasp as the raters contend. To begin with, rating services do not set out to locate the same percentage of plumbers with three children, Irishmen who own cars, elderly people on pensions, schoolteachers with incomes of over $5,000, and so on, as actually exist in the total population. That method, known as *quota* sampling, has inspired such jokes as the one involving the young lady pollster who told a policeman: "It's getting late. Do you know where I can find a nice thirty-year-old man who has left his wife and has lots of money?"

Rating services do not track down unencumbered, rich thirty-year-old men proportionate to their number in the population and then ask them questions. They assume that the proper proportion of such men will turn up among their respondents because of the way the respondents are selected, which is by *random* sampling. This technique, which stems from the laws of probability, owes its development to intensive work by research specialists within the U.S. Bureau of the Census. With random sampling, the Census Bureau has discovered, it can gather information from a small group of people that will very closely resemble information revealed by a full-scale census. No happenstance, this tendency is explained by the theory behind random sampling, which dictates that if all items in a group are afforded an equal opportunity to be selected, a sampling of the group will turn up the items in their proper proportion. Various factors determine whether their resemblance to the whole picture will be rough or precise.

A. C. Nielsen, Sr., has demonstrated the validity of this concept to dubious businessmen by filling a bowl with small ball bearings, one brass ball to every ten of steel, and inviting doubters to scoop out bearings at random. Nine times out of ten, their yield of brass to steel is only 2 per cent different from the actual proportion in the bowl. Clearly impressive. With this same equipment, however, Nielsen could also demonstrate, if he chose, how to violate the theory of random sampling. By placing a significant number of the bearings at the bottom of the bowl, he would destroy their equal chance of being selected. If he put enough of them at the bottom, his samples would be seriously enough distorted so that they would not be representative of the entire bowl.

Nielsen should not find this distortion difficult to manage because *both his and the other rating services accomplish it every day.* That is what the Madow Report revealed, and what has been ignored by those who have used the report to maintain that ratings are "technically sound."

The amount of distortion varies, but the reason is always the same—the raters, like the pollers who elected Thomas E. Dewey President in 1948, do not give everyone an equal chance to be polled. They begin work with the best of technicians' intentions, but before long the distorting factors are at work beside them. This is how it happens:

No matter what the method of securing viewer information, all raters start by preparing their random samples. Those who use telephones define telephone homes as their "universe," and users of meters, diaries, or personal interviews employ maps to locate households. Then, because people are people and not milk in a tank car, the troubles begin.

Consider the meter users (Nielsen and ARB), who according to the Madow Report, face "serious problems of co-operation." Since meter installations are expensive, these services try to persuade their sample selectees to allow the device into their homes for an indefinite period. The Madow Report found that only "about 70 per cent of the originally designated homes will permit installation of the meters." For other reasons, the report then reduced this figure to 67 per cent. This means that a full third of the true random group is bypassed.

When the method is the personal interview (Pulse), there are more problems—interviewer or respondent errors, poorly formulated questions, language difficulties, refusals to co-operate, and absences from the home. These tribulations, the Madow Report disclosed, reduce the responding number of eligible homes to about 63 per cent, which excludes over a third of those whose inhabitants should have been interviewed.

Users of the telephone method (Trendex, and ARB in the placement of many of its diaries) fare no better, the report found. Because only 70 per cent of American homes can be reached through published telephone directories, and because only 85 to 90 per cent of those who answer will cooperate, the effective information figure is 60 to 63 per cent, further diminished by the raters' exclusion of toll-call areas. With this method, therefore, 40 per cent to half the true random group is excluded.

And when rating services employ the diary method (Nielsen, ARB), the Madow group found, "usable reports can be expected from about 57 per cent of the original random group."

In view of these serious distortions of the original random samples, it is no exaggeration to say that the rating services, which rebut critics on grounds that they simply do not understand scientific random sampling, are not using scientific random sampling at all.

When questioned about the gravity of the Madow findings, the services' replies vary. Nielsen's vice-president, Warren N. Cordell, is not surprisingly the boldest; he tends to demean the ability of the statistical investigaters. "I believe," Cordell says, "that the Madow Committee endeavored to do a very serious and scholarly job of appraising the broadcast measurement services, but that the limitations and the involvement of this field made it a difficult assignment, which they themselves admit in the preface of their report." The American Research Bureau's James W. Seiler agrees that "any lack of randomness in a sample is a serious problem," but adds that the Madow Report did not overstate the case "from the point of view of pure research methods." For "practical business decisions," Seiler feels, ARB's deficiencies are not significant. Sydney Roslow, of The Pulse, states flatly that the Madow Committee "is not correct" in its estimate that his firm's personal interview technique reaches only 63 per cent of the original random sample. Since the largest gap in interview research is caused by not-at-homes, Roslow once used a system of revisits, but, he says, "we almost went broke doing it."

Whatever these explanations are worth, the rating services' enthusiasm for distorted samples is not shared by the grandfather of the random sampling technique, the U.S. Bureau of the Census. The services have repeatedly contended that if they are to be criticized, so is the Census Bureau, but William N. Hurwitz, chief of the Bureau's statistical research division, indicates that he would not be caught with such samples in his countinghouse. "In every sample survey," he says, "one would expect some non-interviews and other sources of biases. However, non-response rates ranging from 35 to 45 per cent do not meet our standards."

Since broadcasters' intelligence is not in question, the explanation for their embrace of flimsy rating figures lies elsewhere. It can be found in the networks' decision to restrict the range of programming, making it more or less uniform in appeal. With such a schedule, ratings don't have to be very sensitive. A few leading attractions will stand apart at the top, and a few public affairs programs, cultural programs, and utterly inept entertainment shows will weight the bottom. The vast majority of the remainder will lie evenly distributed in the middle range; the programs don't differ enough to affect careful *or* sloppy ratings significantly.

Ratings, in short, are measuring degrees of sameness, not something meaningful. It does not require a Descartes, after all, to conclude that an opera, or a foreign-policy discussion, will be outdrawn by almost any form of light entertainment.

It does require a special mentality, though, to use such inappropriate figures as a justification of moronic programming. Advertisers want shows that will appeal to as many people as possible, and networks provide them because they want the advertising. The networks then point to apparent differences in rating figures and declare: We're giving the people what they want; they vote every half-hour with effective balloting devices—the channel selector and the on-off dial.

Since room for candidates in television is limited, however, those who are least popular are steadily ruled off the ballot. The result: Most of the candidates come from the same party and we have a television dictatorship.

Totalitarian television, as jointly ruled by ABC, CBS, and NBC, has increasingly robbed us of the right of free choice; the instances are numerous and shocking. Consider the shabby case of *The Voice of Firestone,* which began on NBC Radio in 1928 and introduced millions to Gladys Swarthout, Thomas L. Thomas, and others. In 1949 the program was extended to television and soon went out over the largest live network on the air. When NBC added an affiliate, Firestone immediately ordered it despite initially small audiences. In 1953 David Sarnoff said NBC had "a deep sense of pride in being able to share in this anniversary with . . . a company which for a quarter of a century has been bringing a fine and wholesome broadcast series to American homes." Firestone had by then spent $40,000,000 with NBC and was its oldest customer.

Barely four months after Sarnoff's statement, *The Voice of Firestone* was knocked out of its 8:30 to 9 P.M. period on Mondays. It was being "clobbered" by Arthur Godfrey's ratings on CBS and was replaced by Sid Caesar's show (which was later killed by Lawrence Welk's ratings on ABC). NBC offered to keep the musical program, but only in non-prime time or in the Sunday afternoon "cultural ghetto." Firestone declined these pigeonholes and negotiated with ABC, which was then hungry for a "classy" show. The network accepted the program for the Monday evening time period and Firestone sponsored it fifty-two weeks a year for three years, in return for which ABC granted one-year renewal options. In 1957, though, Firestone reduced its television budget and ordered only thirty-nine programs. ABC, with its Hollywood action series, was then emerging as a competitor to CBS and NBC.

With Firestone shorn of its renewal rights, ABC told the company in February, 1959, that its show could no longer have the 9 to 9:30 P.M. period (to which it had moved). The network suggested the 10 P.M. period (in which audiences are smaller), complete with a report entitled, "A Study to Determine Whether *The Voice of Firestone* Would Reach a Higher Audience at Monday, 10 P.M., than Monday, 9 P.M." It requires little imagination to guess what the report concluded, and Firestone would have none of it, nor of other proposals that would push it closer to midnight. It did not think much, either, of a CBS proposal to award it a Sunday afternoon niche and only four "special" prime-time hours a year.

The Voice of Firestone, a good-music candidate, was forced off the television ballot. ABC replaced it with a husky brute named *Adventures in Paradise,* which started at 8:30 and continued for an hour. Before long, ABC's Monday evening prime-time ballot read: *Cheyenne, The Rifleman, Surfside Six,* and *Ben Casey.* Early in 1962, while ABC was shining its tarnished image, Firestone was invited back; this time it hastened to accept the 10 P.M. time period.

Omnibus was also bad-pennied by the networks despite a stellar record of achievement: Joseph E. Welch on capital punishment, and on the Constitution; Peter Ustinov in "The Life of Samuel Johnson"; Leonard Bernstein explaining the meaning of opera; Gene Kelly in "Dancing Is a Man's Game," and other excellent programs. The show's producer, Robert Saudek, said he placed his faith not in ratings but "in the well-conceived idea, the well-written word, the well-spent dollar." *Omnibus* is off the ballot, too.

In addition to producing these undemocratic effects, ratings cause a tremendous waste of talent. Producers, writers, and performers are channeled into nonsensical projects or left to stare out the window. Sometimes they are permitted to create a worthwhile project, but then the project is placed on a shelf instead of on the air. An abysmal example of this process involved *The Robert Herridge Theater,* which was produced at a cost of almost $400,000 by CBS Films, Inc., but has never appeared on the network of its corporate parent.

The show was born in 1958, in the office of Sam Cook Digges, who was then general manager of WCBS-TV, CBS's owned-and-operated station in New York. Digges, while declining to agree with television's severest critics, had nevertheless shown consideration for what he calls "the minority tastes of the viewing public." He originated WCBS-TV's *Sunrise Semester,* an early morning college course for credit whose basic format has since been utilized by both the station's parent, CBS, and by NBC. Digges's station had also been carrying *Camera Three,* a brilliant local series produced in association with the New York State Education Department (and hidden away on Sunday mornings); Herridge was not only the originator of *Camera Three* but had produced and directed many of its finest episodes. The "literary conscience of the medium," as *Variety* called him, Herridge had also produced such *Studio One* dramas as Steinbeck's "Flight" and Conrad Aiken's "Mr. Arcularis."

Digges was aware that Herridge had left CBS because of inaction and was negotiating with NBC. Then Digges was promoted to a vice-presidency at CBS Films and had an opportunity to act. He sold the idea for a dramatic series by Herridge to the CBS stations division, of which CBS Films is a part, and received a budget a third the size of a network show's. But at least an effort would be made to program for "minority tastes."

Herridge made twenty-six filmed shows, some of which were fair but most of which ranged from very good to stunning. I had to dry my eyes after seeing "A Trip to Czardis," Edwin Granberry's story of two boys' last visit to their father; one is too young to understand that his father is not ill but is shortly to be hanged. Herridge also made Shirley Jackson's remarkable "The Lottery," a chilling commentary on man's inhumanity to man. And he did a western, "The Gunfighter," that made the conventional bang-bang resemble a Keystone Cops brawl.

It may be discerned from these synopses, however, that much of *The Robert Herridge Theater* suffered from an unforgivable Madison Avenue fault known as "downbeat," a misnomer for "thought-provoking." The shows rose from the wasteland through their ability to evoke deep emotional reaction; their daddies were not idiots, their mommies' thoughts transcended the breakfast-food problem, and their children were not preposterous little monsters.

These were fatal defects in any plan to gather high ratings. One sponsor looked, pronounced the death sentence—"Depressing. Aren't there any happy ones?"—and has since found joy with *National Velvet, The Tab Hunter Show,* the *Garry Moore Show, Whispering Smith,* and *The Barbara Stanwyck Theatre.* Men from advertising agencies saw screenings of the series and invariably felt it should be on the air—if someone other than their clients would sponsor it. At one point, Digges wrote directly to the heads of major corporations, suggesting that television needed "men of courage," and received abuse from their ad agencies for his audacity in going over their heads. CBS Films offered the series to all three networks, but was turned down—even by the programming board of parent CBS. Finally, when it syndicated the series—offered it to individual stations—its own salesmen made such comments as, "Herridge didn't use his head. You can't stop these shows for commercials. They're too good."

As a result of such mental slavery, *The Robert Herridge Theater* was presented on Canadian television before it appeared on a single station in the United States. And when "The Lottery" was shown there, a major newspaper controversy developed from Vancouver to Toronto over the story's theme, which was attacked and defended heatedly in hundreds of letters to editors. (Have you written a letter lately about Pete's treatment of Gladys's mother?) Canadian viewers had been stirred to think, speak, and exchange opinions. The show has been sold in twelve other countries, too, but at the end of 1961 only twenty-five U.S. commercial and two educational stations had taken it. Wherever it has played, critics have been enthusiastic.

And what of Robert Herridge? In 1960, he worked with writer Gore Vidal on an Omnibus-type program to be called *Monograph;* it never reached the production stage. A year later, he obtained a temporary release from CBS to produce some *Bell Telephone Hours* for NBC. Early in 1962, NBC announced it was dropping this musical series. The view from the creative window is gray; where there are no ratings, there is no sunshine.

When the denials of network executives are ignored (a recommended procedure), it can be seen that ratings are the backbone of program decisions. Robert W. Lishman, chief counsel of the House subcommittee that investigated the rigged quiz shows, reported that every producer who testified said that rigging was needed "to command a large audience and therefore a high rating . . . there was a direct relationship between high ratings and the fraud and deception practiced on those programs." The producers of *Tic Tac Dough, The $64,000 Question,* and *The $64,000 Challenge* called ratings the "primary" motivation for rigging. And a subcommittee member concluded that some quizzes were dropped prior to the investigation only because they "did not maintain their ratings."

Rating fever ran so high that when Steve Allen beat Ed Sullivan five times during their contention on Sunday evenings, there was "such rejoicing and hollering," Allen says, "that you would have thought I was a war hero." Phil Silvers recalls the epilogue to a rating triumph over Milton Berle: "When I walked out of the CBS elevator the morning after, all the secretaries rose to their feet and applauded. There, in one dramatic nutshell, was an indication to me of the height of frenzy to which the rating race had climbed."

In face of such foolishness, and in view of what we know

and suspect about the quality of some rating numbers, I choose to stake out a position with David Sarnoff, who has not yet denied that in 1953 he told NBC's affiliates: "Our industry from the outset has been plagued by rating systems which do not say what they mean and do not mean what they say."

And I am not alone. The occupant of at least one "Nielsen home" shares this attitude. This man is conducting an amusing game with Nielsen that the rating service can't appreciate because it isn't in on the fun. A resident of Chicago, he allowed Nielsen to attach an Audimeter to his television—not to cooperate but because he felt that ratings were ridiculous and deserved some sabotage, which he is engaged in. Our man on a mission, who reverently refers to his electronic program checker as "my little bug," watches only high-quality programs. In this way, he casts bullet votes for opera, occasional good drama, and the better public affairs programs. He tunes in a good program even when he chooses not to watch it; he knows that the mighty Audimeter measures only tuning, not seeing. He is a happy man. He has no illusions about the effect his small vote is having on programming, but he does have a modicum of satisfaction.

Can many viewers who have been robbed by the rating dictatorship say the same?

14 PAPER TIGERS OF THE POTOMAC

The Federal Communications Commission "presents a somewhat extraordinary spectacle." —James M. Landis, in a report to President Kennedy.

Late on a January afternoon in 1961, Newton Norman Minow, a lawyer from Chicago, emerged from the New Post Office Building in Washington, realized he was not going to find a cab, and trudged up Pennsylvania Avenue, through a snowstorm, to his hotel. Minow had come to the capital two days earlier, on his thirty-fifth birthday, to acquaint himself with his new job as chairman of the Federal Communications Commission, an agency that is supposed to regulate the broadcasting industry but rarely has.

Sixteen weeks later, having confirmed at close range what he had suspected from a distance, Minow stood at a rostrum in the Sheraton-Park Hotel and prepared to infuriate the delegates to the annual convention of the National Association of Broadcasters. These were men who had attended many conventions, heard scores of speakers, and usually applauded out of politeness and boredom. Few orators had said anything extraordinary, memorable, or, most important, troublesome.

True, an earlier FCC chairman, the never vague James

Lawrence Fly, had exasperatedly told broadcasting's leadership of its resemblance to "a dead mackerel in the moonlight—it both shines and stinks." But broadcasting had survived Fly handily, as it has the few other commissioners who have suggested moderation in indecency.

Thus it was that on May 9, 1961, the industry waited with curiosity, if not exactly apprehension, for an indication of how nettlesome this Newton Minow promised to be. Readers who wish to savor an extended digest of his remarks may consult Appendix A. Suffice it to say here that this was Minow's "vast wasteland" speech. "I have confidence in your health," he commented after noting broadcasting's Gargantuan profits, "but not in your product. . . . When television is good, nothing—not the theater, not the magazines or newspapers—nothing is better. But when television is bad, nothing is worse. I invite you to sit down in front of your television set when your station goes on the air and stay there without a book, magazine, newspaper, profit and loss sheet or rating book to distract you—and keep your eyes glued to that set until the station signs off. I can assure you that you will observe a vast wasteland."

Perhaps because he did not believe that a normal, red-blooded station owner could bear to watch his own channel for a full day, Minow recapitulated a typical schedule for his suddenly squirming auditors. They would be exposed, he said, to "a procession of game shows, violence, audience participation shows, formula comedies about totally unbelievable families, blood and thunder, mayhem, violence, sadism, murder, western badmen, western good men, private eyes, gangsters, more violence, and cartoons. And, endlessly, commercials—many screaming, cajoling, and offending. And most of all, boredom."

With applause decreasing at the approximate rate these truths were reaching the NAB members, Minow reached a point in his bill of particulars that was painfully embarrassing, and therefore particularly angering. "Is there one person in this room," he asked, "who claims that broadcasting can't do better?" In the baleful silence that followed, the chairman smiled, looking more like a chubby Wally Cox than Hercules at the stable door. He had fired the first salvo in a war that should have been declared a generation earlier, that will not end for some time, and whose outcome will affect all of our lives.

The broadcasting industry's conduct toward the Federal Communications Commission recalls a schoolteacher's approach to a class in which it was once my lot to sit. This clever woman opened each day's learning adventure in a spirit of unprovoked assault. She strode the classroom with a ruler in hand and smote every student mightily, in turn. "That's for doing nothing," she would explain. "Now do something!" The method struck me as extreme, but it is true that we pupils always behaved like lambs.

Since the creation of the FCC, broadcasters have repeatedly assailed their regulators for nothing in order to discourage them from doing something. Almost without exception, the Commission's members have responded by behaving like lambs. "In recent years," *Advertising Age* has commented, "many FCC members have sounded as if they felt their jobs depended on a vote of confidence from the NAB."

While querulousness is not necessarily a virtue in the federal agency business, neither is obsequiousness, and, as the most servile congregation on the banks of the Potomac, the FCC has established a record of sorts in collecting insults from frustrated and outraged citizens. The commissioners have conducted themselves in such a way, in fact, as to generate confusion over their agency's *raison d'être*. Is it a people's watchdog, or a fife-and-drum corps for the broadcasting industry? On the rare occasions when it has growled, the industry has arranged for its teeth to be ground down in short order. And when it has functioned as an industry promoter, its members have been lured into ethical traps, outright scandal, and personal disaster. When the Hoover Commission studied the FCC, it noted "the possibility that some members of the Commission's staff have sought to curry favor with the industry in order to obtain more lucrative positions." This bipartisan group also said, in diplomatic understatement, that at times the FCC "appears to have confused private interests with the public interest."

The last time an honest and intelligent man studied the machinations of the agency, he recoiled in stupefaction. This was James M. Landis, once dean of the Harvard Law School, a flinty one-man emergency squad whose services the government has periodically made use of. Landis was commissioned in 1960 by a Senate subcommittee to look into the workings of the federal regulatory agencies, and he did not like what he found. In a report to President-elect Kennedy, he said the FCC

> . . . presents a somewhat extraordinary spectacle. Despite considerable technical excellence on the part of its staff, the Commission has drifted, vacillated, and stalled in almost every major area. It seems incapable of policy planning, of disposing within a reasonable period of time of the business before it, of fashioning procedures that are effective to deal with its problems. . . . A strong suspicion also exists that far too great an influence is exercised over the Commission by the networks. . . .

This low estate is at least partly the result of the FCC's second-class status in Washington. Established in 1934, it has never had a home of its own and to this day utilizes what room it can get in the New Post Office Building, which is not very new. These quarters are so inadequate that it has been forced to rent additional space in private Washington buildings. The Commission has no facilities for regular communication with the public; its releases are mimeographed for and picked up by the trade press, which means that a citizen interested in broadcasting must buy *Broadcasting*. The agency is so thoroughly isolated from the listeners and viewers it is supposed to represent that it even publishes a bulletin telling them what it won't supply in the way of information and directing them to firms that will, for a fee.

The Commission's persistent ineffectiveness is related, predictably, to money. The opportunity to become a money-making broadcaster is restricted by the physical capacity, or incapacity, of the broadcasting spectrum; there is room for only a certain number of radio and television frequencies on the air. As almost everyone seems to appreciate, this is a natural phenomenon and not a devilish plot of the New Deal, the Fair Deal, or even the New Frontier. It has no connection with Barry Goldwater, Nikita Khrushchev, or Souvanna Phouma. It *is* connected, though, with the need for regulation. Since the air waves are a limited natural resource, their use must be governed to prevent anarchic interference and insure public benefit. Therefore, a license is valuable to mutually dependent parties—the broadcaster who provides a service (and who profits through the sale of air time for advertising) and the public that uses the service.

This interdependence creates a dilemma as soon as a broadcaster violates the terms under which his license was issued. (We are now talking about something that goes on every day.) If he were to be penalized by suspension or revocation, the public would be simultaneously penalized by a deprivation of service. The license, a temporary franchise, derives from public property, but the transmitting facility is private property.

Because of this awkward admixture of human and property rights, until recently a unique arrangement in world broadcasting, the FCC has traditionally been reluctant to punish malfeasance and non-feasance by pronouncing the "death penalty"—revocation of or refusal to renew a station's license. As dinosaurically as 1932, Henry A. Bellows, who had graduated (financially and otherwise) from the Federal Radio Commission to a vice-presidency of the Columbia Broadcasting System, was berating a proposal to arm the FCC with "new and alarming powers to suspend stations" for brief periods. He pointed out, logically enough, that a suspension would inevitably lead to cancellation of advertising contracts and undoubtedly to the ruin of a station. The FCC did not get this power, and, despite repeated attempts to write it into the Communications Act, the Commission still does not have it.

It is an inescapable truth, however, that the only broadcasters who could be affected by such punitive power are those who might violate the provisions of their licenses—that is, might break the law; all others would bask in unchallengeable grace. The public, the object of the law's concern, could only benefit, a factor that would seem to have relevance. If a television station were a profitable operation (which almost all are), and its license were to be suspended for tawdry service (which it should be), and it collapsed financially, then a more responsible licensee would quickly present himself and a brief deprivation of poor service would result in a presumably permanent gain of improved service.

Good free-enterprise thinking? Broadcasters don't think so; therefore, this viewpoint has never prevailed at the FCC, whose job it is to enforce the Communications Act of 1934, which requires that broadcasting be regulated to promote the "public interest, convenience, and necessity."

Under normal procedure, station licenses are granted for three years, a period which makes it possible for a broadcaster to settle down and program properly despite any early difficulties he might encounter, and which also makes it possible for the FCC to review his performance within a reasonable length of time. What can a rational regulatory body do with a person who abuses his license? It can revoke it or refuse to renew it on expiration; this provision is written into the law. But what does an irrational agency do with a person who abuses his license? It fails to revoke, and it renews regularly by shuffling papers, yawning, and affixing the official seal. The knowledgeable Dean Roscoe Barrow of the University of Cincinnati Law School emerged from an exhaustive study of broadcasting for the Commission with the comment, "They should pump some life into the license renewal process and hold broadcasters to the promises they make. But it takes a great deal of fortitude for the regulators to do this."

By doing nothing, the Federal Comatose Commission violates the law itself, and that is what it did as a routine matter for twenty-five years. The routine was mildly interrupted in 1960, seven months after William P. Rogers, then U.S. Attorney General, issued a blistering report on FCC inaction. The Commission then notified each broadcaster that he was obliged to consult with his community's leaders in order to determine its programming needs. Although this requirement left much room for ambiguous compliance, the Commission did refuse a new license to an FM applicant when it simply copied an existing station's programming proposals and submitted them as its own.

In 1961, the FCC took stronger action. When KORD, a radio station in Pasco, Washington, applied for a renewal of its license, the application was set down for a hearing because there was almost no resemblance between KORD's original promises and the programming it had presented. The station protested, in effect and with good logic, that it was unfair for the FCC suddenly to enforce the law by singling it out. The Commission reconsidered and had to agree, thus confirming that it had been rubber-stamping violated licenses for years. But in agreeing, it gave KORD only a one-year renewal and notified it that failure to live up to programming promises would constitute grounds for refusal to renew a license in the future. In a widely publicized action, it then sent copies of its "KORD letter" to every radio and television station in the country.

The warning was clear that the FCC was finally on its feet, fighting for enforcement of the Communications Act. Or was it clear? *Television Digest,* a Washington trade paper, said: "Only time will tell whether the Commission is kidding." If it *was* kidding and now retreats from this position, few people will be able to take the FCC seriously for a long time. If broadcasters are forced to adhere to their promises, bedrock minimum requirements for public service will be met. But such requirements have no bearing on the quality of entertainment programming, which is what is really wrong with television.

To balance the FCC's lengthy history of inaction, it is worth noting some cases in which it *has* taken action. The last one lies in a musty closet of radio history; it is important because everything the FCC does, or doesn't do, about television springs from what it did and didn't do about radio. The case involved such blatant misconduct that it could not have been ignored longer than it was. The miscreant was a whiskered highwayman of the 1920's, known, not quite accurately, as "Doctor" John R. Brinkley, specialist in male rejuvenation. Brinkley set up shop in Milford, Kansas, with the object of reinvigorating the men of the nation through the implantation of goat glands. Since the line between hope and gullibility is vague, the imaginative surgeon made a fortune, if not a more virile populace. In the course of his escapade, Brinkley established KFKB, a radio station over which he dispensed medical advice and licentiousness. Without the benefit of seeing or laying hands on patients, he read their letters and then prescribed quackish potions which he compounded, numbered, and offered for sale. In one broadcast, Brinkley said:

> Now here is a letter from a dear mother—a dear little mother who holds to her breast a babe of nine months. She should take No. 2 and—yes, No. 17—and she will be helped. Brinkley's 2 and 17. She should order them from the Milford Drug Company, Milford, Kansas, and they shall be sent to you, Mother—collect. May the Lord guard and protect you, Mother. The postage will be prepaid.

Between 1923 and 1930, KFKB's "Medical Question Box" diagnosed most ailments, from fallen arches to cancer. On one broadcast alone, Brinkley handled forty-four different complaints, in each case prescribing from one to ten of his numbers-game medicinals. He also brought an air of informality to his discussions, as when a woman in Olathe complained that she was having too many children. Brinkley clutched his microphone and told his correspondent:

> I suggest you have your husband sterilized, and then you will be safe, providing you don't get out in anybody else's cow pasture and get in with some other bull.

The Federal Radio Commission, founded in 1927, did nothing about Brinkley until (1) the *Kansas City Star* dramatically exposed him, (2) the Kansas Medical Board unfrocked him, and (3) the American Medical Association opposed the renewal of KFKB's license. The Commission thereupon held a hearing, the wild and woolly nature of which may be imagined, and finally refused to renew, but only by a vote of three to two. Moreover, the Commission permitted the swindler to continue his dangerous broadcasts while he appealed to the courts; this enabled Brinkley, by the time the Commission was upheld, to sell KFKB to a Wichita insurance company for $90,000.

In 1937, the FCC stirred itself over complaints that NBC had transmitted sexual suggestiveness during a sketch presented by Mae West, the celebrated stripper, and Edgar Bergen's dummy, Charlie McCarthy. When congressmen became aroused by letters from offended constituents, the Commission delved into this weighty matter and ultimately concluded that the "Adam and Eve" sketch had been "vulgar and indecent." It dispatched a stern letter of reprimand to NBC and to each affiliate that had carried the program, with the warning that it would have this heinous crime in mind when the stations' licenses came up for renewal. All licenses were renewed, of course, and that was, ho-hum, the end of that.

Eleven years later, after the expenditure of numerous lives in a war against fascism, the Commission received complaints that a Los Angeles radio station, KMPC, had been slanting its news reports to coincide with the anti-Semitic sentiments of its owner, George A. Richards. Among those making the charges were two newsmen who had once been in KMPC's employ, and among those demanding that the FCC investigate were the American Jewish Congress, the National Association of Radio News Directors, the American Federation of Radio Artists, the Democratic State Central Committee of California, and a number of congressmen.

The FCC ordered a public hearing in November, 1948, but with the observance of numerous legal niceties, the hearing did not commence until March, 1950. By Christmas of that year, one hundred and thirteen days had been consumed with the taking of testimony, much of which was extremely incriminating. The hearing examiner (that is, the second hearing examiner; the first died in the interim) then went off to deliberate, but before he could divest himself of an opinion, broadcaster Richards also died. Whereupon, in June, 1951, the examiner delivered an initial decision in which he recommended that the proceedings be dismissed. If this seems astounding, the reader should consider the reaction of those who had complained of KMPC's conduct three and a half years earlier. They were dumfounded, as was the FCC's general counsel, who took exception to the decision. The lawyers for Richards's estate, calm in the face of inexplicable triumph, applied for a transfer of Richards's licenses (he also owned stations in Cleveland and Detroit) to his widow. The Commission granted this request in December, 1951, in an action reminiscent of the FRC's decision in the Brinkley case. Mrs. Richards sold two of the stations shortly afterward and the case was closed without serious loss to the Richards family estate.

The accumulating effect of such decisions has paved the way for informal acceptance of the doctrine that a broadcaster should not be dislodged from his *publicly franchised position* for misconduct without allowing him first to drain the final drop of profit. The question is not complicated: Is a broadcaster receiving a temporary license, or a permanent deed to a frequency? The law says license; the FCC makes it a deed.

During this lengthy and fitful period of somnolence, the FCC did indicate that it was at least vigilant of plots to destroy America through broadcast subversion, or something. When an unidentified party told the Commission that a Toledo broadcaster was a member of the Communist Party and had advocated violent overthrow of the government, it leaped to horse and instituted an investigation that was protracted and extravagant in the type of testimony received. The object of scrutiny was Edward Oliver Lamb, a wealthy native of Toledo, a graduate of Dartmouth College and of the Yale, Harvard, and Western Reserve Law Schools, a corporation lawyer who was interested in both capital and labor, a candidate for office on both the Republican and Democratic tickets, a publisher whose newspaper consistently carried anti-Communist editorials, the author of a book, *The Planned Economy in Soviet Russia,* and a man whose radio stations' programming did not depart from the usual pattern. Lamb involuntarily consumed three years of the Commission's time, during which it was routinely approving the licenses of similarly programmed stations, before a hearing examiner recommended that his license be renewed. The agency's Broadcast Bureau—incredibly, many thought—objected and attempted to prolong the case, but the commissioners finally dropped the matter. The money expended must have been staggering.

The commissioners' tardy notice of Goat-Gland Brinkley's patent quackery, their alacrity, on the other hand, in damning Mae West's and Edgar Bergen's peccadillo, their pettifoggery in dealing with the anti-Semitism case, and their dance of fear in The Communist Capers of Toledo suggest to the vulgarly spoken that this Commission hasn't often known what the hell to do with our money and its time and energy. It ought to meet the youngster I once heard educating a policeman in Central Park. The boy was trying to play on some new grass seed and the officer was bent on expelling him. "G'wan," the clear-thinking child lectured, "whyntcha go catch a raper?"

The FCC had an opportunity to collar some enormous scoundrels when, in 1957, two national magazines and a New York newspaper suggested, as directly as they could within the libel laws, that the television quiz shows were fraudulent. But the chairman of the FCC, John C. Doerfer, like the presidents of CBS and NBC, somehow missed these allegations. It was the middle of the following year before the news filtered into the Commission's offices in far-off Washingtonland; one day a secretary opened the morning mail and discovered an affidavit from a CBS quiz-show contestant who had been wronged. Bouncing to its racket-busting feet, the Commission located a typewriter and wrote a letter of its own. It said, in effect, Dear CBS: What's transpiring, honorable sirs? CBS replied that, well, there had been a modicum of unpleasantness on the *Dotto* show, which it had been unaware of, to be sure, but in any event the program had been sent packing and measures taken to bolt the doors against further nefariousness. "We got an immediate response from the networks that they were going to take care of that themselves," Chairman Doerfer later testified, inaccurately. The FCC did not even write to NBC, which carried a nighttime version of *Dotto,* for another six months, because no one had waved a specific complaint before its official nose.

Doerfer was an illuminating witness before a House subcommittee that did the FCC's work for it by investigating the quiz scandals. As President Eisenhower's first appointee to the FCC, he had acted in such a way that *Advertising Age* was later prompted to remark: "In his public statements he managed to leave the impression that he was more concerned about curbing the FCC than he was in curbing the broadcasters who were out of line." If the quiz shows were out of line, Doerfer didn't notice. He felt no overwhelming curiosity when *Dotto* was taken off the air while more important hoodwinkers—*Twenty-One, The $64,000 Question,* and *The $64,000 Challenge*—remained.

A detective who fails to seek out a culprit because of stupidity has the right to expect pity along with the scorn he merits, but what of a detective who explains that, with substantial evidence of fraud in hand, he doesn't have the *authority* to track down a wrongdoer? That was Doerfer's position; he seated himself before the congressional investigators after the quiz scandals had broken into the open and declared that the FCC might have violated the Constitution if it had insisted that crooked quiz shows be taken off the air. This was the exchange:

Q. . . . What constitutional provision do you have in mind?

A. Freedom of speech.

Q. Freedom of speech?

A. Freedom of press. The First Amendment to the Constitution.

Q. You mean you take that as a blanket justification to permit the American people to be deceived for a period of a year or eighteen months without ever reporting it to the Congress?

A. I don't take that as a blanket. I am merely presenting to you the various considerations which have thrown substantial doubt into precipitous action on the part of the Commission. To tamper with our cherished freedom of speech is not a simple proposition. It takes a good deal of study.

Q. [*Another Congressman*]: . . . has the Commission the authority to impose . . . regulations which would prevent fraud or irregularities in presenting programs of skill or knowledge?

A. There is a great deal of doubt connected with that . . .

Q. You could require that they be honest, could you not?

A. Strange to say, I doubt that.

Three months after he delivered these extraordinary and self-serving views, Doerfer was strongly contradicted by U.S. Attorney General Rogers, who reported to President Eisenhower that the FCC had all the authority it needed "to eradicate most, if not all, of the deceptive and corrupt practices" that the congressional committee had learned of. Moreover, Rogers declared, the Commission had investigatory powers "fully as great" as those of the committee and could have conducted its own probe of the mess. Two months after *that,* it emerged that Chairman Doerfer had spent some of his time inappropriately while the fraud was occurring. He had vacationed aboard the yacht of George B. Storer, holder of several FCC licenses for radio and television stations. When Doerfer contended that Storer's hospitality was limited because the yacht did not stray far from the dock, the *Baltimore Sun* promulgated "Doerfer's Law": the extent to which a regulator can be influenced aboard an industry yacht varies inversely with the shallowness of the water. President Eisenhower testily suggested that his appointee resign. He did, and went to work for a Bethesda, Maryland, plastics company of which Storer was a stockholder.

John Doerfer's yachting non-trip was probably more inopportune than dastardly—it came at a time when scandal was in the air, and it might have been overlooked in more pacific days. The fact is, he was fired for the wrong reason: the President should have let him out the day he officially proclaimed that while the FCC was supposed to regulate broadcasting, it could not consider the nature of programming, which *is* broadcasting. Few commissioners have ever taken a contrary stand, however; most have rubber-stamped their way through their tenures, tacitly bowing to pressures that are varied, heavy, and ever present. These pressures have led to three evils: (1) the fear or unwillingness of commissioners to carry out their mandate, (2) the improper relations between, or outright financial involvement with, existing or potential licensees, and (3) the perpetuation of time-killing procedures that prevent the Commission from performing effectively, should it desire to.

James M. Landis has pointed out that all federal regulatory agencies are subjected to a "daily machine-gun-like impact" of industry lobbying, and the broadcasting lobby has some of the biggest guns on Capitol Hill; Newton Minow noted its omnipresence shortly after he arrived in Washington when he said he had "no illusions about the influence the industry wields in this town." The industry does not issue written orders to FCC commissioners and employees, of course; this is the age of subtlety, and of bonhomie at the nineteenth hole of the Congressional Country Club.

The lure of industry jobs, for one thing, is obvious, and an uncomfortable number of commissioners have responded to it by abandoning the modestly rewarded field of public service for the greener fields of private broadcasting. Since the creation of the Federal Radio Commission in 1927, five commissioners have taken industry positions (some as vice-presidents of CBS and NBC); Congress finally barred FCC members from accepting industry jobs during the unexpired portion of their terms even if they resigned. But other commissioners have gone into station ownership; one quit to practice law—and represent broadcasters before the Commission; one became an officer of a broadcasting company after his first term and is now serving a second term; and the regulators' chief engineer from 1930 to 1935 moved to RCA as a vice-president.

Because of this game of musical chairs, almost a dozen-and-a-half men have been FCC chairmen since 1927. A normal term of office is seven years, but over forty men have served as members. Such treadmilling is admirable in a hamster but it is not in a regulatory agency. It not only destroys continuity, but is as much notice as a reasonably astute man needs that industry steak may be made available at any moment to a gentle, needy paper tiger.

In view of numerous revelations concerning one-sided, off-the-record presentations that some commissioners have accommodated, it is not difficult to understand why the quality of appointments to the FCC has been criticized. At least a dozen grants of television channels have come under a cloud for this reason, and in one widely publicized case, a commissioner admitted that he had been receiving money through a pipeline whose other end was manned by a television channel-seeker. The commissioner, Richard A. Mack, became involved in 1953, while a member of the Florida Railroad and Public Utilities Commission, with Thurman A. Whiteside, a Miami lawyer. Whiteside gave Mack an interest in an insurance agency that was handling the television account of National Airlines, which was soon to apply for a license to operate

Channel 10 in Miami. Not long after Mack was appointed to the FCC, by President Eisenhower in 1955, he voted for National's subsidiary, Public Service Television, which had three opponents. National won the channel. When the commissioner's financial dependence on Whiteside was revealed, he was forced to resign and both men were indicted for conspiracy. Their first trial ended in a hung jury; Whiteside was acquitted in a second trial, then committed suicide, and Mack has not been tried again because of illness.

More interesting than Mack's involvement was the revelation that two of the other three contestants for Channel 10 had also made back-door approaches to FCC members. As a result of the scandal, National Airlines' license was revoked and Channel 10 given to L. B. Wilson, Inc., the only petitioner that had not tried to exercise improper influence.

Although these messes demonstrate that in the quest for scarce television channels, many licensees abhor competition and employ unethical means of avoiding it, let luridness not lure us from the far greater meaning of the scandals. A license to operate a television station is a license to hunt money in open season; the following table shows television industry profits, before federal income taxes, during the decade 1951–1960:

Year	Profit (*millions*)
1951	$ 41.6
1952	55.5
1953	68.0
1954	90.3
1955	150.2
1956	189.6
1957	160.0
1958	171.9
1959	222.3
1960	244.1

Figure filberts sometimes try to demean this decade profit total of well over a billion and a quarter dollars by pointing to the industry's losses in the period preceding 1951. But the red-ink figures have long since been eradicated by profit ratios of almost 20 per cent of income, which work down to a net profit, *after* taxes, of almost 10 per cent. Few *unregulated* industries could claim such a bonanza. Moreover, the figures related above are based on profit-and-loss statements submitted to the FCC, and it is a celebrated fact that such statements do not reflect the number of dollars taken out of enterprises in the form of ultra-comfortable executive salaries and tax-free expense accounts.

When the networks discuss their share of the take, they employ a device that railroads have found helpful—speak loudly of commuter losses and softly of freight profits. The three networks state with accuracy that their combined profit-to-income ratio in 1960 was 6.7 per cent before federal taxes. There is more to the story, though: their profits have risen from $9,000,000 in 1952 to $95,000,000 in 1960. In addition, their corporate parents own fifteen television stations outright, and these, never doubt, are situated in the choicest cities (market areas) of the nation—New York, Washington, Philadelphia, Pittsburgh, Detroit, Chicago, St. Louis, Los Angeles, and San Francisco. Some of these stations earn over $10,000,000 a year, which accounts for the otherwise odd fact that while they comprise fewer than 3 per cent of all outlets, they earn over 40 per cent of station profits. During the 1950's, network owned-and-operated stations cleared over $300,000,000, while other network operations showed a profit of $200,000,000 more. Total: a half-billion dollars.

The networks need such profit margins, to be sure. How else could CBS scrape together enough money to pay William S. Paley, Frank Stanton, and James Aubrey almost $900,000 in salaries and pensions for one year's work? How else could NBC pay Robert Sarnoff $200,000 a year in salary and "incentive awards?" And where would ABC have raised the wherewithal for Oliver Treyz's $100,000 a year? (These may be treated as self-answering questions.)

Wall Street, in any event, does not seem to fear that there are hard times ahead for television networks. At the end of 1961, one investment firm looked into CBS's future and concluded that its stock was "an excellent buy for long-term appreciation." Even "if there is any further pressure brought to bear on the networks by the FCC for better programming," the securities analysts said, "we do not feel it will adversely affect Columbia's prospects." The prediction for CBS's 1962 net income and profit margin: highest in its history. NBC hit its high in 1961 and shows no signs of disappointing its stockholders in the future.

This avalanche of numbers may explain the zest with which the broadcasters' lobby fights, and usually defeats, attempts to narrow the yawning gap between greed and responsibility. Consider, for example, the game of station speculation, in which a television channel is regarded as a steer, to be bought skinny and cheap, its appearance improved (with promotion money), and then sold high. Only the most remarkable man would, under such circumstances, care what was emanating from his transmitter, so long as it drew large ratings. The speculator is entranced with the opportunity to realize a quick profit on his investment of feed money.

To make such profits possible, though, a station's value must be "bid up," which is exactly what happens. In 1958, the magazine *U.S. News & World Report* unearthed an example of this bidding process that explained the mechanism clearly. An article showed how, in 1948, Company A received a license to construct and operate a television station, whose cost was estimated to be $186,000. Five years later, Company A asked the FCC for permission (which it received) to sell out to Company B. The price was then $2,400,000, of which $1,200,000 represented the value of its physical assets; the other half covered "intangibles." In 1957, Company B asked the FCC for permission (which it received) to sell out to Company C.

By then the price was $6,300,000, of which only $1,500,000 represented the value of physical assets.

In this actual case, the approved bidding-up process increased the station's value 3,300 per cent in two sales, although the value of its physical assets had risen by only one-fourth that amount. The "intangible" three-fourths consisted largely of the FCC-granted license to operate; a public property was being marketed by a private interest at a fabulous profit, with the continuing approval of a public agency.

In such free-wheeling circumstances, it is not surprising that station speculators are legion. Of approximately four hundred and fifty radio and television stations that changed hands during 1960, for $200,000,000, about half had been owned less than three years. Seven television outlets, the transfer of whose licenses was duly approved by the FCC, brought in over $1,000,000 each; one sold for $3,000,000, and one for $4,000,000. Educational interests had to pay over $6,000,000 for Channel 13 in New York; this, the *least* profitable of seven stations in New York, had originally been purchased for $3,000,000.

When the FCC decided to stop talking about trafficking and slow it down, it collided with the ever-vigilant patriots of the industry, Patrick Henry types who would rather be dead than lose their liberty to collect commissions and fees in station sales. Finally, in early 1962, the Commission ruled that when a station was offered for sale before it had been held three years, a full-dress hearing would automatically be held on the transaction. Since hearings slow the gambling action, this reasonable and belated decision caused unhappiness among a number of lawyers, station brokers, and broadcasters, who alleged an "abridgment of free enterprise," whatever that means.

Other methods have been employed to subvert the fuzzy-enough requirement of the Communications Act that broadcasting be conducted in the "public interest, convenience, and necessity," and one in particular reveals the amount of public money that is wasted by lobby-nurtured ineffectualness in regulation. The problem again involves trafficking. When a contest for a new television channel develops, the FCC holds a "comparative hearing" in which, theoretically at least, each contestant strives to demonstrate that he would provide a better service than any of his adversaries. In ludicrous practice, dusty lawyers of the FCC trail fill out their clients' forms so that differences in contesting programming proposals are, for realistic purposes, indistinguishable. "The man who gets the station," Clifford J. Durr, a former FCC member, has said, "is often the man willing to stretch the truth the farthest." In any event, the Commission then makes its Solomon's decision, which all too frequently is a Hobson's choice.

But if a wily operator secures a television station, then does what he had planned to do all along—get in and out fast—the FCC is completely powerless. It must approve the license transfer unless it can show that the sale would not be in the public interest. A new comparative hearing may not be held because, in 1952, *Congress actually forbade it.* Thus the time and money expended on the original comparative hearing are washed away. The emasculation of 1952 was a product of one of the most predatory lobbying campaigns seen on Capitol Hill. (The Communications Act was so plundered that FCC members were even prohibited from consulting with many of their key staff members on pending cases, a crippling ban that was not lifted until 1961.)

Congressional bills are periodically introduced to empower the FCC to order a new comparative hearing in such cases, but that kind of legislation seems as passage-proof as other kinds that would force broadcasting to behave. Keeping a firm hold on reality, though, the value of such legislation must be considered in face of the Commission's own practice of granting licenses and renewals with all the marksmanship of a boy playing pin the tail on the donkey. Perhaps it is an indication of how dreary the entire situation is when remedial legislation can only be regarded as a white cane and not the restoration of eyesight.

If the FCC sometimes seems to be handicapped by congressional reticence, there is a reason: Congress contains some of the best friends broadcasting could wish for. Congressmen established the regulatory agencies as an arm of the *legislative* branch, they are fond of saying at those coincidental moments when someone is trying to make the agencies function. Example: Station owners do not pay a nickel—not even a license fee—in return for the right to place their cash registers on public property, despite repeated pleas from the Budget Bureau that the regulated help defray the cost of essential regulation. When, in 1954, the FCC set out to recover a modest fraction of its budget, broadcasters evinced displeasure and the Senate Commerce Committee crisply told the Commission to drop the matter. It did. When Chairman Minow suggested in 1961 that applicants pay $600 for a television license, the chairman of the House Commerce Committee, Oren Harris, frowned, and Minow's colleagues voted him down. When President Truman submitted a plan in 1950 to take the creak out of the FCC's machinery by reorganizing it, Congress defeated the proposal. When President Kennedy submitted a reorganization plan eleven years later, Congress trounced it—while approving the streamlining of other regulatory agencies. (Contributing to this debacle were some of the lawyers who specialize in practice before the FCC. These men are steadily squeezing the exaggeration out of a contention that a broadcaster can maneuver more days in FCC hearing rooms than can a condemned man in courtrooms. One of them became so fervent in his defense of the Constitution that he likened the President's reorganization proposal to one of Hitler's gambits for seizing power. If the FCC is ever truly streamlined, with the right of redress amply safeguarded, lawyers will be far and away the most crestfallen patriots in the District of Columbia.)

It is true that Congress created the federal agencies, and is given to protecting them with its collective fury from the designs of the White House and other centers of conspiracy. It is at least equally true that congressmen should emulate Caesar's wife as much as possible. Twenty-four members of Congress as well as the Vice-President of the United States have a personal or family financial interest in commercial radio or television stations through stock ownership or a director's seat.*

Such connections have led to peculiar conduct. In 1943, for example, Representative Eugene Cox of Georgia inspired one of many pointless congressional investigations of the FCC. When it was noted that Cox had been voted $2,500 in the stock of a broadcasting company in his state, and that he had used his official position to help the company secure a radio license, Cox lost little time in charging the Commission with "terroristic control of all media of communications." The FCC was the "nastiest nest of rats in the country," he said, and what was more, the commissioners had "Communist affiliations." The investigation cost a lot of money and produced nothing but short-lived petty sensations.

In view of current zeal in unearthing conflicts of interest among government officials, it is puzzling that congressmen perceive no conflict in legislating about businesses in whose profits they or theirs share. Where certain congressmen are concerned, puzzlement gives way to outright distress. Warren G. Magnuson is an example. A man who has described himself as an "old frontiersman," Magnuson owns 10,000 shares in a Seattle radio and television property. As chairman of the Senate Commerce Committee, he is also the most influential

* Senators Clinton P. Anderson (New Mexico), Olin D. Johnston (South Carolina), B. Everett Jordan (North Carolina), Robert S. Kerr (Oklahoma), Warren G. Magnuson (Washington), Winston L. Prouty (Vermont), A. Willis Robertson (West Virginia), John J. Sparkman (Alabama), and Herman A. Talmadge (Georgia); Representatives J. Floyd Breeding (Kansas), Donald C. Bruce (Indiana), Thomas B. Curtis (Missouri), John W. Davis (Georgia), James J. Delaney (New York), L. H. Fountain (North Carolina), Porter Hardy, Jr. (Virginia), Paul C. Jones, Sr. (Missouri), Eugene J. Keogh (New York), Richard E. Lankford (Maryland), George H. Mahon (Texas), Albert M. Rains (Alabama), William W. Scranton (Pennsylvania), Morris K. Udall (Arizona), and Phil Weaver (Nebraska).

man in broadcasting affairs on the Senate side of Capitol Hill. It was Magnuson's committee that, in 1954, bade the FCC drop its plans to charge fees for the costs of regulation, and that, in 1960, was instrumental in halving an FCC request for funds with which to monitor television stations more closely. Trade magazines regard the senator as the "strongest industry friend in Congress." When Magnuson's committee was questioning Newton Minow during hearings on his nomination, *Television Daily* said he "virtually directed" the chairman-designate to rely on television's "self-policing" efforts instead of on more stringent regulation. Said *Sponsor:* "Magnuson made it clear he would continue to be broadcasting's most powerful friend on Capitol Hill."

Oren Harris, Magnuson's opposite number in the House, notified the FCC in April, 1957, that he had bought a 25 per cent share in a television station in El Dorado, Arkansas (his home state), for $5,000. Less than one year later, Harris announced that he had sold his share "because of the constant and continuous harassment in certain press circles, accompanied by accusations, implications, insinuations, and innuendoes." Jack Gould of the *New York Times*, for one, had pointed out that the Representative initially responsible for broadcasting legislation had a financial interest in broadcasting.

Six months later, Harris conceded that he had intervened with the FCC on behalf of an Arkansas radio station owner who was upset over the possibility that the FCC would grant a license to another broadcaster in his area and thus increase his competition. After the station owner wrote to the FCC, Harris asked the agency for a copy of its reply. He also asked the FCC to explain its policy on the economic ability of an area to sustain competition—and to use the Arkansas case as a model.

Then there is the Representative from Indianapolis, Donald C. Bruce, elected to Congress while business manager of a radio station. Bruce's nineteen years in broadcasting drew him to the Washington convention of the National Association of Broadcasters at which Newton Minow made his "vast wasteland" suggestion. Bruce rose in the House and proclaimed that he had never heard "such an arrogant, overbearing violation of the concept of the American system." Was he speaking as a broadcaster, or as a congressman prepared to consider broadcasting legislation with all due neutrality and detachment?

When the Eighty-seventh Congress lost Lyndon Johnson as Senate Majority Leader, the upper chamber gained as its presiding officer a man whose family controls, or has a significant investment in, five Texas television stations. The Vice-President's wife, Lady Bird, is vice-president, board chairman, and 60 per cent owner of the LBJ Company, which would be affected by any legislation affecting broadcasting. No one has suggested that Johnson spends his time making unethical suggestions in regard to broadcasting legislation, but this does not shake off a serious headache that begs for relief. Congressmen are famous, if that is the word, for intervening with members of the presumably independent regulatory agencies. The FCC has revealed that in 1958 alone its members received over nine hundred letters (plus an untabulated number of telephone calls) from congressmen in connection with pending matters; many of these contacts represented direct intercession for constituents. It would be difficult for a congressman to be unaware of the not so subtle effect of his credentials, and it would be impossible for a commissioner to be unaware that Congress controls the FCC's budget and can confirm or reject its appointees.

The double standard under which congressmen wear dark glasses while seeking motes in their brothers' eyes has offended some of their colleagues. Senators Clifford P. Case and Maurine Neuberger persist in introducing a full-disclosure bill "to promote public confidence" which would require congressmen to report regularly on their income-producing transactions, and, perhaps more importantly, would spread on the record all oral or written communications from congressmen to commissioners. Senators Case and Neuberger persist, but Congress resists.

Such sentiments lead many people to hope that the Federal Communications Commission will remake television. Inspired by Minow's criticisms, and by intermittent encouragement of his stand from President Kennedy, they impatiently await the day when television will join the world and entertain with inspiration and craftsmanship, stimulate with wit and intelligence, inform with courage and perception—during hours convenient for most of the audience.

These good people shall be disappointed; their conception of Minow's aim is faulty. They would like to think that he is telling a little white lie—that he is indeed a censor while denying it out of necessity. Minow is a lawyer, charged with carrying out the imperfect, outdated, and shallow Communications Act. Neither he nor any other FCC member has indicated a regulator's concern with the heart of the television problem—the entertainment programming that in the long run fashions thought and molds the national culture and purpose. This dominant segment of the medium will continue to pour drivel. All that Minow has proposed to do is force the industry to adhere to minimum standards, and these will not lift television very far out of the muck.

There are four major reasons for this dreary condition:

The first is the absence of a national policy proclaiming a necessary and urgent credo: Broadcasting is now the most penetrating force in the land. What is broadcast is public business. Therefore, public policy demands that broadcasting be useful, not wasteful. Anyone who believes such a policy will be proclaimed by the White House in the imaginable future might as well take hashish because he is suffering the discomfort while missing the pleasure. This issue is what a Washington correspondent would call political dynamite—it would crystallize flag wavers, rugged individualists, extreme right-wingers, demagogues, and sincere conservatives into an army of opposition, and it would jeopardize any number of peculiar congressional deals under which much legislation is passed. It is doubtful that the Administration, even if it were so inclined, would place effective broadcast legislation before matters it considers more pressing.

This problem is linked to the second reason for our abysmal condition. Congressmen control the FCC through their absolute control over its funds and the Senate's power to approve or block appointments of commissioners. They have repeatedly indicated that they do not wish their regulatory agency to interfere seriously with broadcasters' obligations to the stockholders. The chairmen of the Senate and House Commerce Committees have made plain that radical departures from the suffocating norm will be attended to on Capitol Hill, where there are few radicals.

The third reason for a bearish outlook stems from our willingness to prohibit the FCC from interfering with "free speech" in broadcasting while allowing advertisers to apply thought control every day. If government censorship is unlawful, why should it be lawful for television—operating under grants of public property—to be censored by soap peddlers, cigarette makers, and patent medicine hawkers? This policy can be justified only if we concede that the medium's merchandising role *is* essential to the health of the national economy and therefore has priority over television's cultural and informational functions. If we concede this, we are also saying that we have simply become too rich to afford anything but tawdriness.

Finally, militating against significant improvement is the very composition of the Federal Communications Commission. It is made up of seven men who divide on substantive issues and often subdivide on pettifogging details. They illustrate the power of a stalemated group to produce ineffective regulation.

NEWTON N. MINOW achieved national prominence with his "vast wasteland" speech in May, 1961. Three weeks later, his predecessor on the FCC, Charles H. King, made a speech of his own in which he recalled a prediction that the commissioners "would try to improve the quality of television, that they would make some brave speeches and go through some muscle-flexing motions, but as far as actual results were concerned, they would be just spinning their wheels. Mr. Minow sure proved me right about the brave speeches. I wonder if he can prove me wrong about the wheels spinning."

Minow is what he is supposed to be—a man with a limited mission of reform. His road is strewn with obstacles and his chances of gaining effective traction are questionable. Since he was thrust into a scandalous situation, any cleanup he can accomplish will inevitably be confused with genuine improvement; the measure of the man will lie in his own disinclination to settle for featherdusting.

Thirty-four years old when he was nominated as chairman, Minow was graduated from Northwestern University to a clerkship with Chief Justice Fred M. Vinson, became administrative assistant to Governor Adlai Stevenson of Illinois, worked in Stevenson's two campaigns for the Presidency and in President Kennedy's campaign in 1960. While a law partner of Stevenson's in Chicago, he was counsel to an educational group, the Midwest Council for Airborne Television, and represented Encyclopædia Britannica Films, Inc., which is also involved in educational television. His term expires in 1968, by which time the regulated industry will be able to judge the validity of an implied prediction by an official of the National Association of Broadcasters: "We've had tough FCC chairmen before and we've lived through them."

ROSEL H. HYDE, the senior commissioner in length of service, was appointed and reappointed by President Truman in 1946 and 1952 and reappointed again by President Eisenhower in 1959. In his sixties, Hyde is a veteran government employee who was general counsel of the FCC when he was given a commissioner's seat.

Since he will be prominent on the television scene until 1966, at least, so will extreme conservatism. Hyde and Minow sit side by side during Commission meetings and chat pleasantly, but they represent the poles of attitude toward the government's role in broadcasting. "I think it is unfortunate that the public is being led to look to the FCC for fulfillment of its program interest," Hyde says. He believes government should be seen and not heard, if it is not seen too much. Broadcasting, he has said, "must be an unimpeded and unsubservient communications service." This position has led him to vote against measures to inhibit speculation in station sales and to give the Commission more power to demand that stations adhere to their programming promises. He has used the word "dictator" in connection with strong regulation, and has suggested that a firm FCC course could lead to a form of government thought control.

Hyde has even campaigned among industry groups against the "Minow position." Leaving little to the imagination, he told broadcasters in Idaho, his home state, "I make the suggestion, with concern for the future of broadcasting, that operators of stations haven't made their works or their position adequately understood . . . or that their demonstration of the advantages of the free enterprise system should have improved attention." Since the trade magazine *Broadcasting* rarely bets on imagination, it translated Hyde's remarks in this way: "Mr. Hyde said broadcasters haven't had guts enough to fight for their honor and their freedom. They have been willing to let the government steal both."

Hyde once demonstrated his hands-off position while acting as chairman during Minow's absence. The FCC was taking testimony from officials of the National Broadcasting Company, and its attorney, Ashbrook P. Bryant, was uncovering damaging information on the extent of advertisers' control of programming when Hyde abruptly shut off the line of questioning; Bryant retired from active participation in the NBC proceedings in clear but impotent protest.

TUNIS A. M. CRAVEN will retire from the FCC in 1963 at the age of seventy, a departure that is eagerly awaited by many inasmuch as he is Rosel Hyde's ideological ally. Craven is a radio engineer who was originally appointed by President Roosevelt in 1937; when his term expired he declined reappointment in order to accept a vice-presidency of the Cowles Broadcasting Company. During this period he was also a director of the National Association of Broadcasters. In 1949 he was a member of a firm of consulting radio engineers in Washington, and in 1956, President Eisenhower appointed him to a second term as a commissioner.

James Lawrence Fly once recalled Craven as "always taking the position that the Commission is just an electronic traffic cop." He wants the Commission to be careful to avoid "throttling of initiative, creative thinking, and the legal rights and duties of licensees in violation of the censorship provisions." He votes that way, too.

JOHN S. CROSS was, originally, another Eisenhower appointee; he replaced Commissioner Richard A. Mack, who resigned in the Miami Channel 10 "influence" case. An Alabaman in his late fifties, Cross's value is said to lie in diplomatic and engineering experience gained in the State Department's telecommunications division; his strength lies in support from Oren Harris, the House Commerce chairman, and the rest of the congressional delegation from his adopted state, Arkansas.

It is a rare day in Washington when Cross works for stronger regulation. Occasionally he growls at an industry witness, but it often follows that the witness has not been assiduous in getting the industry's position on the record. When this has been accomplished, Cross usually subsides.

ROBERT T. BARTLEY, a Texan, an intimate of Vice-President Johnson and a nephew of the late House Speaker, Sam Rayburn, worked for a congressional committee and federal regulatory agencies before becoming a vice-president of the Yankee Network. In 1943, Bartley directed "government relations" for the NAB, and five years later became Rayburn's administrative assistant; he held that job when President Truman appointed him to the FCC in 1952. President Eisenhower reappointed him in 1958.

Bartley is a quiet man in his early fifties who baffles observers because his votes do not always jibe with his public utterances. He has said that the FCC must "be an affirmative defender of the public's right to the best possible communications service." He has conceded, too, that there has been a "whittling away of the powers of the Commission." Yet Bartley is also a "firm believer in self-regulation," which has been a palpable failure; his lengthy association with leading politicians may have taught him the art of cakewalking. He exhibits concern over monopoly situations and trafficking in licenses, but if and when decisions on programming performance hang on one vote—tough decisions, that is—Bartley's vote is not expected to land on the "Minow side" often enough to guarantee a majority.

FREDERICK W. FORD, who served as FCC chairman for one year before Minow was installed (after the resignation of John Doerfer), was appointed by President Eisenhower in 1957. He was a lawyer in West Virginia before entering government employment in 1939. He has served in a number of federal agencies, commissions, and departments, including the FCC. In his early fifties, Ford has rejected the argument that a viewer's rights are secured by turning off the television set if programming is putrid, and he has said that a broadcaster cannot "raise a cry of deprivation of free speech if he is compelled to prove that there is something more than naked commercial selfishness in his purpose."

Ford generally matches his votes with his words; he worked for a revitalization of the Commission during his brief tenure as chairman and initiated a number of positive measures, for whose inheritance Minow has publicly thanked him.

ROBERT E. LEE was twice appointed by President Eisenhower despite his close association with Senator Joseph R. McCarthy, whose "man in the FBI" he was often called. He was an FBI special agent in 1938, administrative assistant to J. Edgar

Hoover in 1941, and later the agency's chief clerk. Originally a Chicagoan and an auditor, Lee is just fifty and has often expressed a preference for self-regulation over a firm government hand.

Yet, so peculiar is this FCC, Lee has been voting with Minow and Ford on many programming issues. Why? According to one corridor theory, his intense enthusiasm for UHF has brought about an informal, unwritten bargain: Lee votes for Minow-Ford programming positions and they support his campaign for UHF, which they also want.

This shifting lineup, whose unpredictability is increased by the absence of a coherent communications policy from the White House and firm support from Congress, explains why the FCC is not going to clear the slum and erect the dream city of television. With luck, the Commission will induce the squatter-proprietors of broadcasting to make emergency repairs —information programming will be grudgingly added in prime time, annoying and misleading commercials will decrease but not disappear, a few symphony orchestras and ballet troupes will discover some employment, sponsor control of entertainment will be exercised more discreetly, and there will be less writing of frank, incriminating memos that can be subpoenaed and made public.

What hope is there of doing better than this? The possibility of a government network is so remote that it can be excluded from serious consideration. And that may be just as well since it is doubtful that Congress would give money *and* an artistically free hand to a government television authority. The specter of a congressman charging that O'Neill is smut, or that discussion of *all* sides of world issues amounts to Communist propaganda, is too depressing to contemplate. The point is moot in any event: There is no room for a government network within the constricted VHF television system.

This is probably the place to say, though, that a handful of people in broadcasting *are* casting about for solutions that might alleviate our distress before the century closes. One of them—an exceptionally prominent, intelligent, and nevertheless powerless man—told me of a hope that indicated his desperation. "One of the three networks could emerge as a real hero overnight," he said, "simply by recognizing that the time is ripe for a radical change in broadcasting's thinking. It could steal the show—win big audiences—by suddenly devoting itself to intelligent, exciting television. That network would be away out in front, and it would make money!"

"Do you see any early possibility of such a development?" I asked.

"No," he replied.

The only serviceable plan I have heard is one being circulated by a few knowledgeable and sincere men; they also contend that a real breakthrough could be accomplished right now, within the three-network VHF system, and they have a scheme. They propose that a new, loosely formed network be organized by a group of multi-station owners. Financing their venture co-operatively (and these are companies with tremendous resources), they could produce interesting, high-quality programs and compete with the existing networks for station acceptances.

This plan is based on some extremely practical considerations: (1) Since large numbers of upper-income "opinion leaders" have already been lost to rattle-brained programming, they have also been lost to advertisers. (2) This audience could be "recaptured" for television because the group broadcasters' stations penetrate the leading thirty-five to forty markets (population centers), which are what major advertisers are most interested in anyway.

"You can see," one exponent said, "that this is a down-to-earth idea. There's money in it. Even though some of the group broadcasters are notorious for their disinterest in intelligent and tasteful programming, they are famous for their interest in money. They could make *more* money by being first with a fresh approach. Their thirty-five markets would soon expand to fifty or sixty and then they'd have it made."

I like this plan, and others see much merit in it, too. But my travels through the land of television leave me without conviction that it will rise from the pad of hopefulness. The necessary signs of innovation are simply not evident.

It is conceivable, in other words—perhaps likely—that television may be permitted to go right on declining and falling indefinitely, at least insofar as declining-and-falling time is unlimited in the big-screen megaton age.

The difficult moment is at hand, therefore, to consider what, if anything, can be accomplished by a beleaguered viewer bent on a rescue mission. A word of caution, though: Anyone searching for an instant miracle solution, conveniently packaged, should turn back now; the road ahead is bumpy.

15 THE PEACOCK BLUES

"This year, the wasteland comes to you in living color." —Bob Hope.

The Federal Communications Commission has had many opportunities to demonstrate vast powers of vacillation, but in no case has it acted with more clear-cut indecisiveness than in dealing with color television. As a result, color broadcasting today is less a product of public policy than of commercial warfare. The winners program in color, the losers do not, and the public be damned.

The Radio Corporation of America and its offspring, the National Broadcasting Company, have been shading their eyes from the dazzling dawn of the color era since 1954, but viewers seem to be less light sensitive. RCA says, more or less continuously, "This is the year for color!" and NBC dutifully agrees. So NBC schedules more color programming, and RCA, which manufactures 95 per cent of all color television sets, schedules more sales expectations. Some day, the color era may actually be here.

NBC advances its cause with the best means it has—color transmission. The network has presented "Color Day, U.S.A.,"

"Color Weekend," "The Most Colorful Night of the Year," a "Festival of Color," and a vainglorious peacock. In 1961, it began to offer *Walt Disney's Wonderful World of Color,* a series whose opening show included a half-hour campaign for color television that must have been interesting to, at most, 1.5 per cent of viewers. The rest didn't have color television sets.

The dawn of the color era is being preceded by the longest winter night south of Hammerfest, Norway. At the end of 1961—after eight years of vigorous promotion—fewer than 800,000 color sets resided in American homes as against almost 55,000,000 black and whites. People watch the splendiferous NBC bird unfurl its plumage, then replace their old monochrome sets with new monochrome sets. This suggests a question: Do people like to see peacocks in black and white?

Probably not. There must be other reasons to account for what resembles a mass passive resistance movement. In view of all the unsociable opinions that have already been expressed about the grubby state of programming, I almost hesitate to suggest what these reasons might be. Fortunately, however, others have spoken. The trade magazine, *Television Age,* has noted that, "With black and white set sales having leveled off, with critics decrying routine programming, with reports of declining audiences, it's little wonder that color is winning new adherents [within the industry]." Another ear-to-the-ground organ, *Television,* explains that "the development of black and white television has reached a plateau. The curves of equipment manufacturing, audience size, and advertising volume are apt to stay just about where they are unless they are kicked hard by something new and powerful. Color is the only force now available with that much kick in it."

One might argue, of course, that exciting programming has "kick," too, but the benefits of arguing with trade magazines are dubious. It need only be observed, perhaps, that few non-morons would cry themselves to sleep if they could not see *The Price Is Right* in color, while the inability of the vast majority to see *The Moon and Sixpence* in color was a genuine loss. When NBC presented Laurence Olivier as Gauguin, whose life *was* color, it created a magnificent episode in the history of television and provided an incentive for the purchase of a color set. When it transmits dreary game shows in color *every day,* monochrome's thirty variations of gray are expensive enough. Bob Hope has not been able to resist this observation: "Newton Minow accused television of being a vast wasteland. RCA met the challenge. This year, the wasteland comes to you in living color."

The cost of color sets is a serious obstacle to their sale, but cost does not seem to tell the entire story. RCA's 1954 set was priced at $1,000 and sold like a lead balloon. By 1956, the cheapest model sold for $495, which accounts for the finding that businessmen, executives, and professionals make up 60 per cent of color-set owners. (They comprise 20 per cent of the population.) It does not explain, though, why so many more families that can afford color don't buy it, unless one accepts the premise that these people are simply unmoved by the prospect of being bored in a variety of shades by what they're already being bored with in basic black and white. There is a logic here that may be unbeatable—outside the RCA Building.

Logic has not been the primary characteristic of the development of color. A lengthy struggle for power between RCA and CBS culminated in adoption of the current system, and it was in this struggle that the Federal Communications Commission flipped, flopped, and frittered away an opportunity to solve some of television's major problems.

When the color issue first came before the FCC, the television industry was still young enough to be engaging in disputes over who would control what. The color controversy was therefore accompanied by numerous references to the public interest that masked the noise of the patent-holders in the background. It is nevertheless conceivable that in 1946, when CBS requested permission to transmit commercially in color, the Commission, at one stroke, could have created a truly competitive national television service. It could have installed television in the ultra-high frequencies, where seventy channels are available, instead of in its current cramped home in the very high frequencies, which provide only twelve channels.

CBS's color was created by a mechanical-disk system, and it was incompatible—black and white sets could not receive the programs. So few television receivers of any kind existed at that time, though, that this problem could have been safely ignored; American television would simply have been color television from the beginning. Moreover, since CBS was then interested in using the ultra-high frequency wave lengths, UHF broadcasting would have been established. Neat package? Zenith and the Cowles Broadcasting Company thought so, and they supported CBS.

On the other hand, RCA, Du Mont, and Philco felt otherwise. These firms contended that the development of an electronic, compatible system was just around the corner, and that color should await an "orderly transition" from a black and white start. There are a number of ways of translating the phrase "orderly transition." The one I like best reads, "First sell millions of black and white sets, then replace them with color receivers."

The FCC resolved the dispute with the sort of reasoning that has made it an object of curiosity. CBS's color system would have required sixteen-megacycle channels, a circumstance that would have reduced the number of potential channels in the UHF band from seventy to twenty-seven. The FCC, explaining that it wished to conserve as much of the UHF spectrum as possible, therefore turned CBS down. It then proceeded, as we shall soon see, to allow UHF to be throttled.

CBS pressed the point by initiating color broadcasts, in 1949, with an improved system that required a channel width of only six megacycles. As may be imagined, this development pleased neither RCA nor most other receiver manufacturers.

RCA quickly notified the FCC that it had developed a compatible, electronic system. The Commission decided, though, that CBS's system was superior and that, furthermore, its color could be received in black and white—if set manufacturers would make their receivers flexible enough. The manufacturers responded without enthusiasm, but in October, 1950, the commissioners went ahead and adopted the CBS system. During the two and a half years that intervened between their decisions, however, millions of black and white receivers had been sold, and these would not be able to receive the CBS transmissions. The national cost of replacement would now be higher, but at least the road to universal color was finally clear.

Well, not exactly clear. RCA obtained an injunction that delayed the start of CBS color broadcasts for eight months, and many more incompatible receivers were sold. And when CBS's color sets (produced by a firm it acquired) eventually reached retail stores, it developed that the rest of the receiver industry was not about to produce sets of its own. The final blow came from the Director of Defense Mobilization, who closed off CBS's production because of a materials conservation problem stemming from the Korean War. The restriction was lifted seven months later, but by then CBS had been overpowered. RCA settled down to the improvement of its own color system, the FCC adopted it in December, 1953, as a *fait accompli,* and to this day RCA owns the basic patents on every color television tube manufactured in the United States and sells almost all the sets. The nation has been saturated with black and white and the campaign is on to bring about an "orderly transition" to color.

In the circumstances, NBC displayed its peacock before over 1,500 hours of programming during 1961, while ABC and CBS have indicated a fondness for monochrome. NBC's chairman, Robert Sarnoff, presses for the popularization of color, but he does it from grounds that seem strange. He does not believe, he says, that networks should wait for color demand.

Instead, he feels, they "should do all they can to create the demand in the first place." Inasmuch as NBC has rarely created a demand for thought-provoking black and white television, Sarnoff's sudden passion for pioneering needs elucidation. He provided it when he explained that the network business is "facing a profit squeeze. Increasing revenues will be difficult. Color television will help enormously to raise from that plateau and to create more television advertising dollars."

Sarnoff's concern for the company's welfare is understandable, as is the desire of advertisers to depict headaches and running noses in color, but does it follow that the multitudes should feel that their duty is to be the first on the block to own current models of color television sets? NBC offers reassurance against obsolescence when it declares that "there is nothing in the foreseeable future to indicate any drastic changes that would obsolete today's sets," but an opening up of the UHF channels could conceivably lead to a revamped color system. One can only hope that a new system would be compatible with existing sets.

This problem goes back to a report prepared in 1959 by a leading FCC engineer, William C. Boese, and a number of his colleagues. Boese, who assumed responsibility for the startling ideas presented in the report, reviewed the technological advances of electronic communications and suggested that in settling for current techniques we could become saddled with less than the best. He wondered, in thirty closely packed pages of data and reasoning, whether the creation of a new and better color process—to be used on ultra-high frequencies—would provide a genuine motivation for a mass swing to the higher broadcasting band. And his discussion of recently acquired technical knowledge in the field of electronics did nothing to dim the prospect that such a system could be developed.

Boese's paper was submitted to the commissioners, who handled it as they would dynamite; they discussed it, agreed it should not be publicized, and dropped the subject. In 1961, though, Jerome B. Wiesner, President Kennedy's special science advisor, rekindled interest in the proposition by noting that the basic technical standards of television should be reviewed in the event that the medium moves to UHF. "We would be missing a golden opportunity if we just use these frequencies for a replica of the present system," Wiesner said. The reason, like engineer Boese's, lies in the tremendous knowledge that has been gained as a result of and since World War II, both in information theory and electronics technology.

It takes little imagination to sense that such proposals face difficult days. Many millions of dollars are involved, as they are in the campaigns to promote Pay TV and to keep television imprisoned in the twelve-channel very high frequencies. These are explosive, anti-monopolistic issues, and it is worth examining the way in which the Federal Communications Commission has, and has not, handled them so far.

16 PAY TV: TRAP OR TREAT?

"*. . . network television as we know it today cannot survive if pay television is successful.*" *—Frank Stanton.*

It is rumored that the first chain of motion-picture theaters in the United States was formed by two popcorn manufacturers who walked into a crowded nickelodeon in the 1920's and exclaimed, "What a marvelous way to sell popcorn!" So they opened movie houses. When radio appeared, they said, "Don't worry. People won't stay home. They can't get our popcorn there." When television arrived, the theater owner–popcorn sellers were stirred, but they still believed that popcorn and progress were linked to the silver screen. At the first mention of *pay* television, however, they became deranged. During lucid periods, they screamed, "Anybody crazy enough to put coins in a television slot is crazy enough to make his *own* popcorn! This is a threat to fundamental American freedoms!"

In their frenetic struggle against pay television, theater owners resemble the man Finley Peter Dunne had in mind when "Mr. Dooley" commented on the nature of sudden, suffocating piousness:

> I don't think they'se anny such thing as hypocrisy in th' wurruld. They can't be. If ye'd turn on th' gas in th' darkest

> heart ye'd find it had a good raison for th' worst things it done, a good varchous raison, like needin' th' money or punishin' th' wicked or tachin' people a lesson to be more careful, or protectin' th' liberties iv mankind, or needin' th' money.

Theater owners are against pay television because movies wouldn't make money—in theaters; this is a compelling reason for their opposition, but it does not compel those who don't make money out of theaters. The exhibitors therefore offer a five-foot shelf of other grounds. Men who have rarely demonstrated compassion for the morals or intellectual sensibilities of the young, the old, or the middle-aged suddenly ooze with solicitousness. Pay television, they declare, would kill "free" television and thereby oppress the poor. And after "free" television was dead, we would all have to pay for the same programs we were getting without coinboxes in our living rooms. And, additionally, pay television's transmission of obscenities in movies and plays would be offensive.

These themes and others have been stated in resourceful variation by Marcus Cohn, as a legal counsel for the organized threatened, the Theater Owners of America, Inc. Cohn concedes that his clients dislike competition, but in his wisdom he finds that there is also "a basic patriotic issue involved."

"The only people who want pay television," he has said, "are those phony elite snobs who can't stand the idea that they are watching the same shows that the masses watch. They write articles for *Harper's* or *The Atlantic* telling how pay television will bring us Schopenhauer and violin recitals. Is that what Americans want?" In a strange bedfellowship with the other mortal enemy of pay television, the "free television" industry, Cohn has thus adopted a favored network tactic: demolition by exaggeration. As networks have implied that anti-democratic eggheads are bent on replacing all diversion with esoterica, Cohn alleges that pay television would promote an exclusive diet of philosophy and high-brow music. Mr. In Between has been shot down again.

Cohn has also unearthed what he calls a "more human issue." "Say you watch the ballet on Sunday afternoon with your children for fifty cents," he hypothesizes. "Beautiful. Then your child goes to school the next day and finds her schoolmates couldn't see the ballet because they didn't have the fifty cents. Is this fair?"

For my money, Cohn has scored a point there, although to accept it one must overlook a radical premise that the filthy rich aren't the only ones entitled to flaming tarts and fifty-cent ballet. I am prepared to ignore that implication because of the possibility that Cohn's cautionary fantasy of Little Miss Affluence vs. Little Miss Misery could come to life. I believe the conflict would be solved, but the *solution* is frightening. Considering the democratic spirit of our children, it is not difficult to predict that once Miss Affluence realized the emotional scar she was inscribing, she would invite all the Miss Miseries she knew to sit before her daddy's coinbox television. Daddy would then try to find a seat, trip over nineteen Miss Miseries who were sponging on his fifty cents, and cry, "What the hell is this anyway—Carnegie Hall?" Embittered, the Little Miss Miseries would slink back to their coinless slums and the seeds of real political trouble would be planted in future members of the League of Women Voters.

This seems a more pressing threat to American freedoms than the possibility of neighborhood theater owners having to find another way of making a living. But if there is a feeling that the fantasies are equally preposterous, the proper conclusion may be that theater owners' complaints against pay television are loud but only noisy. They have not indicated a concern with authentic dangers that, within a few years, could make a pay-as-you-see system a repetition of what we have today—but to be paid for in cash.

Because of the popular belief that television is free, the term *pay* is not altogether fair. Today's viewer not only pays when he buys television-advertised tooth paste and cake mixes, but he buys and maintains his set. $15,000,000,000 worth of receivers were in homes at the end of 1961. In addition he gives his attention, and if attention is not a valuable commodity, stockholders of America's biggest corporations ought to find out why their directors spend so much money attracting it. We have *indirect* pay television now; the kind that would demand coins or bring a periodic bill is *subscription* television. There are few exercises less rewarding than threading a needle with a fine semantic difference, but in this case the needle has a point: The misnomer "free" has been wielded with jack-handle delicacy.

Now that that is clear, we may avoid inevitable confusion by continuing to refer to the current system as free television and the subscription system as pay.

Most of the differences in methods of sending and receiving pay programs are related to ways of scrambling and unscrambling pictures and voices. The basic difference lies in whether programs are transmitted over the air, or by wire from studio to each home. Firms that use the air waves are under the jurisdiction of the Federal Communications Commission. For the moment, at least, "closed-circuit" companies are outside government regulation; theirs is a private arrangement utilizing a blank channel on the home receiver.

The giant of the air systems is the Zenith Radio Corporation, whose late founder, Eugene F. McDonald, maintained in 1931 that television would have to be financed by a "home box office," rather than by advertising, if it were to provide good programming. Zenith formally entered pay television in 1951, when it conducted a limited experiment in Chicago by displaying movies, at $1 apiece, to three hundred subscribers. Its opponents contend that this experiment failed; Zenith says it was a rousing success, noting that when the test ended almost all subscribers indicated they would continue if the system became permanent, and that two hundred and ninety-nine of the three hundred paid their bills even though they had been told at the start that they could refuse if the service was unsatisfactory.

A year later, Zenith panicked the broadcasting industry by notifying the FCC it was ready to stage a full-scale experiment. Gentle folk may feel it was a breach of manners to present such an issue to a regulatory agency that had rarely won even an orange ribbon for courage, but business is business, as we know. So there was the FCC, caught between pressures that threatened to rip the television establishment apart. The Commission could handle the caterwauls of theater owners—anyone could do that—but an industry that regarded the air waves as its private property was quite another matter.

The networks' bellows were heard as far away as Capitol Hill, where CBS's Frank Stanton used a congressional hearing as a sounding board for a famous oration that suggested a causal relationship between pay television and cold, torn feet. He told the House Commerce Committee, "To watch pay television for two-thirds of the number of hours that it now actually watches free television, the average family would have to pay $473 a year. This is seven times what [it] spends annually on shoes." He went on to suggest other dangers to life and limb: "This is three times what it spends on all medical and dental bills, plus all drugs and medicines, plus all cosmetics and shaving supplies, plus all dentifrices." Stanton also blew a shrill note on his ever handy horn of democracy when he warned that television, "now a unifying force, will be divisive" because a pay system would "fence off the best for the carriage trade." But the CBS president was at his vivid mightiest when he seemed to be portraying the chilblained American family, huddled in darkness, sores running, teeth rotting, without lipsticks or razor blades. This was far more graphic stuff than that offered by Robert Sarnoff of NBC, who only indicated that pay television might cause another great depression. "Keep in mind," Sarnoff pointed out, "what the ultimate effect might be on an instrument of communications that, through its commercial messages, has become a prime catalyst in the creation of new mass consumption desires in a nation that consumes its way to prosperity, to growth and strength."

The National Association of Broadcasters, not to be outdone in protecting the mass consumer from commercial-less television, warned that pay viewers "could create a brand-new caste system, the well-heeled looker and the coin-shy nonlooker."

NBC and CBS were careful to make clear, however, that despite the monstrous crime that pay television represented, they would, if necessary, commit it, too. Sarnoff said "economic necessity" would force his network to change horses, and Stanton used the identical phrase and added, "We could expect to operate profitably under a system of pay television."

During an extended period of debate, or din, the FCC studied the problem. Oh, how it studied. For five years it pondered; during this time a half-dozen new commissioners took their seats, and they pondered, too. The American people, on the other hand, were spared a factual appraisal of the proposals. Except for those few who were exposed to thoughtful journals, viewers got their information from broadcasters, who played on an understandable resentment: People who had bought television sets on the premise that programs would be "free" were disturbed at the thought of having to put coins in slots. Those who had never concerned themselves with what went on behind their channel selectors were suddenly struck with the truth of the proposition that the air waves were public property. When television stations urged them to protest to their congressmen against schemes to pick their pockets, they responded with enthusiastic indignation. Some stations presented dramatizations of the most lachrymose scenes since Eliza crossed the ice. These were contained in a widely disseminated script entitled "Now It Can Be Tolled," whose leading character, the "pay viewer of the year," had fed over $5,000 into pay slots within one year. The power of televised one-sidedness was attested to by Senator Russell Long of Louisiana, who told his colleagues of his mail:

> If my information is correct, the public was told that it would cost as much as $700 a year in order to see programs which are presently being presented free over KNOE-TV [Monroe]. Hearing only one side of the argument, the public became terribly alarmed and I have received more than 12,000 communications as a result of the programs of this single station. By contrast, on the other side of the state, in Shreveport, Louisiana, station KSLA-TV presented a television debate in which a spokesman for the Columbia Broadcasting System debated an advocate of pay television. So far as I have been able to determine, the broadcast in which both sides were heard did not generate a single letter. . . .

In the House, a congressman declared that the issue was whether NBC, ABC, and CBS, who were "only competing within a monopoly they jointly share," should be allowed "to coerce Congress into arbitrarily rejecting any new idea that poses any measure of competition to these vested interests." The broadcasters' campaign, he said, was "a frightening demonstration of network power to influence the very workings of our national government."

The FCC was aware, of course, of the abuses to which the air waves were subjected. Chairman John Doerfer told broadcasters that their presentation of pay television's pros and cons reminded him of that famous work, "An Unbiased and Unprejudiced History of the War Between the States From the Southern Point of View." Eventually the Commission chided a couple of stations for their unfairness; no further action was taken.

When the FCC pulled itself together and announced it would accept applications for pay experiments, it revealed the extreme pressure under which it had been functioning, but proclaimed itself fearless—more or less. "Proponents, claiming large benefits to the public from the introduction of a broad new financial base and added programming resources . . ." the Commission said, "urge the immediate, definitive authorization of subscription broadcasting by television stations with a minimum of restricting conditions. Opponents, raising the spectre of a gravely impaired free television service, insist that the only proper course for the Commission is to forbid the service or to refer it to Congress. We believe the proper course for the Commission does not lie at either extreme." The agency took the middle road; it said that demonstrations of the new service could be made—under highly limiting conditions. Despite these restrictions, Zenith announced that it would apply for the inauguration of its service, Phonevision, in Hartford, Connecticut.

Congress emitted a roar of disapproval. Twenty-two hostile bills, some flatly prohibiting pay television, were introduced, and wind on Capitol Hill approached gale force. Representative J. Floyd Breeding of Kansas, a broadcasting stockholder, testified against the innovation before a House committee, and letters were again ground out in the hustings; if many read like carbon copies of many others, such is the way of coincidence. In the midst of the clamor, in early 1958, CBS showed that threats to its financial health had not affected its ability to be gracious. The network arranged a magnificent party for representatives of its affiliated stations around the country. Where else to stage such an affair than in the nation's capital? Who else to invite but hundreds of government officials, members of regulatory commissions, and congressmen? And how to seat the assembled but in state groups, with local broadcasters cheek by jowl with local legislators? Phil Silvers made jokes, and Patti Page made throaty noises, broadcasters murmured to senators and representatives of various perils. It was a well-regulated ball, punctuated by the melodies of state anthems. Doubtlessly, no one had to be so gauche as to remind congressmen that this was an election year and that their hosts could be of assistance with all sorts of home-ground publicity.

In February, 1958, on the eve of pay television's establishment in Hartford, the House Commerce Committee (chairman: Oren Harris) formally requested the FCC to reverse itself and delay action on subscription tests. The Commission buckled, but on the way to its knees announced that if Congress failed to legislate on the matter it would proceed with applications immediately after adjournment. Even before adjournment, however, the commissioners assured Representative Harris that they would not act before the next Congress could hold hearings. The next Congress did not hold hearings, but the FCC held discussions with Harris, following which it finally decided to proceed with pay applications, but under even stronger restrictions than it had originally imposed. Nevertheless, Zenith proceeded with its proposed experiment in Hartford, the unfolding of which will do much to convince the public that pay television is either an attractive or dreadful proposition. If the broadcasting lobby had been out of town, the public would already have made its decision.

One of Phonevision's heartiest well-wishers is the International Telemeter Company, backers of a pay television system that has been able to operate in studios rather than courtrooms; it has been offering movies, plays, operas, musical comedies, comedy routines, and sports events to viewers since February, 1960. But not to American viewers. To escape the delaying tactics of American theater owners, Telemeter, a division of Paramount Pictures, crossed the border into a suburb of Toronto. There are movie houses in Canada, to be sure, but Paramount owns 51 per cent of the largest chain, Famous Players, Ltd., with which few distributors are inclined to argue.

Since Telemeter plans to extend its service to a section of New York City, an area of the West Coast, Little Rock, Arkansas, and another American site, its Canadian working model is of special interest. Telemeter is a wire system under which programs leave a Toronto studio over a coaxial cable carried by telephone poles; feeder lines then split off into homes in the West Toronto suburb of Etobicoke. Of 12,000 homes in the area, almost 6,000 subscribe to the "theater in the home" service.

Sitting on the subscriber's television, and connected to it, is the Telemeter attachment, a neatly styled box that reveals the price (or "admission fee") required for an attraction, receives coins, and indicates the subscriber's credit if he overpays because he doesn't have exact change. He may also pre-pay if he fears his wife will spend the money on shoes for the children. The little box permits him, in addition, to select one of three programs transmitted simultaneously over the cable. (Telemeter is searching for a way to send as many as a dozen shows at the same time.) The selected attraction then appears on Channel 5, which is otherwise blank in Toronto. (News, music, and some local public service programming are free.)

Etobicoke meets a major requirement for a good pay-television testing ground: its incomes are distributed among the working class in new-homes developments, the professional-managerial class, and wealthy groups. Nor is the suburb television-starved and susceptible to easy promises; in addition to Telemeter's Channel(s) 5A, 5B, and 5C, all three U.S. networks are clearly received from Buffalo and there is service from a Canadian Broadcasting Corporation station in Toronto and from two independent stations in Toronto and Windsor. If Paramount's experiment is ultimately successful, no one will be able to say the test was rigged.

Moreover, Telemeter provides a working test of the pay-television promoters' heady pledges. If residents of Etobicoke were to read some U.S. television trade magazines, they might infer that they were being taken in. Instead, they put coins into their contraptions and see some Hollywood B-pictures, the superior (new and old) Hollywood pictures, foreign films, previously blacked-out football and hockey games, productions from Broadway, and "specials."

After two years of the experiment, movies are still far too dominant, but it should also be said that during one week, Telemeter's subscribers were able to watch *Bridge to the Sun,*

Guns of Navarone, Babes in Toyland, Pajama Game, Love Is a Many Splendored Thing, and *Comancheros,* all during their first-run phase in local theaters. Since shows are presented twice on the same night and repeated on other nights, subscribers could watch all six if they wished to pay the fee of $1 to $1.25 each. Considering the cost of single-admission movie tickets, plus transportation and baby-sitting expenses, these rates for a family (and friends?) are considered attractive.

A decrease in movies and an increase in theatrical productions is partially dependent on time. Telemeter is avoiding entanglements with attractions that may now appear on free television, and it will need time to create its own fare. Among specials it has offered, though, was "An Evening With Bob Newhart," before the comedian embarked on his own free-television series. Newhart presented a half-hour of routines, was spelled by Leon Bibb, a top-drawer folk singer, and returned for another half-hour. "Pay television never had a better argument," commented a Toronto reviewer; approximately a third of Telemeter's subscribers paid $1.25 to see the show, and while that resulted in a losing venture, the tape went into a "library" for distribution among other pay areas as they open.

There have also been, for $1.25 or $1.50 each, an off-Broadway production of *Hedda Gabler* and stagings of *Show Girl,* with Carol Channing, taped at a special performance in New York, and of *The Second City Revue,* from Chicago. Telemeter's greatest triumph, however, came with its presentation of Gian-Carlo Menotti's *The Consul.* Jon Ruddy, the critic of the *Toronto Telegram,* said he "sat down last night to an evening of pay television and for more than two hours enjoyed a dramatic masterpiece uninterrupted by commercial messages." Intermissions occurred where they were called for by the author, at which points the screen became blank; a curtain-riser buzzer sounded when the play was about to resume. In his report on the event, Jack Gould of the *New York Times* used a precise word—civilized.

As critic Ruddy also observed of *The Consul,* however, the absence of commercials was enjoyable but of secondary importance. "When and if the Telemeter system becomes a national reality," he warned, "the quality of its productions will account for success or failure. To compete with free television, it must offer shows of importance. We can get the trivia for nothing."

Many people are none the less eager to buy pay television almost sight unseen. Understandably, these are the viewers who were deprived of service when the networks sold out programming to the food and drug peddlers; the deprived are now moved by desperation.

But a perverse feature of the law of unbridled supply and demand holds that whenever eager people stand in line with money in their hands—and have nowhere else to go—they are ripe for plucking. That is the danger amid the bliss of pay television's lavish promises. Because of the monopolistic way in which the air waves are now being used, it is conceivable that (1) the networks' prediction of a free-program blackout will come true, (2) the networks themselves will become dominant in pay television without radically altering their programming, (3) we will have bad programming *plus* commercials, and (4) we will pay cash for such a disaster. Net gain: zero.

This may all happen because television is trapped in a narrow section of the air waves known as the very high frequency band, in which there are only twelve channels. Earlier mentioned as another part of the available spectrum is the *ultra* high frequency band, which has seventy channels. Altogether, the VHF band will yield something over five hundred stations around the country, while the UHF band has room for over 1,300. But while over four hundred and fifty commercial VHF stations are in operation—a near-saturation figure, since a number of V's have been reserved for educational uses—fewer than one hundred U's, or 6 per cent of the number possible, are operating.

This strange situation has produced a strikingly inadequate television service. Of the nation's two hundred and seventy-two "television markets," *almost half are restricted to one station; another quarter have only two stations; only one-fifth have three stations, and fewer than twenty cities have four or more stations.* (Outlets must be kept apart because of interference problems; this accounts for the numerous blanks on channel selector dials.)

The inadequacy of the arrangement is so glaring that many important cities cannot even receive the full program schedules of the three networks. Newton Minow illustrated this practical problem when he referred to CBS's especially newsworthy interview with President Eisenhower in 1961. "It was on at the same hour as two popular entertainment shows," Minow said. "As it happened, President Eisenhower was then in Augusta, Georgia—a two-station market—and his program was not to be seen there. At the last minute, when it was realized that [he was there], some special arrangements were made. So if President Eisenhower had not happened to be in Augusta that day, the 280,000 television homes in the Augusta area would never have had a chance to see this splendid public service program. This is one reason why we need more television in this country—more stations, more outlets, more voices."

The FCC has known since the early 1940's that the VHF band could not provide sufficient channels for a competitive nation-wide television service. There are a number of reasons why we have none the less been saddled with the V band, but few of them are immune to challenge. For over twenty years, engineering considerations have been advanced as the cause of U's neglect, but little was done for a long time to apply our legendary American know-how to the problem. U transmissions do not carry as far as V and are more subject to "shadowing" by terrain and other physical features, but these faults have also been exaggerated into a mythology. Many engineers believe that UHF can now provide a *better* service than we have. The equipment to accomplish this is here today, but so are the vested interests in the V band.

The mess was hatched in 1941, when the FCC, after leaning on the receiver-manufacturing industry for advice, authorized the start of commercial television broadcasting in the VHF band. NBC and CBS opened stations in New York that year, and others would have followed if the onset of World War II had not prevented the construction of both stations and receivers. The FCC, already aware of the dead-end nature of the VHF frequencies, used this "freeze" period to search, it said, for a more sensible way to allocate channels when materials again became available. Once more, though, the receiver industry strongly influenced the proceedings, with set-manufacturing RCA favoring VHF and non-manufacturing CBS plumping for UHF. RCA does not lose many of these combats.

The Federal Communications Commission had an opportunity at this point to establish a clear policy favoring UHF with a minimum cost to consumers inasmuch as only 7,000 television sets were then in circulation. (In any event, those who owned sets during the early 1940's could have withstood the financial shock of replacing them.) But the Commission constructed an odd syllogism: television must ultimately reside in the UHF band; the industry wants to start in the VHF band; therefore, we will use the VHF band.

With this decisive stroke, the FCC sent consumers out to buy VHF receivers while affirming that VHF could not be a permanent system. In so doing, it signaled the receiver industry that there was little point in manufacturing slightly higher-cost UHF receivers. The industry understood, and the consumer, all unaware, contributed to his own undoing.

RCA was not content; it wanted assurance that the VHF operation would be "stabilized" and strengthened—if necessary by taking some spectrum from government services. The requirements of business led the corporation to tell the FCC that "there must no longer be uncertainty about the frequencies to be used by this service." Du Mont, another set manufacturer, suggested that the FM frequencies be raided for more VHF television space. Weep for FM; first the AM broadcasters buried it and then Du Mont proposed robbing the grave so the land could be made more profitable. Somehow, the FCC managed to resist further violence to FM (which did not revive again until AM radio had disgraced itself with raucousness).

By 1948, with the devoted assistance of the receiver industry, the FCC found itself at the end of the dead-end VHF road. It wanted to allocate more V channels by narrowing the distance between stations, but suddenly learned of various interference problems that pointed to the need for greater, not smaller, separation. Badgered and harassed by the problem they had created for themselves, the commissioners, in September, 1948, issued their historic "big freeze" order under which they halted consideration of applications for new television stations. Rather typically, it was estimated that the freeze would last six to nine months; the thaw came almost four years later, in July, 1952, when the Commission (courage—the worst is still ahead!) set out to encourage the development of a UHF system. It opened up the seventy U channels and allocated them to licensees.

The odds against UHF were now insurmountable. During the freeze, the coaxial cable had been installed and network operations had begun. Almost 20,000,000 VHF-only sets had been sold, with a replacement value of over $5,000,000,000. And the cost of converting a set so it could receive UHF programming ranged from $10 to $60—when it worked. Nevertheless, the Commission doggedly initiated a plan to mix U stations into areas already dominated by V's. True, hundreds of communities that had been without any television service could now get it, but in large population centers, intermixture never had a chance. The networks helped defeat it—not out of monopolistic maliciousness, they would explain, but because advertisers find it economical to reach for only the most thickly populated areas and networks exist to serve advertisers.

When the networks did grant affiliations to U stations, they soon found that a nearby, more powerful V outlet was cheaper in terms of cost-per-thousand audience charge to sponsors. The networks owned U stations themselves, too, but eventually sold or closed them. Before long, the peak number of one hundred and twenty-four U stations, achieved in 1954, had declined to the eighties (where it stands today). Business policy had defeated national policy.

With the debacle complete, the FCC set out, in 1955, to review all its allocations once more. A year later it announced it would like to transfer all of television to UHF—but wasn't convinced yet that this would be technically feasible. As a start, it began the laborious process of "de-intermixing"—making every area either all-V or all-U. To do this, it removed a number of UHF stations from areas in which they were unsuccessfully competing with VHF's, but from 1956 through 1961, *only one VHF station was changed over to UHF*. In 1958, Professor Edward L. Bowles, who had been studying the tangled situation for a Senate committee, concluded that the Commission had abdicated authority in the allocation of television channels and "appeared powerless to anticipate, evaluate, or deal decisively" with the problems involved.

The damage has been extensive. Twenty-five areas that once received UHF service now lack a local station, and fifty-eight more no longer have the choice of service they once enjoyed. Moreover, hundreds of other areas have never had even a quasi-competitive service because few investors have been inclined to place their heads in the UHF noose.

This, then, is the cost of "monopoly competition" in television. The networks, protected from true competition, vie *among each other* for shares of the advertising pie, and do it with advertiser ingredients—formula and blandness.

As Newton Minow has said, however, "Fortunately, this is not a hopeless case." The hope of the latterly invigorated FCC lies in new legislation requiring every television set to be capable of receiving *all* channels. (Only 6,000,000 of 55,000,-

000 sets can now receive UHF.) Since the life of a set is estimated at five to six years, such legislation could bring about an inexpensive transition to a combined UHF-VHF system, containing eighty-two channels. As existing receivers failed, they would be replaced by the all-channel type. Then, when combined UHF-VHF broadcasting began, full reception would be possible. The all-channel receivers will cost slightly more than current types, but as Minow has pointed out, "This is a small price to pay for unlocking another seventy channels."

In addition to inspiring true competition, the availability of a large number of channels would help prevent pay television from repeating history and becoming an equally destructive *cash* monopoly. With over-the-air subscription systems, every program requiring payment blocks out a channel over which free programs could be sent. If pay television becomes successful while television is still trapped in the VHF band, and the networks switch to pay programming (as they will want to), both the newcomers and the networks will be free to compete within the same limited, deadening sphere that exists now. The glorious promises of the promoters will be remembered but not realized. It does not seem in the public interest, therefore, for the FCC to allow an over-the-air pay system to operate on a VHF channel. It has not yet done so, but where pressures are strong, past performance is worth noting.

In the case of the wired pay systems, the FCC has no jurisdiction. Yet it is conceivable that they will some day affect the availability of programming to free stations. If they, too, should be regulated, the FCC would be the logical agency for the job, but it cannot assume such a function without a revision of the Communications Act.

The time is overdue, therefore, for a modern restatement of national policy in regard to the *entire* broadcasting industry. There are a number of forms such a declaration could take, but an Executive Order from the President would be one method. Such an Order would be based on the need for a planned, coherent approach to the most penetrating method of communications yet devised. The alternative would be legislation, and the spectacle of the broadcasting lobby operating on Capitol Hill is not appealing.

These considerations being relatively long-range in application and effect, it would seem valuable to return to the present, where troubles are bad enough and may—never fear—become worse.

17 THE GREAT FLAG-WAVING ORGY

"Freedom of speech does not mean freedom to fool the people." —Newton N. Minow.

A popular corridor game in Washington involves guessing how long a maverick will last. When Newton Minow, the maverick chairman of the Federal Communications Commission, delivered his "vast wasteland" indictment of television, he became the prime target of the broadcasting lobby, and therefore of the guessers' interest. At about the same time, the players began quoting odds on the survival of LeRoy Collins as president of the National Association of Broadcasters. This was odd. Collins's stock should have gained each time Minow's lost a point, yet their movements paralleled. As went Minow, the guessers in the corridors maintained, so would go Collins. At Churchill Downs they would be called an entry.

In Collins's office hangs a piece of art that should embarrass him; the fact that it doesn't explains his attitude toward his relations with the Devil, Newton Minow. The art is the original drawing of a cartoon by Herblock (Herbert Block) of the *Washington Post*, depicting a gulch town of the Old West. A band of unsavory roughnecks is scowling at three newcomers fresh off the stagecoach. One is a retiring damsel, appropriately representing the public interest; her companions, adorned in the frock coat and string tie of the big city, are Minow and Collins, who are warning the assembled, as a duet: "Gentlemen, this here town is due for some changes."

This juxtaposition should nettle Collins because the National Association of Broadcasters has traditionally regarded critics of its membership as night-riding vigilantes, subverters of the Republic, and, in general, vipers. The FCC, despite its persistent refusal to reform broadcasting, is The Confounded Enemy.

Collins, perhaps on the theory that Newton Minow didn't invent the institution of truth, seems unconcerned. More heretically, he has broken the long-standing rule of conduct under which NAB leaders are supposed to go to any lengths to avoid leading. As a veteran of Florida politics, he is accustomed to the ways of backwoods politicians, who rarely disguise their feelings behind subtlety or diplomacy. He has bluntly declared that any group that pays him $75,000 a year, plus expenses, is going to get its money's worth, even if leadership wasn't what it thought it was buying.

Few broadcasters have reacted hoarsely in public to this challenge, and, in fact, not many have even privately informed Collins that they don't appreciate his giving aid and comfort to the enemy. Between themselves and behind his back, broadcasting "politicians" confer on methods of restraining their leader.

In reality, Collins is engaged in a Rooseveltian maneuver—he is trying to save a system from its own excesses. The insistence of the NAB's members on squeezing the top dollar out of their franchises has led television into squalor, and Collins knows that even indulgent Americans have their limits. He is attempting to promulgate this truth, which is why some of his associates are quite certain that they hired the wrong man. They have rarely had to deal with reality and are unaccustomed to its occasional discomforts.

This country grocer's son came to the broadcasters' association with an appreciation of the power of television. After working his way through law offices and the Florida Legislature, and serving a bob-tailed term as Governor, he sought election to a full term in 1956 and had occasion to use the medium most dramatically. As he and his opponent were about to verbalize over a Miami channel one evening, an assistant dashed into the studio with a newspaper. Backers of Collins's rival had published an advertisement declaring that the Governor had been so routed in the debate that he had ducked out of town immediately afterward. Since the paper was already on the streets and he had not yet been on the air, Collins advanced on the cameras waving the ad, stole the show, and later carried Miami (Dade County) with a big enough margin to offset his opponent's heavy rural vote.

Four years later, at the Democratic national convention in Los Angeles, Collins starred as chairman. Constantly on camera, he displayed a winning personality and a firm competence; some say that this performance convinced the National Association of Broadcasters that he would make an excellent emissary to the public. He got the job, even though Philip Graham, publisher of the *Washington Post,* cautioned an NAB selection committee, "If they want a Mickey Mouse, they had better stay away from Collins."

When the tall, lean, leathery-faced politician brought his gracious mannerisms to the NAB, he found it a house of uneasy alliances between broadcasters with clashing interests. Small radio stations were mistrustful of big, and FM broadcasters, with a technically superior service, had been crippled by the inhabitants of the dominant AM band. Radio men without a television station resented the medium that had made off with their advertising, and ultra-high frequency telecasters were operating under economic handicaps fashioned by powerful very high frequency interests. This was the NAB, a conglomeration of business rivals who could be united on one issue if on no other—opposition to any attempt by "government bureaucrats" to interfere with "free broadcasting." On this point, they salivated in unison and on signal.

Shortly after taking office in January, 1961, Collins observed protocol by paying his respects to the members of the Federal Communications Bar Association, lawyer-champions of constitutionality for broadcasters in trouble. He relieved himself of a number of bland pleasantries appropriate for the marionette role that Edwin H. James, executive editor of the trade magazine *Television*, once described as the inheritance of the association's sachems:

> NAB members are accustomed to the tradition that presidents speak publicly on one of two themes: (1) broadcasting is wonderful; (2) it can be wrecked by government control. On occasions that demand long speeches, it has been permissible to combine those themes and amplify them with references to the sanctity of free enterprise.

As it developed, however, Collins was, like many a decent poker player, hiding a powerhouse. He was spending his days and nights studying the condition of broadcasting in preparation for a February appearance before the NAB board of directors. He shocked them. "To start with," he said, "I believe broadcasting is in serious trouble, that its public favor is dangerously low." He implied that broadcasters were long on alibis and short on reform: "There is little to be gained now by arguing that there is more 'good' programming than 'bad' programming, for a large part of the public is convinced that there is not enough 'good' and too much 'bad'. . . . Broadcasters, I feel, should stand firmly on the proposition that nothing in their business which is wrong can be excused and left unattended. Further, it is their business to correct it."

A month later, Collins attacked the weather-beaten rationalization that what is popular is necessarily good. "In fact," he said, "the public interest cannot be served adequately through entertainment alone, any more than man can live by bread alone."

The gnashing of teeth was heard over clear channels from

as far south and west as Georgia and North Dakota. NAB board members fumed because Collins insisted on making public his remarks to them, and various state associations talked of withdrawing from the NAB. When rumors of a planned "rump convention" reached Washington, bearers of peace pipes set out from headquarters to pacify the head-hunters in the provinces. They explained that Collins, with a sensitive finger on the congressional pulse, was merely trying to convince broadcasting that it had to do better to avoid more stringent regulation. These attempts at enlightenment were somewhat successful and the open furor ebbed. At heart, though, most broadcasters still wanted their leader to stable his white horse and confine himself to rocking-chair utterances about the best, most patriotic little old broadcasting system this world had ever seen.

As a practiced politician, Collins thus approached the NAB's "wasteland" convention with extreme care. Fellow Democrat Newton Minow did not send over a copy of his own trenchant remarks before their delivery, but the NAB's informational lines were intricate enough to produce the text. Collins was surprised at the sharpness of Minow's attack, but the chairman's tone did not affect his own. Having completed the shock stage of his offensive, Collins had already adjusted his dials to a gentler pitch. Setting aside direct attacks on evil, he indicated its omnipresence by repeatedly and pointedly suggesting improvements. He thought it would be the decent thing, for instance, if network-affiliated stations stopped blacking out public affairs programs so they could schedule action-adventure films sponsored by Joe's local furniture store or Pete's crossroads garage. But Collins also felt it essential to restate his disinclination to play the puppet. "If you want someone gently to paddle NAB's boat into the stagnant pockets of still water," he said, "then you do not want me—nor I, you."

The man with the soft accent and quick, nervous movements continued to develop his unpopular themes—going so far at one point as to suggest what is at the heart of the television problem: "... we should not expect the FCC to close its eyes to abuses in programming reflecting a gross lack of qualifications to enjoy the license privileges.... America simply does not have the time any more to accept anything less than the best from broadcasting." On another occasion, he revealed a keen perception of the paramount issue. "If we mean business about this democratic system of ours," he said, "the improvement of broadcasting is going to have to come through the resources and efforts of the broadcasting profession itself, and not through governmental dictation."

There the Governor stated the dilemma that faces broadcasting and the Federal Communications Commission. If the television industry forces the United States Government to spell out the words *good* and *bad* in programming, many people in this watchful world will conclude that free-enterprise democracy either failed to find a way to control its predatory elements, or that no way but force was possible. This, of course, is a shabby reason to improve—broadcasting should do its job so we the American people can benefit, not so that other people will not sneer—but such are the realities of today's life. If the government is forced by extreme misconduct to take "free" broadcasting by the ear and shake it, the defeat will be the fault of the broadcasters and the repercussions will be unpleasant. But at least the profits will still be handsome.

The hypocrisy of the television industry lies in its cries of "censorship," which, it seeks to have believed, is what Newton Minow likes most to bring home to his children at night. Broadcasters have traditionally selected farfetched terminology to describe anything they are not attracted to. Back in the 1930's, the government schemers were deemed to possess a "mania for power." As an overwrought NAB president then saw it: "Broadcasting in the United States today stands in grave jeopardy. Politically powerful and efficiently organized groups, actuated by selfishness and with a mania for power, are now busily at work plotting the complete destruction of the industry we have pioneered and developed."

Destruction is no less imminent nowadays, of course; only the claim has been updated. "Censorship" was the most heard word at a reception staged by the NAB for the benefit of the thirsty only a few hours after Minow's wasteland speech in May, 1961. Congressmen were conspicuous by their attendance, and it is to marvel that any of them still had lapels when they surrendered their cocktail glasses and departed. Squads of broadcasters pounced on the legislators and disgorged indignation over Minow's threats to the First Amendment, property rights, the First Amendment, the right to make a buck, the First Amendment, the right to unchallenged license renewals, and the First Amendment.

Such extravagant concern should not be ignored, if only because public reaction to Minow's speech was sharply dissimilar; congratulatory letters and telegrams outpointed criticisms by fifty to one. Broadcasters retort that their position is founded in the bedrock of the law and not in hair-pulling; the applicable legalities are therefore fit for examination. They deal with two major questions: (1) Who owns the air waves? and (2) Does the FCC have the right to consider not only when and where the air waves are used, but *how* they are used?

In the Neanderthal days of broadcasting no one questioned that the air waves were public property; they were described by Herbert Hoover, Secretary of Commerce during the 1920's and all-time champion of rugged individualism, as one of the people's most precious resources. The wording of the Communications Act of 1934 made this concept explicit in specifically prohibiting private ownership of broadcast frequencies through Section 301:

> . . . to provide for the use of such channels, but not the ownership thereof, by persons for limited periods of time, under licenses granted by Federal authority, and no such

> license shall be construed to create any right beyond the terms, conditions, and period of the license.

A process of attrition conducted by lawyers and lobbyists, in combination with the inaction of the Comatose Commission, has permitted the broadcasting industry to chip away steadily at this fundamental doctrine until, for practical purposes, it has been nullified. At a 1959 conference of the Center for the Study of Democratic Institutions, Robert Maynard Hutchins, president of the Fund for the Republic, asked, "What happened to the old idea that you didn't have a property in radio or television—that you had nothing but a revocable license?" James Lawrence Fly, the battle-scarred one-time chairman of the FCC, replied, "That is still the basic principle, but actually an ordinary guy who has a radio or TV license has just as much permanence as a fee simple deed to the Empire State Building." Clifford J. Durr, who allied himself with Fly while serving on the FCC, declared, "You need to reiterate over and over again the idea that broadcasting frequencies are public property, even if it has been said ninety-nine times before. The people don't know; they don't understand that this is not the property of the broadcasters."

In real life, it has become their property. When CBS pays $20,000,000 for a broadcasting property whose land and plant are worth about $5,000,000, as it did in Philadelphia, one can be assured the network carefully examined the possibility that it might not always win renewal of a license to operate, and that it decided this was not a matter that required sleeping pills.

Emboldened by what it has accomplished, the industry is now sniping at the very legality of the concept of public ownership. Its acrobatic lawyers can offer arguments, for example, that differentiate between a privilege (a license) and a *valuable* privilege (a license embellished by a costly television station). When a broadcaster brings a transmitting facility to his franchise, they maintain, his valuable privilege takes on the character of a *property right,* and he can no longer be evicted as easily from *his* home. Although such cerebration suggests that the hand is quicker than the eye, the idea was given credence by none less than a recent chairman of the FCC, John Doerfer, who said, "I can't see the distinction between a valuable privilege and a property right." It is not surprising, then, that lawyers advance this disastrous position in face of a stricture in all broadcasting licenses which they must have read to their clients. It states that an applicant "hereby waives any claim to the use of any particular frequency . . . because of the previous use of the same . . ." Could any quitclaim be more ironclad—or more ignored?

Newton Minow, lawyer and once legal counsel for educational television interests, is not unaware of the ground that was given away before he joined the FCC. He faces the problem in the only way he can. When asked what he thought of the argument for proprietary ownership, he replied, "Well, it's a case of the chicken and the egg. You can't use one without the other. You can build the equipment, but unfortunately, if you don't have a license you can't go on the air." But broadcasters are already on the air, and their licenses to continue are still being rubber-stamped. This is the practice that must be halted by a courageous response to the second question in dispute: Can the FCC consider the quality of programming a station has offered when ruling on a license renewal application?

Broadcasters would restate the question: Does the FCC have the power of censorship? This is a game—flog the funny straw man—for which the men of television have enthusiasm. After a few rounds of it, they feel more patriotic while counting the receipts.

The use of the word *censorship* in this debate muddies the waters because it represents an allegation. Since it is treated as a fact, though, whatever legal position broadcasting can muster stems from it. Therefore, the industry usually fires as its opening gun the language of Section 326 of the Communications Act:

> Nothing in this Act shall be understood or construed to give the Commission the power of censorship . . . and no regulation or condition shall be promulgated or fixed by the Commission which shall interfere with the right of free speech . . .

Numerous court decisions are then cited, such as a Supreme Court observation that "Congress has from the first emphatically forbidden the Commission to exercise any power of censorship over radio communication." * The canker that gnaws, however, is that in most of these cases the courts were also affirming the Commission's right to consider programming, which is what broadcasters call censorship. The lawyers are therefore driven to rhetoric. When the eminent Whitney North Seymour, a past president of the American Bar Association, was engaged as special counsel by the NAB to present its view to the FCC, his brief cited cases whose familiarity was guaranteed to put a commissioner to sleep. The brief then descended into a recital of standard broadcaster arguments:

> Those with special views about what the public ought to see, hear, or enjoy should first persuade the public to want them. . . . Whatever may be said in the abstract about the superiority of symphonies or panel discussions over westerns or whodunits, the Commission is not entitled to say to tired farmers, businessmen, or even lawyers, that they must watch or listen to such cultural programs instead of enjoying the kind of entertainment they may prefer, even if their preference saddens some.

The Washington law firm of Daly & Ehrig, which handles broadcasting accounts, has charged that "the establishment of 'guides' for programming is worse than burning the books," and the most prominent of all Washington broadcast attorneys, W. Theodore Pierson, carried the battle directly to Newton Minow. "I say Mr. Minow cannot have it both ways," he announced. "Brilliant, articulate, and sincere person that he is, he cannot free us from our own imperfect taste by binding

* *Farmers Educational and Cooperative Union of America v. WDAY, Inc.*, 360 U. S. 525 (1959).

us to his imperfect taste without denying the principle of freedom upon which our society was built. . . ."

The missing ingredient of these polemics is evidence to demonstrate that the FCC cannot consider programming when reviewing a licensee's performance. The speeches are, rather, public relations performances which may (or may not) cause the populace to demand that people who criticize television be deported to Russia. The industry has consistently found warmth in the Flag when confronted by cold logic. In 1941, the FCC issued its Chain Broadcasting regulations, which, among other things, broke up NBC's Red and Blue networks on grounds that this arrangement stifled competition. NBC felt, naturally, that the American system of broadcasting was being jeopardized. In 1946, the Commission published its Blue Book,* a compendium of outlandish radio practices. Justin Miller, who was then president of the NAB and is now referred to as a wise elder statesman, did not answer the allegations, but he did characterize the Blue Book as "dangerous, subtle poison . . . an effort to discredit free American broadcasting . . . seized upon avidly by crackpots, Communists, and rival advertising media, who proceeded to heap ridicule upon broadcasting and broadcasters generally . . . a reversion to that type of government control and regulation from which our forefathers struggled to escape." In 1958, the Commission issued a rather good study of broadcasting, the Barrow Report, which suggested various modifications of the networks' stranglehold on their affiliates. CBS's Frank Stanton restrained himself from refuting the abuses cited; he did say: "What some men have put together, others are trying to put asunder. There are efforts . . . to atomize, fragmentize, and generally pound the networks into small pieces." Touching? And in 1961, when Newton Minow said what hundreds of thousands were probably beginning to think, NBC's Robert Sarnoff described such notions as constituting "a dangerous, mistaken, illiberal doctrine."

* *Public Service Responsibilities of Broadcast Licensees,* FCC.

Actually, these exercises in doomsaying are muscle-bound substitutes for what broadcasting cannot afford to demand in public: Leave us alone. The regulated industry resents not only the nation's awakened interest in the quality of its product, but any attempt by the FCC to display vigor. This attitude was noted when a roving team of Commission engineers visited Idaho stations to inspect equipment and station logs; although licensees are duty-bound to co-operate with these routine technical investigations, the engineers were preceded at each stop by a missive from the Idaho Broadcasters Association that said, in part:

> Keep your mouth shut and . . . do not volunteer any information unless asked a direct question. . . . If the team hits your station, you are in bad shape.

Perhaps the most miserable aspect of the needless decay of television lies in the fact that, in law, there has rarely been a question of the FCC's right to consider the nature of programming when judging a station's request for license renewal. This authority is so firm, clear, and long-standing that the Commission cannot shift the blame for its refusal to perform. Congress has not often given it support, but neither has it utilized the legal support it already had.

Some of broadcasting's ancient legal jousts with regulation are fascinating because its contentions have not changed. For example, in the 1931 Goat-Gland Brinkley case (Chapter 14), the doughty First Amendment argument was used to show that while the Commission had not used prior restraint, or censorship, it had accomplished the same end through subsequent punishment of Brinkley for his utterances. The court, however, found that the FRC had "merely exercised its undoubted right to take note of appellant's past conduct, which is not censorship." *

A year later, the Radio Commission refused to renew the license of a station that had been used for personal and

* *KFKB Broadcasting Association v. FRC,* 47 F. 2d 671 (1931).

religious attacks. When the station challenged, the court ruled, "In considering an application for a renewal of the license, an important consideration is the past conduct of the applicant, for 'by their fruits ye shall know them.'" *

It was after these cases had been well settled that Congress enacted the Communications Act of 1934, and it is noteworthy that the provisions of the Radio Act under which the Commission had been upheld were carried over to the new law. It is significant, too, that in those days, before broadcasting had become an entrenched big business, the National Association of Broadcasters did not object. Testifying on the proposed new law, the NAB said it was the Commission's "manifest duty" to check on public service, and that "such service necessarily includes the broadcasting of a considerable proportion of programs devoted to education, religion, labor, agriculture, and similar activities concerned with human betterment." In other words, the Commission should care about *what* was broadcast.

In 1940, the Supreme Court was again asked to consider the relationship of regulators to programming, and it ruled that "the character and quality of services" were within their province." † In 1943, when NBC contested the FCC's Chain Broadcasting regulations on several grounds, the Supreme Court minced no words on this point. Writing for the majority, Justice Felix Frankfurter said, in what must irrepressibly be characterized as a historic decision:

> . . . we are asked to regard the Commission as a kind of traffic officer, policing the wavelengths to prevent stations from interfering with each other. But the Act does not restrict the Commission merely to supervision of the traffic. It puts upon the Commission the burden of determining the composition of that traffic. . . . The facilities of radio are limited and therefore precious; they cannot be left to wasteful use without detriment to the public interest. §

* *Trinity Methodist Church, South, v. FRC*, 62 F. 2d 850 (1932).
† *Nelson Brothers v. FCC*, 309 U.S. 470, 475 (1940).
§ *National Broadcasting Company v. U.S.*, 319 U.S. 190 (1943).

There are more citations, but when roses are heaped on roses, the scent remains the same. Besides, the argument must inevitably shake down to a question whose utter ridiculousness should convince the citation-resistant: In considering the composition of broadcasting, what else can the FCC concern itself with *but* programming? What else is broadcasting composed of? As John Crosby once pointed out, the hands-off-programming argument is similar to "asking the Interstate Commerce Commission to regulate the railroads—with the proviso that passenger and freight service is outside its jurisdiction."

It would be thoughtless, of course, to assume that the television industry does not understand this. Edward R. Murrow suggested its real motives when he observed that nothing in the Bill of Rights or the Communications Act said that broadcasters "must increase their net profits each year lest the Republic collapse." And Newton Minow underscored the hypocrisy of it all when he declared that of those who cry, "Censorship! Oh, where will it end?" he would ask, "Responsibility—when will it begin?" He pointed out that freedom of speech "should not be confused with freedom to make promises in order to secure a television license and then freedom to break those promises in order to exploit that license. Freedom of speech does not mean freedom to . . . fool the people."

If broadcasters resist these propositions by pointing to transgressions of the press, the movies, and barbershop art, they may find—probably to everyone's misfortune—as a Fund for the Republic investigator concluded, that "There is apparently a growing trend toward organized social control over media, and this may presage a reinterpretation of the historic American attitudes toward censorship." Walter Lippmann, "believing as I do in freedom of speech and thought," nevertheless sees "no objection in principle to censorship of the mass entertainment of the young." He feels that the dangers to liberty may be "less than the risks of unmanageable violence."

And psychiatrist Fredric Wertham berates those "who think that to allow an industry to seduce children is democratic, while to prevent an industry from seducing children is undemocratic."

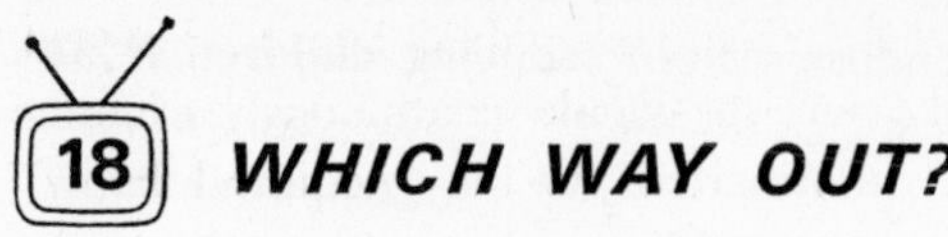

18 WHICH WAY OUT?

"A dozen letters to a sponsor would cause a front-office fit. People would get action in a hurry!" —An advertising man.

Since the 1930's and for sufficient cause, the public has often been exhorted to take a hand in getting a better deal for its eyes and ears. With rare exception, it has declined the invitations. But since this was a predictable reaction, the experiences of those few who *have* tried to accomplish something are worth being aware of. The more informal their approach, the greater has been their impact. Like good whiskies, grand designs can't be hurried.

The most prominent of the ambitious proposals is that advanced by Edward R. Murrow (and, with variations, by John Crosby, former Senator William Benton, and others). Murrow proceeds from the premise that broadcasting can do as much in "informing a troubled, apprehensive but receptive public" as in selling soap, cigarettes, and automobiles. Nor, since his is a truly grand design, does he overlook the rapid growth of stifling newspaper monopolies. He proposes a slow-fused, broad-spectrum therapy in the form of a "National Information Institute," privately financed, whose largest objective would be "to better the whole pattern of information in America."

The institute's working members—public figures, lawyers, journalists, and social scientists—would continuously examine mass communications in America. As they acquired knowledge and acceptance, they could comment with authority on the good and bad in our methods of transmitting information, ideas, and entertainment. The end purpose of Murrow's plan is to stimulate wide discussion of vital issues. The public, he says, would "become more and more aware of what it needs, when it gets it, when it does not get it, and why."

The information institute was first proposed in 1947, when it was conceived by Murrow and a colleague at CBS, Edward Klauber. Murrow restated it at a luncheon of broadcasting executives on his way out of the industry early in 1961, but so far as can be discovered, the waiters were the only ones who took it seriously. Predictability triumphed again.

Back in 1951, Senator Benton, now publisher of the *Encyclopædia Britannica,* proposed a similar idea to his fellow legislators, who were so enthusiastic they held hearings on it for three days before ignoring it. Benton revived his plan in 1960, and he will undoubtedly have many more opportunities to revive it. Essentially, he proposes a citizens' advisory board, appointed by the President, which would act as radio and television's "conscience" and advise the White House, Congress, the FCC, and the public. In the House, Representatives Thomas L. Ashley of Ohio has introduced a bill embodying this concept; under his plan the advisory board would be more closely tied to the FCC, although not under its domination. There might be some point in arguing about this feature if the Ashley bill's chances were not quite so nonexistent. Such legislation would be passed, over the television industry's dead body.

Television's leaders don't like to be trifled with—even by their brothers in arms. When Sigurd S. Larmon, chairman of the Young & Rubicam advertising agency, suggested during the quiz-show scandals that a citizens' committee might be able to suggest reforms, the networks' reaction caused frostbite on Madison Avenue. In full-page newspaper advertisements, NBC rejected "grandiose schemes for television's utopia," and CBS's Frank Stanton invoked his own grandiose semantics. "What is everybody's business is nobody's business," he said, "and eventually becomes government enterprise." Stanton also declared that the networks must "rise or fall on our own performance," but let us resist the temptation to get into *that* again.

There are also some working grand designs for assisting television, chief among them being the Continuing Conference on Communications and the Public Interest, which springs from the Academe. The conference is chaired by Gilbert Seldes of the University of Pennsylvania and contains some of the most knowledgeable and competent broadcasting thinkers in the country, including Charles Siepmann of New York University and Dallas Smythe of the University of Illinois. This group offers excellent suggestions to the Federal Communications Commission: hold local hearings on all applications for new and renewable licenses, charge a fee for the use of the valuable air waves, appoint a "public defender" who can present the Commission with a "systematic, thorough presentation of the needs, preferences, and desires of viewers within a community."

It is of course doubtful that the Continuing Conference will progress more rapidly than inch by inch, as it is doubtful that Congress, the President, a warmhearted millionaire, or a philanthropic foundation will do anything about the other good proposals. Ed Murrow has acidly noted that "vast sums are devoted by foundations and individual philanthropists to education and to many other worthy social causes. Yet the immediate day-to-day impact on men's minds of the radio, the press, television, the movies, and the magazines is of at least equal importance in the critical years now upon us."

One organization the foundations have neglected, despite

appeals, is the National Association for Better Radio and Television, which has been saddled with a monstrous shorthand title—NAFBRAT. Most broadcasters would describe NAFBRAT as unrealistic, impractical, crabby, too demanding, or aspiring to the role of censor. Not true. NAFBRAT is an efficient organization of men and women who are determined to make it as hot as possible for hypocrites and cynical programmers. Financially supported by viewers, it lacks spongy-floored offices in Washington; its national headquarters may be found in a second-story room of the home of Mrs. Clara Logan, in Los Angeles.

Mrs. Logan is a deceptively mild wife and mother of middle age; she is firm and tenacious, as her adversaries know, about things that matter. She became involved in her unusual endeavors in 1943, when she went into a PTA meeting one evening and came out a member of a radio committee. In the course of her work she attended a conference on children's programming and found that while she was discussing quality, the broadcasting delegates were discussing methods of attracting larger audiences. Her irritation and interest increased until, abandoning golf and bridge, she formed a Southern California group of just-plain-listeners. In 1951, at the suggestion of the late Wayne Coy, one of the FCC's conscientious chairmen, the organization adopted its cumbersome name and sought members throughout the nation. It now has about five hundred, many of whom carry out meticulously researched projects guaranteed to give an irresponsible broadcaster a headache.

When one network propagated the amazing theory that crime shows were even better than spinach because they provided children with "emotional outlets for their aggressions," NAFBRAT questioned three hundred pediatricians, psychiatrists, and psychologists, 90 per cent of whom suggested that junior savages were being fashioned. When a Los Angeles television station was offered for sale, NAFBRAT compiled a staggering list of its programming abuses and asked the FCC why the purveyors of such junk should be allowed to earn a profit on their license; the sale was not blocked, but it was delayed, which was enough to send air-wave squatters to the tranquilizer bottles. And when NAFBRAT documents a week in the vast wasteland, it is at least as specific as Newton Minow. Squads of women are assigned to exhaustive channel-watching and careful note-taking. As a result, the organization was able to release a report in 1960 that detailed a black book of crime and horror displayed by Los Angeles's seven channels during one week: one hundred and forty-four murders, one hundred and forty-three attempted murders, fifty-three "justifiable" killings, thirty-six robberies, fourteen druggings, thirteen kidnapings, twelve jail breaks, twelve thefts and burglaries, eleven planned murders, seven tortures, six extortions, five blackmailings, four attempted lynchings, one massacre, one mass murder, one planned mass murder by arson, one mass gun battle, and three posse blood baths in which death occurred with such frequency and confusion that the falling bodies eluded tabulation.

Because of the high quality of the organization's occupationally grisly work, Mrs. Logan has attracted men of outstanding professional reputation to NAFBRAT's board of directors. They include Robert Lewis Shayon of *The Saturday Review*, cartoonist Al Capp, psychiatrist Fredric Wertham, and professors Seldes, Siepmann, and Smythe.* Mrs. Logan participated in a White House Conference on Youth and has testified before congressional committees and the FCC. When she abandons her file-packed room in Los Angeles and arrives in Washington, in the manner of James Stewart, Mrs. Logan presents her audience with a considered, cogent exposure of what is going on, together with suggested remedies. The suggestions are not adopted, of course, but neither were Mr.

* An unabashed public service commercial for NAFBRAT (882 Victoria Avenue, Los Angeles 5, California): Rolls are open to all; the minimum membership fee for one year is five dollars.

Smith's when he went to Washington; he was knocking a vast, dug-in system, and so is she.

NAFBRAT, however, possesses additional strengths—and they display the power of informal, well-targeted action. Its members no longer tell each other how awful programs and commercials are. They tell the people who sponsor the nonsense, and the responses they receive indicate the nervousness that personal missives create in corporate kingdoms. Few business concerns slough letters of criticism or protest suggesting that the writer will be buying noodles or cold tablets from a competitor in the future. The effectiveness of such an approach was demonstrated to Mrs. Logan when she was preparing a list of frequent advertisers for the use of readers of NAFBRAT's quarterly journal. In seeking permission to use a sponsors' address list compiled by a commercial service catering to the television industry, she was not merely refused but lectured on the irreparable harm she might wreak on the American economy. Yes-sirree.

Mrs. Logan's bout with the free-for-us enterprisers was strongly in mind when I discussed the frustrating limitations on viewer action with an advertising agency man who does what he does between 9 A.M. and 5 P.M. but knows better in the evenings. "Our clients aren't very impressed with the opinions of professional critics," he said. "But they're impressed as hell with a letter saying, 'Your —— show last Tuesday night was unfit for public display, and the last package of —— is now in my kitchen.' A dozen letters to a sponsor would cause a front-office fit. People would get action in a hurry!"

Approval of this comment by other candid advertising men leads me, therefore, to suggest a brave and uncomplicated method of convincing sponsors that they should tell the networks they don't really want full-time idiot programming. Drop them a line—not a treatise beginning with the discovery of the wheel, but a simple one- or two-paragraph letter naming the program on which the company's product was advertised, stating the basic objection, and supplying the name or channel number of the station for complete identification. Such letters could mean the beginning of a revision of current attitudes.

Panacea? Hardly. The networks have interred most of the better creative people and the Hollywood hamburger-grinders have tight control of the product. No improvement can be expected overnight. But it is conceivable that control *can* be wrested from the spoilers—not through censorship, by the way, but through the exercise of free speech.

One method of facilitating greater freedom of speech is by making available some obscure information—such as where to send a letter. That is the purpose of Appendix B of this book. In it are listed (1) the products most frequently hawked by television's leading advertisers, and (2) the names and addresses of their manufacturers. Anyone who wishes may match the number beside the product with the number in the company list, write a brief document containing his sentiments, and—for the price of a postage stamp—invoke the true spirit of American democracy. When participated in wholeheartedly, this kind of democracy is a profoundly satisfying sport.

Individual and personalized comments on offensive and tasteless commercials would also affect a sponsor as severely as if he had hammers in his head. (I will confess this hammers-in-the-head idea is not original; we are all products of our culture.)

While the FCC cannot be expected to exercise a truly effective role for some time to come under the best of circumstances, viewers could impress the Commission with the knowledge that they wish it to begin acting with vigor and dispatch, now. Those who are so moved will find Newton Minow's address in Appendix B. He would no doubt share his mail with his colleagues.

Another extension of democracy is feasible; it involves advertising matter that a viewer suspects is misleading or untruthful. The proper agency to alert is the Federal Trade Commission, whose chairman and address may also be found in Appendix B.

To provide diversity for letter writers, Appendix B contains, in addition, the addresses of the three television networks. Their concern for the well-being of the public has been stated so many times that it would be ungracious to omit them from a pleasant evening of television-rescuing. It is not necessary to correspond directly with a network president; when sufficient letters are received, he will hear about them, fear not.

After an intensive study of the television industry, I believe that the above suggestions contain the greatest opportunity for viewers who would like to see the medium rescued before they die. Those who are content to live in vague hope, or who believe that *Pete and Gladys* television is what America needs most are free to continue twirling their dials through the circuit of stupidity and vacuousness.

As the thoughtful Robert Lewis Shayon has remarked, people who don't like what's happening really ought to do something about it soon or quit heckling the television industry and go read a book.

APPENDIX: NEWTON MINOW'S "VAST WASTELAND" SPEECH

Following are highlights from the speech of Newton N. Minow, chairman of the Federal Communications Commission, to the thirty-ninth annual convention of the National Association of Broadcasters, on May 9, 1961:

Your license lets you use the public air waves as trustees for 180,000,000 Americans. The public is your beneficiary. If you want to stay on as trustees, you must deliver a decent return to the public—not only to your stockholders. So, as a representative of the public, your health and your product are among my chief concerns. . . .

I have confidence in your health. But not in your product. . . .

Ours has been called the jet age, the atomic age, the space age. It is also, I submit, the television age. And just as history will decide whether the leaders of today's world employed the atom to destroy the world or rebuild it for mankind's benefit, so will history decide whether today's broadcasters employed their powerful voice to enrich the people or debase them. . . .

When television is good, nothing—not the theater, not the magazines or newspapers—nothing is better. But when television is bad, nothing is worse. I invite you to sit down in front of your television set when your station goes on the air and stay there without a book, magazine, newspaper, profit and loss sheet or rating book to distract you—and keep your eyes glued to that set until the station signs off. I can assure you that you will observe a vast wasteland.

You will see a procession of game shows, violence, audience participation shows, formula comedies about totally unbelievable families, blood and thunder, mayhem, violence, sadism, murder, western badmen, western good men, private eyes, gangsters, more violence, and cartoons. And, endlessly, commercials—many screaming, cajoling, and offending. And most of all, boredom. True, you will see a few things you will enjoy. But they will be very, very few. And if you think I exaggerate, try it. . . .

Gentlemen, your trust accounting with your beneficiaries is overdue. Never have so few owed so much to so many.

Why is so much of television so bad? I have heard many answers: demands of your advertisers; competition for ever higher ratings; the need always to attract a mass audience; the high cost of television programs; the insatiable appetite for programming material—these are some of them. Unquestionably, these are tough problems not susceptible to easy answers.

But I am not convinced that you have tried hard enough to solve them. I do not accept the idea that the present over-all programming is aimed accurately at the public taste. The ratings tell us only that some people have their television sets turned on and of that number, so many are tuned to one channel and so many to another. They don't tell us what the public might watch if they were offered half a dozen additional choices. A rating, at best, is an indication of how many people saw what you gave them. Unfortunately, it does not reveal the depth of the penetration, or the intensity of reaction, and it never reveals what the acceptance would have been if what you gave them had been better—if all the forces of art and creativity and daring and imagination had been unleashed. I believe in the people's good sense and good taste, and I am not convinced that the people's taste is as low as some of you assume.

My concern with the rating services is not with their accuracy. Perhaps they are accurate. I really don't know. What, then, is wrong with the ratings? It's not been their accuracy—it's been their use. . . .

If parents, teachers, and ministers conducted their responsibilities by following the ratings, children would have a steady diet of ice cream, school holidays, and no Sunday School. What about your responsibilities? Is there no room on television to teach, to inform, to uplift, to stretch, to enlarge the capacities of our children? Is there no room for programs deepening their understanding of children in other lands? Is there no room for a children's news show explaining something about the world to them at their level of understanding? Is there no room for reading the great literature of the past, teaching them the great traditions of freedom? There are some fine children's shows, but they are drowned out in the massive doses of cartoons, violence, and more violence. Must these be your trade-marks? Search your consciences and see if you cannot offer more to your young beneficiaries whose future you guide so many hours each and every day.

What about adult programming and ratings? You know, newspaper publishers take popularity ratings, too. The answers are pretty clear: it is almost always the comics, followed by the advice to the lovelorn columns. But, ladies and gentlemen, the news is still on the front page of all newspapers, the editorials are not replaced by more comics, the newspapers have not become one long collection of advice to the lovelorn. Yet newspapers do not need a license from the government to be in business—they do not use public property. But in television—where your responsibilities as public trustees are so plain, the moment that the ratings indicate that westerns are popular there are new imitations of westerns on the air faster than the old coaxial cable could take us from Hollywood to New York. Broadcasting cannot continue to live by the numbers. Ratings ought to be the slave of the broadcaster, not his master. And you and I both know that the rating services themselves would agree.

Let me make clear that what I am talking about is balance. I believe that the public interest is made up of many interests. There are many people in this great country and you must serve all of us. You will get no argument from me if you say that, given a choice between a western and a symphony, more people will watch the western. I like westerns and private eyes, too—but a steady diet for the whole country is obviously not in the public interest. We all know that people would more often prefer to be entertained than stimulated or informed. But your obligations are not satisfied if you look only to popularity as a test of what to broadcast. You are not only in show business; you are free to communicate ideas as well as relaxation. You must provide a wider range of choices, more diversity, more alternatives. It is not enough to cater to the nation's whims—you must also serve the nation's needs. . . .

Tell your sponsors to be less concerned with costs per thousand and more concerned with understanding per millions. And remind your stockholders that an investment in broadcasting is buying a share in public responsibility. . . .

Another and perhaps the most important frontier: television will rapidly join the parade into space. International television will be with us soon. No one knows how long it will be until a broadcast from a studio in New York will be viewed in India as well as in Indiana, will be seen in the Congo as it is seen in Chicago. But as surely as we are meeting here today, that day will come—and once again our world will shrink.

What will the people of other countries think of us when they see our western badmen and good men punching each other in the jaw in between the shooting? What will the Latin American or African child learn of America from our great communications industry? We cannot permit television in its present form to be our voice overseas.

There is your challenge to leadership. You must re-examine

some fundamentals of your industry. You must open your minds and open your hearts to the limitless horizons of tomorrow. . . .

We need imagination in programming, not sterility; creativity, not imitation; experimentation, not conformity; excellence, not mediocrity. Television is filled with creative, imaginative people. You must strive to set them free. . . .

What you gentlemen broadcast through the people's air affects the people's taste, their knowledge, their opinions, their understanding of themselves and of their world. And their future.

The power of instantaneous sight and sound is without precedent in mankind's history. This is an awesome power. It has limitless capabilities for good—and for evil. And it carries with it awesome responsibilities, responsibilities which you and I cannot escape.

Viewers may identify corporate sponsors by locating the name of an advertised product in the alphabetical "Product" table. After each trade-mark is a number that refers to the name of the manufacturer in the "Companies" list.

Letters to networks need not be addressed to specific individuals; they will find their way to the proper parties when addressed as indicated below.

There are so many bureaus and divisions in the Federal Communications Commission and the Federal Trade Commission that viewers would do well to direct letters to the chairmen.

PRODUCTS

AC automotive products (39)
Actin Cough Syrup (20)
Ad detergent (23)
Adorn Hair Spray (40)
Aeromist Deodorizer (4)
Aeroshave (4)
Aerowax (4)
Air-wick deodorizer (53)
Ajax Cleanser (23)
Albers Cereals (18)

Alberto VO5 hair dressing (1)
Alcoa aluminum, Alcoa Wrap (2)
Alka-Seltzer (57)
All detergent (53)
Allstate Insurance (84)
Allsweet Margarine (92)
Alpine Cigarettes (59)
American Family Laundry Soap (73)
Amm-i-dent Toothpaste, Powder (13)
Anacin Tablets (4)
Antizyme Toothpaste (96)
A-1 Almond Candy (33)
Aqua Velva After Shave Lotion (99)
Argo Gloss Starch (26)
Arident Decongestant Tablets (57)
Armour meat products (7)
Armstrong floor, wall coverings (8)
Arrestin Cold Remedy (48)
Arrid Deodorant (19)
Atlas tires, auto batteries (89)
Aunt Jemima products (75)
Avon Cosmetics (9)

Bactine Antiseptic (57)
Baker's chocolate products, Coconut (37)
Ban Deodorant (14)
Banarin Cold Remedy (99)
Band-Aids (48)
Bayer Aspirin, Nasal Spray (90)
Beech-Nut products (12)
Beeman's Chewing Gum (3)
Belair Cigarettes (15)
Best Foods Italian Dressing (26)
Betty Crocker products (38)
Big Top Peanut Butter (73)
Birds Eye foods (37)
Bisodol Powder, Mints (4)
Bis*quick* (38)
Biz Detergent (73)
Black Flag Insecticide (4)
Blatz Beer (67)
Bliss Coffee (37)
Bliss Home Permanent (96)
Blue Bonnet Margarine (88)
Blue Plate food products (44)
Bobbi Pincurl Home Permanent (40)
Bond Street Pipe Tobacco (59)
Bonus Detergent (73)
Bosco Chocolate Syrup (26)
Bravo Detergent (47)
Breakstone dairy products (62)
Breeze Detergent (53)
Breyers Ice Cream (62)
Bridget Detergent (73)
Bromo Quinine (14)
Bromo Seltzer (96)
Brylcreem Hair Dressing (11)
Budweiser Beer (6)
Bufferin tablets (14)
Buick (39)
Busch Bavarian Beer (6)

Calamatum Skin Healer (45)
Calumet Baking Powder (37)
Camay Soap (73)
Camel Cigarettes (80)
Campbell's products (16)
Campho-Phenique (90)
Carnation products (18)
Carter petroleum products (89)
Carter's Little Pills (19)
Cascade Detergent (73)
Cashmere soaps, toiletries (23)
Cavalier Cigarettes (80)
Certs Mints (3)
Charmin paper products (73)
Chase & Sanborn Coffee (88)

Cheer Detergent (73)
Cheerios Cereal (38)
Chef Boy-ar-dee products (4)
Chesterfield Cigarettes (54)
Chevrolet (39)
Chiclets Gum (3)
Chiffon Detergent (7)
Chiffon Pie Filling (37)
Chiquita Canned, Mashed Bananas (4)
Chix Diapers (48)
Chlorodent Toothpaste (53)
Chocks Vitamins (57)
Choice Beauty Bar (23)
Chrysler (21)
Clairol hair products (14)
Clearasil Medication, Soap, Shampoo (81)
Clorets Mints, Gum (3)
Clorox Bleach (73)
Coca-Cola (22)
Cocoa Puffs Chocolate Cereal (38)
Colgate Dental Cream (23)
Colonaid Laxative (19)
Colorcade hair products (40)
Color-Glo Hair Color Rinse (96)
Comet automobiles (34)
Comet Cleanser (73)
Command Hair Dressing (1)
Commander Cigarettes (59)
Conti Shampoo (99)
Continental automobiles (34)
Continental bakery products (25)
Cool Glow Cosmetics (96)
Copper-Tone Suntan Lotion (71)
Corvair automobiles (39)
Coughlets (3)
Count 4 Antacid (14)
Country Corn Flakes, Rice Flakes (38)
Crest Tooth Paste (73)
Crisco (73)
Cut-Rite Wax Paper (83)

Dart automobiles (21)
Dash detergent (73)
Dash Dog Food (7)
Dawn Deodorant Bar (73)
Deep Magic Cleansing Lotion (40)
Delamine Antacid (78)
Delco products (39)
Delsey Bathroom Tissue (51)
Dennison's Canned Foods (4)
Dentu-Creme, Dentu-Grip (13)
Dentyne Chewing Gum (3)
Dermassage Body Rub (23)
Dexol Bleach (70)
Dial products (7)
Dinner-Redy Dinners (53)
Dodge automobiles (21)
Dondril Cough Tablets (4)
Double Danderine (90)
Dove Toilet Soap (53)
Downy Fabric Softener (73)
Dr. Caldwell's Laxative (90)
Dr. Lyons Tooth Powder (90)
Drano (28)
Dream Whip Topping (37)
Dreft Detergent (73)
Drene Shampoo (73)
Driacol Cold Tablets (23)
Drifted Snow Flour (38)
Dristan products (4)
Dromedary products (61)
DuBarry Cosmetics (96)
Duet Margarine (92)
Duke Cigarettes (54)
DuMaurier Cigarettes (15)
Duncan Hines pancake, muffin, Early American, regular, de luxe cake mixes (73)
Duplexin Headache Remedy (4)

du Pont products (29)
Duz Detergent (73)
Dynamo Detergent (23)
D-Zerta products (37)

Eastman Kodak photo equipment (30)
Easy-Off Oven Cleaner, Window Cleaner; Easy-On Spray Starch (4)
El Producto Cigars (24)
Embassy Cigarettes (55)
Energine Products (90)
Eno Antacid (11)
Esquire Boot Polish (76)
Esso petroleum products (89)
Excedrin Pain Reliever (14)

Fab Detergent (23)
Falcon automobiles (34)
Falstaff Beer (31)
Farina Cereal (70)
Fitch products (14)
Fizzies Soft Drink Tablets (96)
Flako pie, muffin mixes (75)
Fleischmann Margarine, Yeast (88)
Fletcher's Castoria (90)
Flit Insecticides (89)
Florient Deodorizer (23)
Fluffo Shortening (73)
Folger's Coffee (32)
Ford (34)
Fortisun Cold Remedy (14)
4-Way Cold Tablets (14)
Franco-American foods (16)
Freezone (4)
Frenchette Salad Dressing (19)
French's food products (35)
Frigidaire (39)
Friskies Dog Food (18)
Frosty O's Cereal (38)

Gain Detergent (73)
Gaines Dog Food (37)
Gem Razor Blades (59)
General Electric products (36)
Genie Household Cleaner (23)
George Washington food products (4)
Geritol (99)
Gillette shaving products (40)
Gleem tooth paste (73)
Glosstex Starch (70)
Gold Medal Flour (38)
Good Luck Margarine (53)
Good Seasons Salad Dressing Mix (37)
Gravy Magic (38)
Gravy Train Dog Food (37)
Green Mint Mouth Wash (13)
Griffin Shoe Polish (4)
Gro-Pup Dog Foods (50)

Haley's M-O Aspirin (90)
Halo Shampoo (23)
Hamms Beer (41)
Handy Andy Cleaner (53)
Heet Liniment (4)
Heinz food products (42)
Helene Curtis products (27)
Hellmann's food products (26)
Hi-C Beverages (58)
Hills Brothers Coffee (43)
Hi-Pro Cereal (38)
H-O Cereals (26)
Hoffman Beverages (67)
Hometown Bread (61)
Hopper's Sudden Beauty Facial Mask (4)
Hostess Cakes (25)
Hotpoint electric products (36)
Hum Detergent (53)
Hunt Club Dog Food (88)
Hunt food products (44)
Hush Deodorant (40)

Imperial automobiles (21)
Imperial Margarine (53)

Imra Depilatory (4)
Instantine Headache Remedy (90)
Instil Stomach Remedy (4)
Ipana Toothpaste (14)
Italianette Salad Dressing (19)
Ivory (73)

Jell-O (37)
Jergen's products (46)
Jif Peanut Butter (73)
Johnson & Johnson products (48)
S. C. Johnson waxes, polishes, cleaners, deodorants (47)
Joy Detergent (73)

Kaiser aluminum, steel, foil (49)
Kan-Kil Insecticide (23)
Karo Syrup (26)
Kasco Dog Food (26)
Kellogg's products (50)
Kendall Dog Food (88)
Ken-L Dog Foods (75)
Kent Cigarettes (55)
Kentucky Kings Cigarettes (15)
Kix Cereal (38)
Kleenex products (51)
Knorr soups (26)
Kolynos Toothpaste (4)
Kool-Aid Beverage Mix (37)
Kool Cigarettes (15)
Kool-Pops (37)
Kraft food products (62)
Kreml Hair Tonic (99)

L&M Cigarettes (54)
Lady Charmin paper products (73)
LaFrance Bluing (37)
Lastic Life Cold Water Soap (4)
Lava Hand Soap (73)
Lavoris Mouth Wash, Oral Spray (81)
Lectric Shave Lotion (99)
Lentheric products (27)
Lestare Bleach (52)
Lestoil (52)
Lifebuoy Soap (53)
Life Cigarettes (15)
Light & Bright Hair Lightener (96)
Lilt Shampoo & Home Permanent (73)
Lincoln automobiles (34)
Linit Liquid Starch (26)
Lip Quick (96)
Lipton soup mixes (53)
Lipton Tea (53)
Liquid Mist Reddi Spray-On Starch (86)
Liquiprin for Children (48)
Listerine products (96)
Log Cabin Syrup (37)
Lucky Strike Cigarettes (5)
Lucky Whip Dessert Topping (53)
Lustre-Creme Shampoo (23)
Lux Detergent, Toilet Soap (53)

M&M Candies (33)
Marlboro Cigarettes (59)
Maxwell House products (37)
Mazola Oil, Margarine (26)
Mennen products (56)
Mercury automobiles (34)
Micrainin Headache Tablets (19)
Milk Bone Dog Foods (61)
Millbrook Bread (61)
Minipoo Dry Shampoo (13)
Minit Rub (14)
Minute Maid frozen juices (58)
Minute Mashed Potatoes (37)

Minute Rice, Tapioca (37)
Morning Evaporated Milk (18)
Morton frozen food products (25)
Mr. Clean Detergent (73)
Mrs. Butterworth's Pancake Syrup (53)
Mum Deodorant (14)
Musterole Chest Rub (71)
Mutual of Omaha Insurance (60)

Nabisco cereals, crackers, cookies (59)
Nair Depilatory (19)
Nebs Pain Reliever (64)
Neet Depilatory (4)
Nervine Liquid, Tablets (57)
Nescafé (63)
Nestlé's products (63)
Newport Cigarettes (55)
Niagara Starch (26)
Nifty Cleanser (53)
Noxzema products (65)
Nucoa Margarine (26)
NuSoft Fabric Softener (26)
Nytol Tablets (13)

Oasis Cigarettes (54)
O-Celo Sponges, Dish Mop (38)
Old Gold Cigarettes (55)
Old Milwaukee Beer (82)
Oldsmobile (39)
One-A-Day Vitamin Tablets (57)
Open Pit Barbecue Sauce (37)
Oxydol Detergent (73)
Oz Peanut Butter (92)

Pace Home Permanent (73)
Painquellizer Tablets (4)
Pal Razor Blades (59)
Pall Mall Cigarettes (5)
Palmolive products (23)
Pamper Shampoo (40)
Pan-O-Gold Chicken (7)
Paper-Mate Pens (40)
Pard Dog Food (92)
Parliament Cigarettes (59)
Party Curl Home Permanent (73)
Patio Soft Drink (68)
Pepsi-Cola (68)
Pepsodent Toothpaste (53)
Pepto-Bismol (64)
Personna Razor Blades (59)
Pertussin Cough Remedy (20)
Pet milk products (69)
Pet-Ritz frozen foods (69)
Philip Morris Cigarettes (59)
Phillies Cigars (10)
Phillips Milk of Magnesia (90)
Pillsbury food products (70)
Pine Bros. Cough Drops (12)
Pinex Cough Syrup (78)
Pin-It Home Permanent (73)
Playtex products (45)
Plymouth automobiles (21)
Poise Roll-On Deodorant (23)
Polaroid Land Camera (72)
Polident Denture Cleaner (13)
Poli-Grip (13)
Pond's products (20)
Pontiac automobiles (39)
Post cereals (37)
Postum (37)
Praise Deodorant Bath Bar (53)
Prell shampoo (73)
Presto food products (26)
Prime Pre-Electric Shave (23)
Prom Home Permanent (40)
Pro-Phy-Lac-Tic toothbrushes (96)
Protein Plus, Wheat Hearts Cereals (38)
Prudential Insurance (74)

Swans Down Cake Mixes (37)
Swanson frozen foods (16)
Swift's foods, dog foods (92)

Tabsin Cold Tablets (57)
Tame Creme Rinse (40)
Tandem Shampoo (14)
Tang Beverage Mix (37)
Tareyton Cigarettes (5)
Tempest automobiles (39)
Tender Leaf Tea (88)
Texaco petroleum products (93)
Thorexin Cough Syrup (40)
Three Little Kittens Cat Food (38)
Thrill Detergent (73)
Thunderbird automobiles (34)
Tide detergent (73)
Tone Furniture Wax (86)
Tonette, Toni Home Permanents (40)
Tootsie Roll Candies (91)
Top Brass Hair Dressing (78)
Treet Canned Meat (7)
Tresemme Hair Coloring (1)
Trig Deodorant (14)
Trix Cereal (38)
Trushay Hand Lotion (14)
Tuffy Scouring Pads (37)
Twinkle Metal Cleaner (28)
Twinkles Cereal (38)
Twirl Home Permanent (40)

Uncle Ben's Rice (33)
Unguentine Ointment (64)
U.S. Steel (95)

V-8 Cocktail vegetable juices (16)
Valcream Hair Dressing (20)
Valiant automobiles (21)
Vam Hair Dressing (23)
Vanish Bowl Cleaner (28)
Vaseline products (20)
Veep Soft Drink (22)
Vel products (23)
Viceroy Cigarettes (15)
Vicks products (81)
Vigran Multiple Vitamins (66)
Vim Detergent (53)
Virisan Nasal Decongestant (96)
Vitalis Hair Tonic (14)

Waldorf Bathroom Tissue (83)
Wash 'n Dri (23)
Webster Cigars (10)
Welch food products (97)
Westinghouse products (98)
Wheaties Cereal (38)
Whirl Shortening (73)
White Cloud Bathroom Tissue (73)
White Rain Lotion Shampoo (40)
Wildroot Cream Oil (23)
Williams shaving products (99)
Willys Jeeps and Trucks (49)
Windex Glass Cleaner (28)
Winston Cigarettes (80)
Wishbone Salad Dressing (53)
Wisk Detergent (53)
Wizard Deodorizer (4)
Wonder bakery products (25)
Wonder Wrap (83)
Wondra Cream Shampoo (73)
Woodbury products (46)
Woolite cold water wash (4)
Wrigley Chewing Gum (100)

York Cigarettes (55)
Yuban Coffee (37)

Zarumin Pain Reliever (99)
Zerex, Zerone Anti-Freeze (29)
Zest Beauty Bar (73)

COMPANIES

1. Alberto-Culver Co.
   2525 W. Armitage Ave.
   Melrose Park, Ill.

2. Aluminum Co. of America
   Alcoa Building
   Pittsburgh 19, Pa.

3. American Chicle Co.
   Thompson & Manley Aves.
   Long Island City 1, N. Y.

4. American Home Products Corp.
   685 3d Ave.
   New York 17, N. Y.

5. American Tobacco Co.
   150 E. 42d St.
   New York 17, N. Y.

6. Anheuser-Busch, Inc.
   721 Pestalozzi St.
   St. Louis 18, Mo.

7. Armour & Co.
   401 N. Wabash
   Chicago 11, Ill.

8. Armstrong Cork Co.
   Lancaster, Pa.

9. Avon Products, Inc.
   30 Rockefeller Plaza
   New York 20, N. Y.

10. Bayuk Cigars, Inc.
    45-45 39th St.
    Long Island City, N. Y.

11. Beecham Products, Inc.
    Clifton, N. J.

12. Beech-Nut Life Savers, Inc.
    477 Madison Ave.
    New York 22, N. Y.

13. Block Drug Co., Inc.
    257 Cornelison Ave.
    Jersey City 2, N. J.

14. Bristol-Myers Co.
    630 5th Ave.
    New York 20, N. Y.

15. Brown & Williamson Tobacco Corp.
    1600 West Hill
    Louisville 1, Ky.

16. Campbell Soup Co.
    375 Memorial Ave.
    Camden 1, N. J.

17. Canadian Breweries, Ltd.
    3950 S. Union St.
    Chicago, Ill.

18. Carnation Co.
    5045 Wilshire Blvd.
    Los Angeles 36, Calif.

19. Carter Products, Inc.
    2 Park Ave.
    New York 16, N. Y.

20. Chesebrough-Pond's, Inc.
    485 Lexington Ave.
    New York 17, N. Y.

21. Chrysler Corp.
    341 Massachusetts Ave.
    Detroit 31, Mich.

22. Coca-Cola Co.
515 Madison Ave.
New York 22, N. Y.

23. Colgate-Palmolive Co.
300 Park Ave.
New York 22, N. Y.

24. Consolidated Cigar Corp.
529 5th Ave.
New York 17, N. Y.

25. Continental Baking Co.
Halstead Ave.
Rye, N. Y.

26. Corn Products Co.
717 5th Ave.
New York 22, N. Y.

27. Helene Curtis Industries, Inc.
4401 W. North Ave.
Chicago 39, Ill.

28. Drackett Co.
5020 Spring Grove Ave.
Cincinnati 32, Ohio

29. E. I. du Pont de Nemours
Wilmington 98, Del.

30. Eastman Kodak Co.
343 State St.
Rochester 4, N. Y.

31. Falstaff Brewing Corp.
5050 Oakland Ave.
St. Louis 10, Mo.

32. J. A. Folger & Co.
330 W. 8th St.
Kansas City, Mo.

33. Food Manufacturers, Inc.
High St.
Hackettstown, N. J.

34. Ford Motor Co.
American Road
Dearborn, Mich.

35. R. T. French Co.
1 Mustard St.
Rochester, N. Y.

36. General Electric Co.
570 Lexington Ave.
New York 22, N. Y.

37. General Foods Corp.
250 North St.
White Plains, N. Y.

38. General Mills, Inc.
9200 Wayzata Blvd.
Minneapolis 26, Minn.

39. General Motors Corp.
General Motors Building
Detroit 2, Mich.

40. Gillette Co.
Gillette Park
Boston 6, Mass.

41. Theo. Hamm Brewing Co.
720 Payne Ave.
St. Paul 1, Minn.

42. H. J. Heinz Co.
1062 Progress St.
Pittsburgh 30, Pa.

43. Hills Bros. Coffee, Inc.
2 Harrison St.
San Francisco 19, Calif.

44. Hunt Foods & Industries, Inc.
1747 W. Commonwealth Ave.
Fullerton, Calif.

45. International Latex Corp.
350 5th Ave.
New York 1, N. Y.

46. Andrew Jergens Co.
2535 Spring Grove
Cincinnati 14, Ohio

47. S. C. Johnson & Son, Inc.
1525 Howe
Racine, Wis.

48. Johnson & Johnson
George & Hamilton Sts.
Brunswick, N. J.

49. Kaiser Industries Corp.
300 Park Ave.
New York 22, N. Y.

50. Kellogg Co.
Battle Creek, Mich.

51. Kimberly-Clark Corp.
250 Park Ave.
New York 17, N. Y.

52. Lestoil Products, Inc.
Holyoke, Mass.

53. Lever Brothers Co.
390 Park Ave.
New York 22, N. Y.

54. Liggett & Myers Tobacco Co., Inc.
630 5th Ave.
New York 20, N. Y.

55. P. Lorillard & Co.
200 E. 42d St.
New York 17, N. Y.

56. Mennen Co.
Hanover Ave.
Morristown, N. J.

57. Miles Laboratories, Inc.
1127 Myrtle
Elkhart, Ind.

58. Minute Maid Corp.
30 Rockefeller Plaza
New York 20, N. Y.

59. Philip Morris, Inc.
100 Park Ave.
New York 17, N. Y.

60. Mutual Benefit Health & Accident Assn.
33d & Farnam Sts.
Omaha 1, Neb.

61. National Biscuit Co.
425 Park Ave.
New York 22, N. Y.

62. National Dairy Products Corp.
260 Madison Ave.
New York 16, N. Y.

63. Nestlé Co., Inc.
2 William St.
White Plains, N. Y.

64. Norwich Pharmacal Co.
Eton Ave.
Norwich, N. Y.

65. Noxzema Chemical Co.
32d & Falls Cliff Rd.
Baltimore 11, Md.

66. Olin Mathieson Chemical Corp.
460 Park Ave.
New York 22, N. Y.

67. Pabst Brewing Co.
Merchandise Mart
Chicago 54, Ill.

68. Pepsi-Cola Co.
500 Park Ave.
New York 21, N. Y.

69. Pet Milk Co.
Arcade Building
St. Louis, Mo.

70. Pillsbury Co.
Pillsbury Building
Minneapolis 2, Minn.

71. Plough, Inc.
3022 Jackson Ave.
Memphis, Tenn.

72. Polaroid Corp.
122 E. 42d St.
New York 17, N. Y.

73. Procter & Gamble Co.
301 E. 6th St.
Cincinnati 1, Ohio

74. Prudential Insurance Co
Newark, N. J.

75. Quaker Oats Co.
345 Merchandise Mart
Chicago 54, Ill.

76. Radio Corp. of America (RCA)
30 Rockefeller Plaza
New York 20, N. Y.

77. Ralston-Purina Co.
835 S. 8th St.
St. Louis 2, Mo.

78. Revlon, Inc.
666 5th Ave.
New York 19, N. Y.

79. Reynolds Metals Co.
Richmond 19, Va.

80. R. J. Reynolds Tobacco Co.
Winston-Salem 1, N. C.

81. Richardson-Merrell, Inc.
122 E. 42d St.
New York 17, N. Y.

82. Jos. E. Schlitz Brewing Co.
235 W. Galena St.
Milwaukee 1, Wis.

83. Scott Paper Co.
Front & Market Sts.
Chester, Pa.

84. Sears, Roebuck & Co.
Homan & Arthington
Chicago 7, Ill.

85. Shell Oil Co.
50 W. 50th St.
New York 20, N. Y.

86. Simoniz Co.
2100 Indiana Ave.
Chicago 16, Ill.

87. Sperry Rand Corp.
30 Rockefeller Plaza
New York 20, N. Y.

88. Standard Brands, Inc.
625 Madison Ave.
New York 22, N. Y.

89. Standard Oil Co. (N. J.)
30 Rockefeller Plaza
New York 20, N. Y.

90. Sterling Drug, Inc.
1450 Broadway
New York 18, N. Y.

91. Sweets Co. of America, Inc.
1515 Willow Ave.
Hoboken, N. J.

92. Swift & Co.
Union Stockyards
Chicago 9, Ill.

93. Texaco, Inc.
135 E. 42d St.
New York 17, N. Y.

94. Robert Hall Clothes, Inc.
333 W. 34th St.
New York 1, N. Y.

95. U.S. Steel Corp.
71 Broadway
New York 6, N. Y.

96. Warner-Lambert Pharmaceutical Co.
201 Tabor Rd.
Morris Plains, N. J.

97. Welch Grape Juice Co.
Westfield, N. Y.

98. Westinghouse Electric Corp.
40 Wall St.
New York, N. Y.

99. J. B. Williams Co., Inc.
711 5th Ave.
New York 22, N. Y.

100. William Wrigley Jr. Co.
410 N. Michigan Ave.
Chicago, Ill.

NETWORKS

ABC Television Network
7 W. 66th St.
New York 23, N. Y.

CBS Television Network
485 Madison Ave.
New York 22, N. Y.

NBC Television Network
30 Rockefeller Plaza
New York 20, N. Y.

FCC

Honorable Newton N. Minow,
Chairman
Federal Communications Commission
New Post Office Building
Washington 25, D.C.

FTC

Honorable Paul Rand Dixon,
Chairman
Federal Trade Commission
Pennsylvania Ave. at Sixth St., NW
Washington 25, D.C.

INDEX

ABOUT THE AUTHOR

HAROLD MEHLING was born in Chicago in 1923, grew up in Los Angeles, and now lives in a suburb of New York with his wife and two children. He has been a newspaperman, has written for television and magazines, and is the author of two earlier books, *The Scandalous Scamps* (1959) and *The Most of Everything* (1960).

Mr. Mehling has written numerous public affairs programs for television. In 1958, his children's show based on the progress of medical research was nominated for an award by the Writers Guild of America.

This book was set in

Caledonia and Univers types by

Harry Sweetman Typesetting Corporation.

It was printed and bound at the press of

The World Publishing Company.

Design is by Larry Kamp.